MY KID BROTHER'S BAND

a.k.a. THE BEATLES!

MY KID BROTHER'S BAND

a.k.a. THE BEATLES!

LOUISE HARRISON

Acclaim Press
MORLEY, MISSOURI

Acclaim Press ™
— *Your Next Great Book* —

P.O. Box 238
Morley, MO 63767
(573) 472-9800
www.acclaimpress.com

Book Design: M. Frene Melton
Cover Design: M. Frene Melton, Emily Blattel

Library of Congress Control Number: 2014901980

Harrison, Louise
My Kid Brother's Band—The Beatles / by Louise Harrison.
    pages cm
ISBN 978-1-938905-52-0 (alk. paper) — ISBN 1-938905-52-0 (alk. paper)
1. Harrison, Louise–Biography. 2. Harrison, George. 1943-2001. 3. Music–Social aspects–North America. 4. Music–Political aspects–20th century. 5. World War, 1939-1945–Children–England–Biography. I. Title.

ML3916. G4103.F7 2013
    [B]–dc23

First Printing 2014
Printed in the United States of America
10 9 8 7 6 5 4 3 2 1

This publication was produced using available information.
The publisher regrets it cannot assume responsibility for errors or omissions.

Photo Credits: All photos are from the Louise Harrison Collection unless otherwise noted.

CONTENTS

DISCLAIMER

It's only me!

I really didn't want to *write* a book or produce a literary masterpiece: I'm not Dickens, Tolstoy, or Hemmingway. I just wanted to tell my story to my Global Family, in my own words, just as I have always done: openly and honestly. I've also included a few "off the wall" ideas and opinions for you to consider, gathered from eight decades of my particular life experiences.

My only reason to become involved in helping to promote a band was simply this: My kid brother was playig lead guitar in a hometown band. As a self-confessed "ham" and a new US resident, I wanted to help.

In 1963 in the United States, I always referred to the band as *My Kid Brother's Band.* Had I used the word "Beetles" people might have associated me with an exterminating business.

My Kid Brother's Band was always my focus. However, everyone else started calling them THE BEATLES!

Louise Harrison

INTRODUCTION

My Kid Brother's Band,
a.k.a. The Beatles!

*H*ello. I am Louise Harrison, sister of Beatle George.
Since 1963, I have received dozens of books about The
Beatles. I seldom inflict upon myself the stress of reading
them unless, in some cases, the author and possibly the
veracity of the content are known to me.

From my perspective, some 65% of "Beatle books" were
written by someone who once spent five minutes in the same
room as a Beatle, or was in the same hotel, or on the same
plane, or even on the same planet. So I find the often fantastic
imagineering of said authors to be a little OFF!

This book, though, is not just about the Boys. During the
years I've interacted with my global family of Beatle people
as the global or flying Mum, many have wanted to know
more about myself. So, since I've nothing to hide, here goes.
I will include my story, interwoven with my experiences and
perspectives as the only biological sister of any Beatle. I also
think it's important for you to know more about our parents
and our upbringing so you can better understand how he
became the man you love and admire.

Quite some time ago I received *The Beatles and Philosophy*,
a compilation of essays by prominent philosophers (edited
by Michael and Steven Baur, published in 2006 by Carus
Publishing Company). Prior to reading this book, I'd
been invited by several ministers to sermons they'd given
regarding the positive values contained in many Beatles'
songs and interviews. So I was interested to see what was
being depicted as their philosophy. When I initially flipped
through the book, I was alarmed to see a subheading "The

Harrison Family Curse." The only curse of which I'd been aware was the universal one, seemingly passed down from generation to generation—"I hope when you grow up, your children will be as ungrateful as you are." So I read about the curse!

Briefly, the curse confirmed what I'd experienced. We Harrison children had been raised by very ethical and honest parents. We were encouraged to treat others with kindness and compassion; to conduct ourselves with integrity, giving thanks to our Creator for any gifts or abilities with which we had been endowed; then to put those gifts and abilities to the best possible use, and never take personal credit if our endeavors led to praises.

In video clips of George receiving awards, you may notice he is embarrassed by the applause; he implores the audience, "please—I can't take it. This is too much." Audiences at my appearances also know that I usually say, "You don't have to applaud, it's only *me*." We obviously adhered to our parents' teachings. The curse part is that since we totally trusted our parents, we assumed that everyone else was equally trustworthy, making us quite vulnerable when we came in contact with con-men and women, predators and manipulators, and all the other unsavory human behavioral types, considered by many to be "par for the curse."

The number of times we Harrisons and the other three Beatles have been taken for a ride bears out the accuracy of this theory. All four young men were raised by straightforward, hardworking parents, and, as one who WAS there before the Fame, I can say with conviction that most of the very public mistakes they made were the direct result of being too trusting. For most of their lives they believed in the sincerity of those who—attracted by their fame and fortune—offered their friendship and *help*. In many cases it was not until the "proverbial knife" was being removed that they realized they had once again been stabbed in the back. So, "The Harrison Family Curse" was briefly considered as a title, and at one point I also considered "Gullibles' Travails," but I realized my parents would not wish me to depict us as victims…so I decided to remain as open as my parents would have wished. Although in these days of out and out corruption, maybe I am stabbing myself in the back, and no one will wish to publish such an unsensational story. Fortunately I have now been introduced to a publisher with the same integrity as our parents.

For years now, Beatles' fans—noting the profusion of other, often erroneous books about The Beatles—have been asking me, "Louise, isn't it about time you told their story from your own personal perspective?" For a few months "It's About Time" was the working title; the next title considered was "The Harrison Hug." However, after input from many friends, I now have the definitive title.

This is how the hug came about. Whenever George and I were reunited after any length of time, we would always give each other a big hug. On one occasion, he said to me, "Pass it on." Since his death, I have been doing just that: passing on his hug and telling people that this hug originally came directly from George. Then, as a Harrison Hug recipient, you are now asked to continue to "pass it on." In this way George's love keeps circulating.

A year or so ago, a lady in Argentina sent an email. She told me she had received a Harrison Hug for her birthday from a fan to whom I'd given the hug in Cleveland in 2003. Also, more recently, another person sent a text saying she has now given her Harrison Hug to people in seventeen different countries—more evidence that George's love circles the globe. Let us keep the love flowing. The world certainly needs it! But, recently I realized there is something more important to consider.

Not only that: Thousands of young fans who wrote letters to The Beatles in the early Beatlemania years know this very well. Mum and Dad, in making the enormous effort to answer the letters, welcomed those youngsters to our extended family with love and kindness. I often received letters from fans delightedly telling me, "I just had a letter from Mum and Dad Harrison."

Again, not only that: When dozens of fans began to arrive on their doorstep, did Mum and Dad turn them away? Not at all; my parents hospitably invited them inside, chatted and signed photos, and served cups of tea and biscuits.

Yet again: Many times, young fans would run away from home to find a Beatle. Mum and Dad would occasionally find a youngster crouching in the flower beds at night and would take them inside, provide them with sandwiches and cocoa, then, after phoning to reassure the parents that their kids were okay, would take the trouble to drive those kids often hundreds of miles to their homes. At times, when the distance was too far, my parents "put them up" for the night.

So you see, the Harrison Hug is much more than just a hug; it says, "We care about you." I realize it didn't **really** start with George and I; it was circling the globe decades earlier! But the most important thing to understand is this:

No one family can claim to have "cornered the market" on love and compassion. Mum and Dad Harrison often told me, and I have no problem repeating this:

"The more love you give, the more you will receive!"

I believe each and every one of us has the capacity to give *love and kindness* to others rather than *hate and fear*. After much thought, discussion and deliberation, the title of the book you hold in your hand came to be. During my efforts in 1963 to gain US radio airplay for my young brother's band, I always referred to them as "My Kid Brother's Band." After all, at that time no one in the United States had heard of The Beatles. I have, and will always think of them as my kid brother's "For Peace/Four Piece Band."

In chapter five you will see that Dad didn't have as much trouble thinking of a name when my kid brother arrived!

I hope you enjoy it. As I write, I imagine the many familiar faces of people I have chatted with, hugged, or signed photos for; in other words, I see my global family and friends. True?

Parts of this book may offend a few, but then no one is required to agree with me. A lot of what I say comes from the same perspective as Monty Python, Bill Maher, Stephen Colbert, Jon Stewart and others of that mind-set, so I hope you chuckle rather than get angry!!! My opinions are my own, based on eight decades of carefully observing trends and events. I'm merely telling what happened and not examining the motives of others. I won't waste my energy holding any grudges. As Bob Dylan said, *"When you ain't got nothing, you ain't got nothing to lose."* True, I may not have worldly goods to lose, but I do still have the integrity taught me by my parents, and that is something I will never give up! My dad lived by—and often quoted—these lines from Shakespeare:

"This above all: to thine own self be true,
And it must follow, as the night the day,
Thou canst not then be false to any man."

We Harrison kids grew up with these values as the firm foundation of our worldview. When we left the nest, the world we encountered as adults was—to quote Monty Python—*"...something completely different."*

MY KID BROTHER'S BAND a.k.a. THE BEATLES!

Chapter Zero

ZERO COMES BEFORE #1

This may be a little unusual, but I decided for my memoir to be more palatable, I needed an appetizer, so before getting to my own life, I will offer a little taste of what is to come. In other words, here's the story of how my kid brother George became the first Beatle to set foot upon, and perform on, American soil.

In 1963, my very brilliant engineer husband and I, with our two Canadian-born children, became permanent resident aliens when, after a long journey from Gagnon in Quebec, we entered the United States at Niagara Falls on March 7.

A couple of months earlier, Mum had sent me the first single released in England by my kid brother's band. The song was called "Love Me Do"; the band was known as The Beatles. My immediate reaction upon playing it the first time was, "Wow! This certainly has a different sound!"

My husband was an innovative mining design engineer whose expertise was in great demand by mining companies throughout North and South America—more about that later in the book. Therefore, when the Midwest coal mining industry had finished gathering surface coal, a procedure known as "strip mining," mining companies were looking for a qualified engineer capable of leading the venture into underground (long-wall) mining. Freeman Coal Company in West Frankfort, Illinois, approached my husband, hired him, and rushed our family through the immigration process.

We headed from Niagara Falls to our new home. However, due to the length of the drive and the lateness of the hour, we stopped in a town called Benton, just six miles north of

West Frankfort, and spent the night in a motel. The next morning, my husband went off to start his new job as the chief mechanical engineer. I was charged with the task of finding us somewhere to live.

With only an English five pound note and a Canadian two dollar bill to my name, I took my two children and walked into town.

I found a local realtor named Aden Summers. With his help, before the day was over, I'd purchased a nice five bedroom house near the high school. The house belonged to Loren Lewis, a local attorney. Weeks later, I discovered he was part of the local Lewis family who had descended from the Lewis of "Lewis and Clark" fame. Loren helped me borrow a down payment of $500 from Russell Davis, the local bank manager, and I agreed to pay $150 dollars a month at 5% simple interest until the $12,000 asking price of the home was paid. I met Loren's aunt, Lillian, wife of the local judge, Everett Lewis. They lived in the house directly across the street from 113 McCann Street, my new home. I also met my next door neighbors, the Whittingtons.

Without saying anything to me, the Lewis and the Whittington families went to work soliciting donations of household furnishings so that we could move into our home whilst waiting for our own furniture to finish its journey from Canada. They also took me to the local utilities to sign up for electricity, water and telephone; these were immediately hooked up. I imagine they must have vouched for me, as I wasn't asked to pay any deposits. During the afternoon, Lillian Lewis took my children to her house and played piano to keep them amused whilst I started to freshen up the empty house.

Suddenly, a mid-sized truck drew up in the driveway laden with a stove, refrigerator, beds, and tables and chairs. By the time my husband's first work day was over, I was able to phone him and explain how to get to our new home. He arrived to a modestly furnished home, complete with a tasty meal of chicken and dumplings provided by Lillian and delicious brownies baked by Leah Whittington.

This was my first full day in the United States, and, considering that my only financial assets amounted to about ten dollars, I guess I truly found the United States to be the land of opportunity! I was overwhelmed by the kindness of these Midwesterners. Of course, I realized many years later what the **secret** was: my engineer husband had arrived to take a very senior and well-paid position at one of the primary employers in the region, so his arrival was considered an asset to the community.

As our small family settled in, we were regarded as rather exotic—we had previously lived in Britain, Canada and Peru, yet apparently in those days very few people from overseas ventured so far into the Midwest.

Meanwhile back in Britain, my kid brother and his band were making more recordings. The next single I received was "Please, Please Me." By then, our furniture had arrived from Canada, and the borrowed furnishings were returned with thanks. However, we did not have a stereo, something quite new at the time. So, off I went to the Benton Square and into Barton and Collins to purchase a stereo player with plenty of storage for albums. Then Mum sent me The Beatles' first album; the English version was "Please, Please Me." Naturally, just as all future Beatles' fans would do, I played the album constantly. We used to joke that it was played so much the tracks became wide enough to drive a train around.

When picking up my husband's weekly work clothes, the driver of our local dry cleaners' van showed great enthusiasm on hearing the album playing indoors. He sat on the porch swing with me saying, "Wow, I have a small band here, and I've never heard anything like this before in my life! This is great." His name was Gabe McCarty. Gabe played a significant part in early Beatle history when, together with his band "The Four Vests," George was to become the first Beatle to play live in the United States.

Here is the story of how that came about:

Throughout 1963, Mum had continued to send me The Beatles' singles as they were released. Being an outgoing Leo

NEMS ENTERPRISES LTD
DIRECTORS: B. AND C. J. EPSTEIN

12-14 WHITECHAPEL, LIVERPOOL, 1   TELEPHONE ROYAL 7895

Reference BE/DW

15th July, 1963.

Dear Lou,

Thank you very much indeed for your letter. It was very good to hear from you and also to note your interest in the BEATLES. I am sending, under separate cover, three copies of their L.P. and four copies of "From Me To You" which I hope will be of some avail. I will really be more than grateful for anything that you can do with the records because we really are very anxious indeed that their records will eventually "break" in the States.

I am also going to take the liberty of enclosing a copy of GERRY and the PACEMAKERS "How Do You Do It" and "I Like It" and also of John and Paul's song which they wrote for BILLY J. KRAMER, "Do You Want to Know a Secret". Perhaps you can do something with this to!

I am also going to ask our London Press Office to send you some photographs of the BEATLES (and if I may, some of the others to).

Finally, many many thanks for your interest and anticipated help.

With best wishes,

Kind regards,
Yours sincerely,
BRIAN EPSTEIN

Mrs. L. Caldwell,
113 McCann Street,
Benton,
Illinois,
U.S.A.

personality, I'd always yearned to be in showbiz. I enjoyed making people laugh and was quite happy to be "on display." So, when my youngest brother became a band member and was actually now creating records, I was delighted! I was a very proud "big sister," new to the United States myself. Yet, I knew that The Beatles' business manager, Brian

Epstein, and his associates were unfamiliar with America's more aggressive marketing of products. So, I took it upon myself to become the unofficial "Research, Development and Promotional" outpost of the newly-minted Beatles. Due to our very comfortable financial situation, I was able to employ competent caregivers for my children whenever I

DIRECTOR
RICHARD L.JAMES

DICK JAMES MUSIC LIMITED
SUITE TWO, 132 CHARING CROSS ROAD, LONDON, W.C.2

TELEPHONE
TEMPLE BAR 1687/8

CABLES
DEJAMUS, LONDON-WC2

DJ/RD

22nd July, 1963.

Mrs. G. Caldwell,
113 McCann Street,
Benton,
Illinois 62812,
U. S. A.

My Dear Mrs. Caldwell,

You will no doubt be surprised to receive this package, but I am sending it at the request of your brother George Harrison of The Beatles.

I understand that several disc-jockeys in your area may be interested in playing this but have experienced difficulty in receiving regular copies from Veejay Records.

Needless to say, I will indeed be most grateful if you can pass these to the important D. J.s in your locale.

Perhaps, if you are not too busy, you may drop me a line giving me an idea of the reaction that The Beatles are receiving in the States. I feel sure that they will break through in a very big way as they are certainly proving to be "world-beaters"!!

Trusting that you are well and George sends his best wishes.

Yours very sincerely,

Dick James.

wished to drive to visit potential radio stations in larger markets. Not one to take any challenge lightly, I subscribed to the *Billboard, Cashbox,* and *Variety* magazines in order to learn more about the American music business. As my research progressed, I imparted this knowledge in fourteen-page, handwritten letters to Brian Epstein each week.

WCIL 218 West Main Street

Phones 167 ~ 765

Carbondale, Illinois

Southern Illinois Broadcasting Partnership

1020 Kilocycles   1000 Watts

July 23, 1963

Miss Louise Caldwell
113 Mc Cann Street
Benton, Illinois

Dear Miss Caldwell:

In regard to your letter of July 17, we would be happy to have a couple copies of "The Beetles" record.

If, after receiving the record, we like it, we should be most happy to give it a few spins on the air.

Send the record to Paul H. McRoy, Record Librarian, WCIL Radio, Carbondale.

Sincerely,

Paul H. McRoy

Paul H. McRoy
Program Director

PHMc/ba

"Voice of Southern Illinois"

AM
1460 Kilocycles
1000 WATTS

FM
97.3 Megacycles
11,000 WATTS

CARMI BROADCASTING COMPANY
P. O. BOX 31 -- CARMI, ILLINOIS
Telephone: Carmi 382-4161

JULY 24, 1963

MRS. LOUISE CALDWELL
113 McCann STREET
BENTON, ILL.

DEAR MRS. CALDWELL,

We were very happy to recieve your letter informing us of the "Beatles" and would very much like to obtain a copy of their latest recording. We will be more than happy to audition and play the tune if we believe it could become a hit. If you are interested we will relay to you our evaluation of the record.

Sincerely yours,

Mike Hassan

Michael A. Hassan
Music Director
WROY

"Where Northern Vigor Meets Southern Hospitality"

He responded by sending me packages of singles and promotional materials, which I took to all the radio stations in the cities within about 200 miles of my home.

One thing Brian and I had in common was the attitude—taught to me by my parents—that just because you had no experience in something, it didn't follow that you couldn't become successful at it (after all, when we are born, we don't

DICK JAMES MUSIC LIMITED

SUITE TWO, 132 CHARING CROSS ROAD, LONDON, W.C.2

DIRECTOR
RICHARD L.JAMES

TELEPHONE
TEMPLE BAR 1687/8

CABLES
DEJAMUS, LONDON-WC2

RD/RD

30th July, 1963.

Mrs. L. Caldwell,
113 McCann Street,
Benton,
Illinois 62812,
U. S. A.

Dear Mrs. Caldwell,

Many thanks for your letter of July the 25th. Dick James is on vacation at the present time but he will reply to your letter upon his return on August the 9th.

Re. your query about radio liscencing, the Beatles "From Me To You" is published in the U. S. by Gil Music Corp. of 1650 Broadway, New York 19, New York, and I am sure Mr. George Pincus would be delighted to help you in this matter.

Please let me know if you require any more records or photos or publicity material as I would be delighted to send it to you.

With all good wishes.

Yours sincerely,

Rosalind Duque.
Secretary.

know how to breathe, but in order to survive, we quickly learn). And so it was that I spent a great deal of time and energy finding potential radio stations, talking to the program directors and trying to find a way to get The Beatles on the air in the United States. To give you an idea of what went on, I've included in this book some of the letters I received from the early British players in the Beatle adventure including George Martin and Dick James. As these letters indicate, my transatlantic participation was a welcome asset!

In the course of my endeavors, I discovered just how different it was to market music in the United States. I was also faced with the prevailing attitude in the predominantly white, male-dominated, Judeo-Christian culture, which according to comedians of the day maintained, that women and children should be seen and not heard. This mindset created an extra obstacle for me because most of the program directors I talked to believed I should be in the kitchen preparing dinner instead of interfering in "men's business." To help rectify this situation, my husband, somewhat sympathetic to my frustration, made a suggestion that I ask Brian to name me an official US Beatles' representative. He reasoned it would be better for me to approach the "men in charge" by saying, "Hello, I am the representative in America of the #1 British rock and roll band." There was never any suggestion (or need) for a salary, just a *title* to provide more credibility than saying, "Please play my kid brother's band's records." Although this idea was encouraged by many of my connections in Britain, Brian declined. This, of course, didn't cause me to miss a beat. After all, it was still *my kid brother's band*, whether or not I, as a mere woman, was considered *official*.

In Britain, performers needed only to be heard and accepted by one entity—the BBC. Once that happened, those performers had access to all the airwaves in the U.K. But, at that time in the United States, there were around 6,000 radio stations, and they each had only a limited outreach, depending on the wattage. Also at that time, the common practice at most radio stations was to "cross the palms with silver" or otherwise make some monetary or material reward to the stations decision maker. I later found out this practice was known as payola and was not considered very ethical (not that *that* stopped anybody).

The first Beatles' singles came to the Unites States via Vee-Jay Records. One day I drove to the address of Vee-Jay in St. Louis, only to find an abandoned, vacant lot at the street address. All of these findings I passed on to Brian, advising him that without the financial and influential backing of one of the major record companies, our little band might as well be nowhere men!

Because I'd joined a record club run by either RCA or Columbia, I'd learned they and Capitol records were the "top three" players in this industry. Concerned, I urged Brian in my weekly letters to go after one of the big three. Later I learned that although Capitol was part of EMI, they refused to accept my kid brother's band for many months.

I'd also become aware that the major TV show of the era was the *Ed Sullivan Show*, and I made a joke of PS'ing my letters each week with the message, "Get them on the *Ed Sullivan Show!*" Brian obviously took my finding to heart; he began to shop for better record labels, but you might be able to imagine my dismay when I received the letter shown on the next page.

"Oh, golly," I thought, *"this label is no better than Vee-Jay, but I suppose Philadelphia sounded pretty impressive to Brian over in England."*

He was determined, as was I, to get these lads to the "toppermost of the poppermost!," the ambition they themselves expressed.

During this time, I was also in touch with George on a weekly basis. At first I didn't reveal much about my correspondence with Brian, as I didn't want my brother to get any false hopes—which at that point in time could well have floundered. However, around this time the people at EMI, The Beatles' record company, and NEMS, Brian Epstein's family business, must have mentioned my involvement to George; he then had them start sending me even more promotional materials.

In one of his letters, he told me he had a couple of weeks free in September, and—with enough money to buy a transatlantic air ticket—he suggested coming to visit me to meet his first nephew, my six-year-old son and his niece, my almost four-year-old daughter. George first suggested that he and Ringo would travel together.

You can now read this letter in *George Harrison: Living in the Material World,* by Olivia Harrison, the companion book to the Martin Scorsese documentary of the same name. I personally no longer have many of George's letters, because

PER AIR MAIL

Miss L. Caldwell,
113, McCann Street,
BENTON,
Illinois

NEMS ENTERPRISES LTD
DIRECTORS: B. AND C. J. EPSTEIN

24 MOORFIELDS, LIVERPOOL, 2   TELEPHONE CENtral 0793

BE/AT

23rd August, 1963

Dear Louise,

Just very briefly a note to acknowledge your last letter.
I am going into everything you say very carefully. I have
already instructed persons concerned to change release of
the BEATLES' disc to another label. 'She Loves You' will
definitely not go out on Vee Jay. More news soon. xx

Yours sincerely,
BRIAN EPSTEIN

Miss L. Caldwell,
113, McCann Street,
BENTON,
Illinois

AIR MAIL   xx It's going
out on
SWAN Records
PHILADELPHIA

29

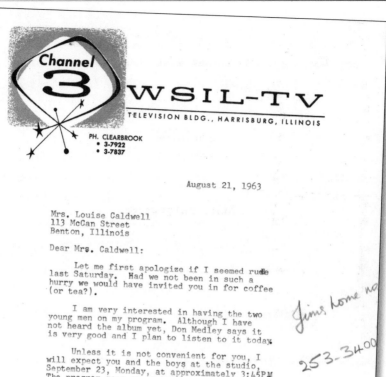

August 21, 1963

Mrs. Louise Caldwell
113 McCan Street
Benton, Illinois

Dear Mrs. Caldwell:

Let me first apologize if I seemed rude last Saturday. Had we not been in such a hurry we would have invited you in for coffee (or tea?).

I am very interested in having the two young men on my program. Although I have not heard the album yet, Don Medley says it is very good and I plan to listen to it today.

Unless it is not convenient for you, I will expect you and the boys at the studio, September 23, Monday, at approximately 3:45PM. The program goes on at 4:00.

Sincerely,

Jim Cox

James H. Cox
"The Hour"

Jim's home no
253-3400

in the '80s I returned to him most of the letters he'd written to me over the years. The intent was to protect his privacy. But since some of those letters are now being published, I can feel okay about sharing this charming incident with you.

Back when my son was born, I had received a letter from George, who at that time was only about 14-years-old. This 1957 letter started out saying, ""Dear Lou, I don't have anything to do right now, so I thought I'd write to you and tell you how chuffed I am to know that I am now an uncle. I am learning to play the guitar, and when my nephew grows up, I will teach him." Unfortunately, due to The Beatles' saga, those lessons never materialized, much to my late son's dismay. But, my son may have caught up with his Uncle George in 2010.

Naturally, I was delighted at the prospect of seeing my brother and introducing him to my children. Pleased that both George and Ringo were going to visit, I renewed my promotional efforts to include a TV appearance by the two lads. The letter on page 30 shows the result of that effort.

When I told George I'd secured a TV date for them, Ringo told him, "If she is going to make us work, I'm not going!" And so it was that George and our middle brother, Peter, came to the United States instead. I cancelled the TV date but was persuaded to do it myself at a later time.

During that summer, an American singer named Del Shannon, who'd been on tour in England, released a cover version of The Beatles' latest #1 "From Me to You." In the States, his version made it to #17 on the charts, and I, taking my Beatles' copy, redoubled my efforts to get the radio stations to play the original. I did successfuly win WFRX, a small station in West Frankfort whose owner gave the record to his daughter, Marcia, to play on her Saturday afternoon Teen Show. *(See photo on page 201.)* George visited her to thank her during his vacation. I also contacted major publications to alert them to The Beatles phenomenon. Here's one of the replies:

TIME *The Weekly Newsmagazine*

Your thought of TIME was very much appreciated. However, as we depend on our world-wide staff of full-time and part-time correspondents for most of the news that appears in our pages, we are rarely able to accept suggestions from other sources. Under the circumstances, we trust you will understand why we cannot use yours.

Eugenia Dooley
For the Editors

As September drew near, the excitement mounted for my children, who were soon to meet two of their uncles. They were already very familiar with The Beatles, since I had been playing their singles, "Love Me Do," "Please, Please Me," and "From Me to You," along with the English version of the "Please, Please Me" album, which had been #1 in England since the first week it was released and remained #1 for an entire year until the release of their second album, replacing it at #1.

Our five-bedroom home was spiffed up ready for the visit. The downstairs back bedroom was readied with two single beds for Uncles Peter and George. The day of their arrival, at Lambert Field Airport in St. Louis, was momentous. We drove to the airport, and at our designated meeting place beneath the *Spirit of St. Louis,* my children met their uncles for the first time.

One incident I recall was there were a number of people outside the airport with signs protesting against the proposed legislation in the United States to afford equal rights to minorities. Although Britain had been involved in slavery in the previous century, there was currently no hostility in Britain between people of different racial backgrounds. George commented on the hateful attitudes toward minorities in the States by saying he'd overheard this comment by an American male on the flight: "I've nothing against _____ [imagine the N-word here]; I think everyone should own one." Later I learned that this remark was regarded as a common "joke" in those days.

I should mention, during their tours in the '60s, The Beatles refused to play for segregated audiences and have always held the positive view that *We Are All Equal.*

Although much progress was made on this matter in the '60s, it seems racism has in the 21st century, once again reared its ugly head. I'm afraid our species is regressing! (When you consider the brutal treatment and total opposition to his policies our *half black* president is enduring, without any regard to the damage their actions are having on the entire country, can you even IMAGINE how those same misguided folks would treat a *100% black* president?)

However, on that day we were all happy. Arriving at 113 McCann Street, we were greeted with great enthusiasm by our six-month-old German shepherd, Sheba. As children, we never had a pet; in Britain in that era most people could not afford the extra costs. Also, there was not even enough food for people due to rationing and other factors. So, Peter and George were quite delighted to see that my children had the pleasure of sharing a big bundle of love named Sheba.

As Peter and George settled in for their two-week holiday, they found to their delight that their nephew had a playroom complete with a very extensive Lionel electric train set. Naturally, the good salary my husband earned made it possible for us to enjoy a pretty high standard of living. Peter and George, due to a wartime childhood, had never had such a luxurious toy. They spent hours with the children, concocting scenarios involving the trains, the villages, and all the other additions to this wonderful set-up. But, we also spent time outdoors!

Earlier that year, we had bought a fairly large two-room orange canvas tent and had enjoyed camping weekends at the nearby plentiful campsites in southern Illinois. During my brothers' visit, we went camping at Garden of the Gods, Pounds Hollow, Lake Glendale, and, possibly Big Springs in Missouri. George had bought a silent movie camera to record his trip and I have some of this footage.

We particularly enjoyed the evenings seated around the campfire. New to my brothers was the roasting of hot dogs and marshmallows. George was fascinated by the more exotic insect life to be found in the States than in Britain. He had at first noticed this lovely green leaf that—to his amazement—began to walk around. So he spent some time filming this leaf-bug walking on a tree. Later the same evening whilst we were chatting around the fire, a twig fell on George's arm, and when he went to brush it off, it too, started to run! In astonishment he yelled, "I wish these bugs would own-up!" This one was known as a stick insect. Apart from the insects in disguise, we had a wonderfully relaxing couple of weeks.

DICK JAMES MUSIC LIMITED

TELEPHONE
TEMPLE BAR 1687/8

CABLES
DEJAMUS, LONDON·W·C2

DIRECTOR
RICHARD L.JAMES

SUITE TWO, 132 CHARING CROSS ROAD, LONDON, W.C.2

RD/RD

8th August, 1963.

Mrs. Louise Caldwell,
113 McCann Street,
Benton,
Illinois 62812,
U. S. A.

Dear Mrs. Caldwell,

Many thanks for the letter. As you can see, I have enclosed photos, publicity sheets and the sheet music you asked for. Please let me know if you would like anything else.

I have just seen in one of our "trade" papers - The New Musical Express - that the boys "FROM ME TO YOU" is No. 116 in "Billboard", so here's hoping it makes it!! If it gets into the Top 100 it will mean so much to the Beatles as this is one of their biggest ambitions.

The reason that Del Shannon's version came out in the States first was that it was recorded in England. Dick wouldn't give the publication rights to an American publisher until the Beatles' version was released so that no-one could be issued with a recording liscence and "hurt" the boys' record, but, because Del Shannon's version was made over here, it could and was released in the States first. In answer to your question, the U. S. release is usually about a month or so after the English one.

I think its a great idea about you becoming the U.S. rep and keep "bashing" away at Brian until he agrees.

Everytime I read of you sitting by the swimmingpool or of 99° heat I turn a beautiful shade of pale pea-green as the weather over here is UGH!!! It's hot but not sunny and the general feeling is like being wrapped up in thick airless blankets. On top of this it rained all last weekend which was August Bank Holiday Monday. Last week we had four whole hot sunny days, but when you are in the office what good is that!

By the way, congratulations on the new Kennedy!

Bardstown.
Box 222
Rhill Penn

When we returned from our first camping trip, my brothers and I went shopping, first of all to the Benton Square. George mentioned that he'd heard a lot about T-bone steaks and suggested we buy some to bar-b-que. This was of course in the days before he became a vegetarian. We left the square and proceeded along East Main Street to the local grocery store. After selecting the steaks, George reached into his back pocket and offered to go ahead and pay for them. In horror he realized

RD/RD   -2-   8th August, 1963.

Dick is still in Belgium and from what I hear doesn't want to come back. He will be in the office on Monday and on the following Sunday, the 18th, I am off for two weeks to Italy. So if you don't hear for a little while it's not because we will have forgotten you.

I am glad the kids (hark at me, an old lady of 20) like the Beatles and tell them their opinion of the L.P. is shared over here. It's been No. 1 in the L.P. charts so long people think it's a permanent fixture!! They are also No. 1 in the E.P. charts and we are hoping that these two positions will hold out until the release of their single as it would be fab for them to be No. 1 in all three charts!!!

The new single is being released on August the 23rd and is called "SHE LOVES YOU" c/w "I'LL GET YOU". It's really gear and the advance sales alone should make it a wacking great big No. 1. As soon as I can I'll send you a disc and the sheet music.

Write soon as its great to hear what's happening over the overside.

With all good wishes.

Yours very sincerly,

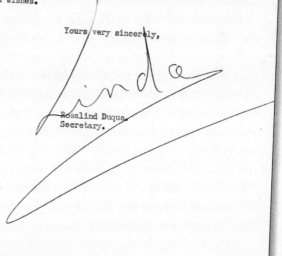

Rosalind Duque.
Secretary.

his billfold was gone; it contained all four hundred dollars of his remaining cash. He'd been hoping to buy a Rickenbacker guitar, so the loss of his wallet was a big blow! Speedily, he and Peter rushed back to the square to see if they could find the missing wallet. He remembered that he still had it whilst filming the "time and temperature clock" above the bank.

But, as they frantically rushed back, a youth was rushing from the square trying to find us to return the wallet.

Apparently, a youngster named C.J. Parris had been looking out of a second floor window above one of the stores when he noticed our little group. Intrigued with George's (to the American mind) unusual hair-do, he watched closely. He noticed the wallet fall out of George's pocket as he was filming the scene. C.J. sent a friend of his to retrieve the wallet and go find the "long-haired stranger" and return it to him. George was overjoyed when all his holiday funds were so quickly returned. He exclaimed, "Wow, I can't think of many places where I could have lost so much money and had it all returned to me!" He gave the boy a reward, and thereafter praised the honesty of the people of the Heartland. The following February, I was to return from *The Ed Sullivan Show* in New York to Benton with an autographed gift as a special "thank you" for C.J. Parris.

Once Gabe, the musician/dry cleaning van driver, heard that George was coming to the States, he made sure that he and his band members could meet him. His lead guitarist was Kenny Welsh, then in his early thirties. He had played at the Grand Ole Opry in Nashville. Young George, at 20, was a mere five years into his guitar playing career, so was very impressed and gratified to have access, however briefly, to such an accomplished musician. Together they sat in our living room, Kenny patiently teaching chords and various other techniques, all of which are a complete mystery to me. I remember George saying to me, "I wonder if I can ever be as good of a player as Kenny."

A year or so later a really comical incident was connected to THAT remark. When The Beatles were making their first movie, *A Hard Day's Night,* there was a complex guitar riff running through the title song. When Kenny heard it he exclaimed to me, *"WOW, your kid brother has REALLY come a long way with his playing!"* I happily passed this complimentary remark on to George during one of our phone calls. However, George burst out laughing and said, *"I'm sorry to disappoint you all... but I played that riff at normal speed and George Martin doubled the speed for the actual sound track and record!!! I'm still a long way from being as good as Kenny."*

Honesty Thy name is Harrison!

Besides camping with our family, George and Peter also did some sight-seeing with Gabe during this vacation. One of their most enjoyable outings was to an A&W root beer place whose servers were shapely girls on roller skates. The same place would later sport a sign claiming that George Harrison had dined there.

One day, Gabe and his buddies took George to a well-stocked music store in Mount Vernon, a larger town some twenty miles north of Benton. George—who was very keen to own a Rickenbacker guitar like the one John used—was thrilled to find one there, but asked the store owner if he would paint the red guitar black for him. A week later, George returned and paid in full for the instrument. The fact that this young lad could afford to pay in full was, especially in those days, quite noteworthy. This store for many years afterwards had a sign saying that George Harrison bought a guitar there. Note: this guitar was recently sold at auction for over $600,000! *(See photo on page 204.)*

Another novelty my brothers enjoyed was a drive-in movie. They may not exist anymore, but the one we went to was located on Route 37 just north of Marion. As luck would have it, the movie that night was a British offering starring Cliff Richards. Until the arrival of The Beatles on the British music scene, Cliff was THE STAR. We sat in the car, the speaker resting on the open passenger side window, and watched the movie. Well, the comical thing was hearing George every so often saying softly in awe, *"I know him! I've met him! I know him!"* This was surely the first time anyone in our family had actually known a person in a movie. However, it was not to be the last.

There were many Italian miners in the area, and they had a club called The Boneyard Bocce Ball Club. My husband, whose presence was considered to be quite an asset to our community, had been invited to join. Due to his former military service he was also invited to join the American Legion, as well as the Rotary Club.

The Bocce Ball Club was a family friendly place; the men could have a beer, and yet it was OK for their wives and

Copy

113 McCann
Benton
Ill.
62812
Oct 10th.

Dear Mr Connell,

Sorry I have not been able to get to see you, but then I don't suppose a personal visit could add anything to what you already know about "the Beatles".

I am taking the liberty of enclosing their latest disc along with some publicity sheets for your inspection.

From 'Billboard' you should have a fairly good idea that this group is Britain's "hottest disc property" Sept 2½ and I hope you will see your way clear to giving this group an airing – I'm sure you won't be sorry as I know many local teenagers who are hoping to hear them on the air and I'm sure they would soon be popular throughout the country.

Thanks in Advance
Sincerely
Louise Caldwell.

Letter written to the program director at KXOK in St. Louis, October 10, 1963.

children to gather as well. Actually, this was also true of many other establishments in town, including the Legion. I recall one occasion at the Legion. My three-year-old daughter had just learned how to whistle and she went around to all the people in the room saying, "Hey, I know how to whistle, do you wan'na hear?" Naturally, everyone agreed, so she entertained the delighted members and guests. One gentleman, a retired state attorney in his nineties, Joe Hickman, was so taken with her that he mailed her a 1921 Morgan silver dollar, which I understand was quite rare. Unfortunately, it has long since vanished.

Peter and George made several visits to the Bocce Ball Club and met many of our friends. The high school principal and his wife, Sherwood and Ruth Ann Pace, were amused when George referred to the husband as "the headmaster." His wife asked, "Well, does that make me the head *mistress?*" Most Midwesterners found the differences between the British and American words for the same thing to be quite amusing. The head-mistress' birthday occurred during the two-week holiday, and I recall that George sat on a stool with a borrowed guitar and sang "Happy Birthday to You!"

Let us now get to the *really big shew* of that vacation!

A tiny, two-line ad in the local paper announced: "The Four Vests will play on Saturday night at the VFW Club in Eldorado, Illinois." Gabe invited us to come along. My brothers, husband, and two other couples made the approximately thirty-mile trip. The room the band was to perform in was on the second floor. Around the edges of this large room were tables that would seat about ten people. The center of the room was open for dancing, and at the far end was a small stage about eighteen inches high. The Four Vests were pretty popular in the area, and the room was filled to capacity. *(See photo on page 201.)*

The band began to play. Gabe introduced each song, named the writer or singer and also what type of dance, i.e. waltz, quick-step, rumba, tango, etc. People were drinking, smoking, eating, dancing, and generally enjoying themselves. However, to my concern, I noticed that after Gabe's introductions

E.M.I. RECORDS LTD

Controlled by Electric & Musical Industries Ltd—the greatest recording organisation in the World

E.M.I. HOUSE · 20 MANCHESTER SQUARE · LONDON W.1

TEL. HUNter 4488 · Telex No. 22643 · Inland Telegrams EMIRECORD, LONDON TELEX · Cables: EMIRECORD, LONDON, W.1

November 19th. 1963.

Mrs. G. Caldwell,
113, McCann Street,
Benton,
Illinois,
U.S.A.

Dear Mrs. Caldwell,

I saw your brother George on Monday and he asked me to send you a few records. I have sent off to you today their latest single and L.P. and also all the Billy J. Kramer recordings we have made. I included a new record by The Fourmost which I thought you might like to hear.

There are a couple more copies of the new L.P. to come but I will send these over next week - I thought it better not to send too many at once in case you get caught for custom payments.

It is so exciting about the success of the Beatles - it is quite the most amazing thing the amount of excitement they have caused here. We have always been their greatest fans in this office and couldn't be more thrilled and proud.

With best wishes,

Sincerely yours,

Judy Lockhart Smith

STATESIDE · M-G-M · MERCURY · TOP RANK · LIBERTY · UNITED ARTISTS · VERVE RECORDS
AND OF COURSE—E.M.I. TAPE RECORDS AND EMITEX

and at the end of each song when people returned to their seats, there was never any applause. I remember thinking to myself, "Maybe this showbiz stuff isn't so satisfying after all." But, at least all were having fun. George and I did the Twist at one point, and I know I danced a lot.

Toward the end of the evening, Kenny came over to Peter and asked, "Do you think George would get up and do a song with us?" Peter replied, "No, he's on holiday, but...if you were to put a guitar into his hands, I don't think he could resist!" So a few minutes later, Kenny came over to George and, faking an emergency, said, "Hey, could you take over for me for a few minutes? I have to go...." George, always an obliging type, took the instrument and stepped onto the stage. Gabe made an elaborate announcement about George's success with a band in England, but no one was listening; they all were talking amongst themselves, just as they'd done all evening.

After a quick conference about which songs they might be able to pull off together, George stepped to the mike and began to sing. Almost immediately it was as though a lightning bolt had ripped through the room! The chatter stopped and everybody started to yell, applaud, stomp their feet on the ground, and pound their fists on the tables. Fingers at the sides of their mouths, many gave that super loud whistle. Some of the songs included "Teddy Bear," "Green Onions," and "Everybody's Trying to Be My Baby." The roomful of people continued to go wild. When he stepped down from the stage, George was mobbed.

It had been quite a long time since the latest war, so most of the veterans and families were far from being youngsters. One elderly gentleman came over to George and, putting a friendly arm around his shoulder, said, "Son, with the right kind of backing, you could really go places!" Yet another approached Gabe and told him very seriously, "This young fella' trying out for your band.... Well, I think you'd be a fool not to hire him!"

Whenever I tell this story, I usually end by remarking wryly, "Just think, George could have been The Fifth Vest!"

There in a tiny town, before an audience of about 200 people, unbeknownst to anyone present, Beatle History was made when George became the first Beatle to give a (free) live performance in the United States. So, before Harrison and McCartney played in the Unites States, Harrison and McCarty did!!!

Is it OK now, for me to tell you *my* story, starting with Chapter 1?

My story does include much more about my kid brother's band "The Beatles."

Chapter One

W.O.W. –
WELCOME TO OUR WORLD

*H*aving just served the appetizer in chapter Zero, I shall now attempt the more usual format and begin my memoir at my earthly beginning. But, since life is always in the "now moment," you may find as I recount events that "time" and "sequence of events" becomes a little irrelevant. You see, when recalling and writing about the events of my life, many times I have felt compelled to add some present day observations regarding the particular incident or experience. When this happens I enclose the 21st century remarks thus (bla bla...).

Don't worry, I've made it through okay, and I'm sure you will too!

Although I was present, I don't claim to recall this part; I was told about it later. I was born at 3:30 p.m. on a Sunday afternoon, the 16th of August 1931. My parents were living with my maternal grandmother at 47 Cecil Street in Wavertree, Liverpool.

My parents, Harold Hargreaves Harrison and Louise French, both of Wavertree, had met several years earlier in 1927. Here is a brief rundown of their family history as I know it:

Dad's family had lived for quite some time in Liverpool. My grandfather Henry Harrison was, I understand, an architect/builder in Liverpool and several of his well known accomplishments were pointed out as I grew, including the Wellington Road Barracks. He married—I think the maiden name of my paternal grandmother was Thompson. They had seven children before he volunteered to join the army at the start of WWI. He was killed in Mons, Belgium in 1914, leaving his widow to care for their seven children. In those days there were no government "benefits" to assist those left in dire need. She had quite a struggle, but raised them all to be decent citizens. The seven children of whom Dad was the middle child, born in 1909, were two aunts, Lizzie and Janey, and four uncles, known to me as Uncles Harry, Teddy, Billy (Billy lost a leg and an arm during WWII), and Jimmy. Naturally, we never met Grandad Harrison, but knew Dad's mom as Granny Harrison. We visited her quite often as I was growing up.

Mum's family had not been longtime Liverpool residents. John French, my grandfather, came to Liverpool from Dublin when he was 12. Born and raised in County Wexford, he was a descendant of the Normans who moved to Southern Ireland hundreds of years earlier from Normandy in France. Thus, the family name became French, originally spelt Ffrench and they were known as "The Ffrenchies." Apparently prior to the "potato famine," the French family had been fairly wealthy landowners. As an adult in Liverpool, John French worked as a police officer. He married Louise Woolham, who had lived in a smaller town in Lancashire up the coast from Liverpool. They also had seven children, my mom being the middle one born in 1911, and again I had four uncles—Uncles Johnny, George, Jimmy, and Eddy, and two aunts, Kathy and Cissy. My Granddad French lived until I was about 7, and I knew him and Nanny French very well because they lived in Albert Grove and we lived on the next street over. Nanny French died when I was 17.

Naturally, I didn't learn most of what I'm now about to reveal until I was a teenager.

Mum and Dad met in 1927 when she was about 16 and he was 18. Apparently, they were each walking in the park with a group of friends when the two groups converged. Then, one who was known to both groups made introductions and a lively conversation ensued. Harold and his friends were, at that time, employed by the White Star/Cunard Steamship Company, whose cruise ships sailed regularly out of Liverpool. In those days one left school and took a job at age 14, so Louise was already working as a housemaid in one of the grander homes on Queens Drive (which was the area of Liverpool where the wealthy Epstein family of future Beatle fame-resided). One of Harold's pals asked Louise for her address and offered to send her some perfume when he next stopped at a French port. When Louise finished writing her address on a slip of paper, Harold stepped forward, took the address, and said firmly, "No, I will send perfume to her, not you."

Some weeks later, there was great excitement at Louise's home when a package containing perfume arrived from a foreign address. So began what was known in those days as a "courtship." *(See photos on page 193.)* Much of the time Harold was away at sea, and for the next few years they wrote many loving letters to each other. Mum was proud to show me many of those letters as I was growing up.

It must have been around the end of 1930 that Harold was assigned to a six-month world cruise. What this meant to the young couple was that his earnings—including the generous tips he would gather from being a steward in First Class— would give them enough financial security to be married on his return. After bidding each other a tearful and passionate farewell, pledging to be married the following May, Louise learned a few months later—to her horror and dismay—that she was pregnant. I can only imagine what suffering she endured back in those times to be "the good Catholic girl gone wrong." All they could do was to plan a much more hurried wedding ceremony than they had anticipated the moment he returned.

(My younger readers having been raised in an era when every aspect of the reproductive process is known, even to five-year-olds, will not understand that back in the 1920/30s, very little information was imparted to teenagers regarding their own biological functions, much less anything about reproduction. "I will tell you when you are 21" was the theme of the times. The most common information available told that storks delivered babies. Therefore, as she herself told me, even on the day of my birth, Mum was unsure how the "lump" would be removed—she thought "she would be cut open." At my birth Mum was twenty years old. She never told me if the actual birthing process was a relief or not! However, she did make sure that when I became a teen I knew as much as I needed to know so that I would not be "caught unawares" as she was.)

Harold returned in May, and on the eighteenth of May, 1931, they were married by a justice of the peace at a registry office in Liverpool. Following the wedding, they moved in with Dad's mother. I was due to arrive three months later.

Now to the events of my birthday! I was born just in time for afternoon tea. About an hour later as the midwife, Nurse Ryand, was leaving the house, the local Catholic priest arrived. This same midwife assisted at the births of all four of us, including the "later to be famous one"—George.

In response to the priest's question, the nurse pointed to the upstairs bedroom where Mom and Dad were joyfully welcoming me to this world. Full of righteous fury, the priest charged up the stairs and thrust himself into our tableau.

"You and the child will burn in Hell forever!" he yelled at Mom. He kept on ranting and raving whilst the shocked young couple gathered their wits. Mum told me many years later that Dad remained calm but took the priest by the elbow, and—rushing him down the stairs and outside the house—told him, *"You are much more likely to be burning in Hell than either of these two!"*

The reason for the priest's fury was that although Mum was one of his parishioners, due to their embarrassment and haste, my parents were not married in the Catholic Church. Therefore, *not married at all* in the eyes of the church! I did not know of this incident until many years later, yet in some ways it set the stage for my own lifelong dismay at the unfortunate events in much of our world history generated by the prevalence of similar religious intolerance.

Mum told me that at my first Christmas, Dad sent a lovely card from his next cruise to Australia. I will include a copy of his message inside the card in our companion book.

The worldwide Depression that started in the US in 1929 hit Britain late in 1931. Early in 1932, Dad was laid-off from

Cunard because there were no longer affluent people taking cruises. His only income, then, was what they called "the dole" or unemployment. The amount he received was twenty-three shillings per week, out of which they paid ten shillings for rent. Mum told me that whilst she was still nursing me, her main meal of the day was a bouillon/OXO cube melted in a cup of hot water with some dry bread to dip into the "broth."

However, once the economy started to improve, Dad was back at work with Cunard—I think on the *Brittanic*—a sister ship to the *Titanic*. Once Dad was back "at sea," we moved into our own rented house, 12 Arnold Grove. Again the rent was ten shillings per week. My parents were content and Dad's income was adequate for their modest way of life. This was our home for the remainder of my childhood, and the house where all three of my brothers were born—the same house many of my readers will have visited when on the tour of Beatle homes in Liverpool.

Chapter Two

A Global Family

I suppose it was due to my untimely arrival into the Harrison family that my parents felt as though they had been struck by a bolt of lightning. But in any case, Dad's name for me was "Lightning." Throughout my babyhood and subsequent childhood, I apparently injected a great deal of "hurry-up" into most of my activities, sometimes with unfortunate results!

I took my first steps at ten months and at thirteen months sprained my ankle running with a pram/baby carriage. This incident led to the first of many experiences with the Liverpool Children's Hospital emergency department. In today's world, I imagine Mum and Dad would have been suspected as child-abusers, but in truth it was just my rambunctious behavior that was responsible for my numerous injuries. Mum told me years later how amused she had been when during my treatment for the sprain, after a week or so, a nurse told her, "She's just pretending she can't walk. Her sprain is cured, and she can walk now. Wait a minute and I'll prove it."

The nurse told Mum to go to the far side of the room and call me. This she did, but to the dismay of the nurse, I went down on my hands and knees and crawled speedily across the room to Mum.

Mum spent lots of time coaching me, and by the age of two I was reportedly speaking in articulate sentences. The Christmas after my fourth birthday, I was enrolled in school. There was no such thing as kindergarten back then, so I went into the first class. Before I was five I was moved up into the second class, where it was great fun to learn how to read. Back then they used the phonetic system—you know, the sound 'a' is for apple, 'b' is for bat, 'c' is for cat, and so on. It was a much better and more productive system than the "See Jack Run" used in the United States to teach my children.

One of my early memories happened when Harry was about nine months old. Mum and Dad had a box camera, and I was accustomed to being "snapped." Then a couple of weeks later, when the photo was developed, I would see myself on the snap. I often wondered why the snap only showed one moment, and not all the things happening at the time. I guess I was anticipating the advent of the video camera? Anyway, one day Mum told me we were all going into the city to a place called Jerome's to have our "photographs taken."

I was already having sleeping problems due to the prayer we'd been taught at Sunday school and was expected to say each night before going to bed:

"Now I lay me down to sleep, pray the Lord my soul to keep,
If I should die before I wake, pray the Lord my soul to take."

By this stage in my life I had a pretty strong instinct that "my soul" was a rather vital and perhaps important part of me, and if someone was to sneak in and "take it" whilst I was sleeping, I'd be in a mess. Thus began a lifelong problem of not wanting to be "off my guard" by foolishly falling asleep. Having never heard the word photograph before, I thought this "having my photograph *taken*" seemed very ominous. It seemed to my young mind something to avoid at all costs.

We arrived at Jerome's all decked out in our best and entered a long corridor filled with people in line. Most of the time in Liverpool folks are very friendly and talkative, but in this place all were dressed up and silent. Sensing no good outcome, I decided to make my escape. I took off at great speed—I wasn't known as Lightning for nothing— and headed away from Jerome's, which turned out to be in a very high traffic area close to St. George's Hall building and St. John's Gardens, not far from the entrance to the Mersey Tunnel. Mum apparently asked one of the customers to hold

Harry while she chased after me. Back in those days nobody wanted an extra child, so he was in no danger of being stolen. Catching up with me several blocks away, she hauled me back to the dreaded "photograph" place. I will include the subsequent photo, and you will see by my expression that I was not a happy camper. *(See photo on page 196.)* I was not about to allow anything to be "taken" from me without some resistance.

Later that day when Dad was told of my behavior, I was able to tell him what had been going on in my mind, and naturally he explained the whole photograph process to my satisfaction. These days, when having my "photograph taken" with dozens of folks most nights, it's just as well I understand.

Another incident occurred when I was about five, which I totally enjoyed but which gave my Mom a few uneasy moments. It happened when we all went to the zoo located on the outskirts of Liverpool. This was really fascinating. I knew from my conversations with Dad from which countries most of these "non-British" creatures had originated. As was usual in those much safer times, I was allowed to wander wherever my curiosity led me. During my explorations I found a crowd surrounding a wonderful Indian elephant. I knew from Dad's teachings that this was an Indian and not a large floppy eared African elephant. I also knew that Indian elephants were much more domesticated than African elephants. There was a set of steps beside the creature. It had a seat on its back that held about four to six people. I joined the line of people ascending the steps in order to take a ride. Before long I was seated atop this wonderful creature, enjoying a somewhat lurching, wobbly ride, I had to hold on tight to the side of the seat. I could see across the field for quite a distance from my perch. I saw Mum and Harry, calling "Lulu, Lulu, where are you?" So from my vantage point I yelled, "Mum, look up here; here I am!" When she heard me, she looked in astonishment and called "Lulu, whatever are you doing up there?"

I replied quite logically, "Having an elephant ride." Then she asked, "How did you get up there?" Again, my calm reply was, "I climbed up the steps." Apparently there was actually a small fee charged for these rides, but the person collecting the money, seeing my eagerness, had, I guess, given me a free ride. Once again, my Mom, finding me safely enjoying yet another adventure, did not reprimand me or try to stifle my explorer nature.

(In retrospect, it is difficult for me to imagine the dull and uninspiring childhood I might have had with more restrictive parents, or how terrible it must be for children today, when for ominously real reasons, they are taught never to speak to strangers. I'm thankful to have been born into a different era and thankful also to Mum and Dad for allowing me to explore my world, and learn so much—not always pain-free—from my own experiences. I did learn to avoid repeating some, but not all of my most painful experiences.)

By the time I was six I joined the Wavertree Public Library. Outside the library there was a huge rock, or stone, which was actually about three feet high, smooth and shiny. We kids had lots of fun climbing up one side and sliding down the other. Funnily enough, when I was living in New York in the '70s, George would visit often, and during some of our conversations about our childhood, we both remembered sliding down that rock. The legend was that this granite looking rock was a tiny meteor from space and did not consist of any material known on Earth. I don't know if this was true or just myth, but we kids enjoyed the rock tremendously.

I was an avid reader, especially of the Andrew Lang Collection of Fairy Stories. The genre implied that all the beautiful princesses with their handsome princes lived happily ever after. I had no trouble believing the happily-ever-afterwards, because my own parents' marriage confirmed the possibility of long-term marital happiness. So I naturally assumed I was destined for a happy marriage too. Whoops!

Although the library was about a half-mile from my home and the other side of busy High Street, I was always allowed to go on my own to change my books. British children learn early on to be responsible for our own well-being. I guess there was either less paranoia or less crime than now. The books I read had no illustrations, and I would read two or three a week. Because I spent so much time reading, I recall Mum frequently telling me to get my "nose out of the book" and attend to some chore.

One day the librarian became a bit suspicious of my almost daily visits, and she asked, "How old are you? And what are you really doing with all these books?" Raised by totally honest parents, I was taken aback by her question. I told her I was six, which seemed pretty old to me as I had a brother who was merely three. Anyway, she had me read a few pages to her, and she seemed satisfied.

The three-year-old brother in question had arrived on the 20th of July 1934. He was my first brother, Harold James Harrison, known as Harry. At the time of his birth, we were living in our own rented home in Arnold Grove, the next street to where Mum had been raised along with her brothers and sisters,

When Harry arrived, Mum—who through no fault of her own had been brainwashed throughout her childhood by the Roman Catholic Church—was still terrified by the threat of eternal damnation she experienced at my birth. Apparently after those priestly threats that day, my paternal grandmother, Granny Harrison, had taken me to be christened in the Church of England. But in 1934, now that Mum had another child, she wanted to take the opportunity to at least save *me* from that terrible fate by having me, as she believed, "properly" baptized in the TRUE church along with Harry. So, dressed in my best outfit and accompanied by Mum's two older sisters, Auntie Kathy and Auntie Cissy, I was led off to the parish church, Our Lady of Good Hope. *(See photo on page 194.)*

This event turned into somewhat of a fiasco. We were led to the christening font by a bunch of men wearing long black dresses with lacey white tops. They were chanting scary stuff in strange echoing voices. Next thing I knew, one of these men began to pour water over my new baby brother, and Harry started to scream loudly. So what does a protective BIG sister do? What else? "Leave my brother alone!" I yelled and then delivered a hefty kick to the shins of the bully. His reaction was, "It's going to take a lot more than water to get the Devil out of you, young lady!" Then my two aunts lifted me up, and I also was doused with water, then with the bully saying a lot of strange words, was hoisted kicking and screaming into the Catholic religion. I remember all of this very vividly. I'm still glad I kicked him!

Apart from the arrival of my first brother, that year was also notable in Liverpool because of the official opening of the Mersey Tunnel, which was at that time considered quite an extraordinary feat of engineering and sheer determination. Many Irish laborers lost their lives during the very dangerous work on this tunnel. It was about three miles in length and ran under the river from Liverpool to Birkenhead, thus making it possible to go from town to town by road instead of using the ferries across the Mersey. Back in those days, however, very few people had motorcars, so the majority of people still used the ferries in order to cross from Liverpool to the other side of the Mersey. (You may remember a famous song called "Ferry Across the Mersey" recorded by Gerry and the Pacemakers, one of Brian Epstein's "stable" of stars and a song Brian had sent to me to promote.)

During my very early school years we were asked if anyone knew a song to sing. Mum had taught me a delightful little song about dandelions. So, Lou the "ham" offered to sing this song to our class. Here are the fondly remembered words:

"Dandelions, dandelions, like golden stars are you.
Shining in the meadow grass, and sparkling with the dew.
Do you shine up yonder dears all the long night through?
And then come dancing down with the sun,
because the children all love you."

It soon became quite a favorite with the rest of my class because in one of our early childhood games—when we wanted to know "What time is it?" we would find a fully feathered dandelion, and then puff at the seeds until they were completely dispersed. Depending on how many puffs it took, we then said, "It is four o'clock," or whatever the outcome. We knew many people made dandelion tea, and others used the leaves in salads. So, besides telling time, providing beverages and salads *and* being the subject of a child friendly song, dandelions though out my childhood were a source of fun and great happiness.

(I'm afraid my present day experiences living in our modern pesticide paradise cause me to feel great sadness at the status and plight of that sturdy, edible and child-friendly flower. Now, in pesticide commercials we see this brave hardy little flower, struggling up from the earth, making its way through a crack in a concrete driveway, only to have its life rudely and painfully snuffed out by being sprayed with "left over from WWII nerve gas, now re-invented as pesticides." You may be able to imagine my dismay–I can't watch as the commercial goes on to show the poor little plant wither and die right before your eyes. If this was an "abused animal appeal" PSA, the creature would look at you with sad puppy dog eyes and say, "What did I ever do to you?" Unfortunately, there are no agencies to help protect the many often indigenous, hardy plants that our "civilized society" has condemned as weeds. I don't quite understand why so many of our other earthling species designed with a strong survival instinct are "frowned upon" and are designated to be eliminated by society. I was encouraged, however, a few years ago when crossing the border from the US into Canada. There I saw acres and acres of meadows glowing golden in the sunlight full of my dear little dandelions. Maybe they are welcome in other places?)

So once again back to the past:

In my early years, each week I went with Mum and brother Harry to a basement office in the Cunard/White Star Building at the Pier Head in Liverpool to pick up Dad's pay. Martins Bank, on the High Street in Wavertree, was where Mum had her savings account. She made a deposit there each time she managed–through extreme thrift–to save a few shillings or even pounds. When I was quite young, I can remember her showing me her savings book with an amount of over a hundred pounds, quite an achievement in those hard times.

Due to the severe experience of the Depression, she always saved as much as she could. *(See photo on page 198.)*

Dad had first started work with the Cunard/White Star when he was about sixteen or seventeen; his initial intent was to become a purser, a sort of accountant. But very soon he learned that the stewards in First Class made a much better income from generous tips, so he transferred to become a steward.

On his trips to the States, he bought furniture—all art-deco stuff for our home including a rosewood gramophone; he also provided many records. We spent many hours winding up the handle on the side and playing the records of the day. On one of his earlier trips in 1929, he and some of his shipmates visited Chicago, only to arrive there on the day of the St. Valentine's Day Massacre. He had very strong opinions on the foolishness of allowing all and sundry to possess guns. Of course, in Britain even the police did not carry firearms, with consequently less mayhem.

In fact, during my childhood, and actually all my life in Britain, we regarded the bobbies as friends. We did not call our police "cops"; that was thought to be a derogatory expression. As children we were encouraged to search out a bobby "on the beat" if we ever needed help, for instance, to cross a busy street full of traffic. We even had a song that went, "If you want to know the time, ask a policeman. If you want to cross the street, ask a policeman." I took this advice quite often when on my trips to the library. Most bobbies walked the "beat" and were readily available to help all citizens whenever needed. All had those distinctive helmets, and some bobbies rode bikes.

(Writing this in 2014 after the shooting of Arizona senator Gabby Giffords, I wonder if the Brits' courteous attitude toward our law enforcement officers and the discouraging of personal gun ownership may have been more sensible, or safer.)

As I edit this memoir, more horrific shooting "incidents" in the United States are continually taking place. Most folks in the United States acknowledge "guns," particularly assault weapons, really are a problem. Even many who belong to the NRA admit the same. So why can no action be taken? When will the public say "enough is enough"? Not yet obviously, not while there is money to be made on sales of these "toys." Well, since I am not running for office anywhere in the United States, I am not afraid to refer to these matters. Please citizens *think* and perhaps *act*.)

One of Dad's other adventures whilst working with Cunard involved "borrowing" a stagecoach. At family get-togethers, in these "modern days of motor cars," he used to laughingly—in a somewhat proud though shamefaced way—tell us that "once I was arrested for stealing a stagecoach!" Apparently, on one of the cruises, he and his pals—lads in their early twenties— had docked at a seaport on the Mexican coast. They took a trip into Mexico City and had a great time. In the midst of the great time, one of them realized they were due back on board pretty soon. There happened to be a stagecoach with four horses hitched up outside the cantina. Unable to find the driver, they "borrowed" the stagecoach in order to get back to their ship on time. They were apprehended a short while later and briefly arrested. However, after explaining their predicament, their captors facilitated their return to the ship by hastily driving them the remaining distance to the dock. Situations today are not treated so leniently. Perhaps a little more compassion could create less criminals?

Dad and many of his shipmates also found a means to acquire extra income on their trips to the US. Prohibition was in force at that time in the States, which proved very lucrative for organized crime. (As we see today, the criminalization of certain substances also lines the pockets of many predators instead of providing legally taxable revenue, as in the case of both liquor and cigarettes.) Using a concealed compartment onboard ship, Dad and his pals—as did most Britons—saw no harm in having a friendly drink. So, they decided as an "act of charity" to bring liquid aid to the deprived Americans. I don't think that adventure lasted very long, though.

It may have been due to Dad's extensive world travels that Mum was interested in the pen pal section on the back page of a magazine called *Woman's Companion*. She corresponded with people from all over the world. I would sit at Dad's feet whenever he was home and ask him about the places he'd visited: Cape Town, Sydney, Perth, Acapulco, Buenos Aires, Rio de Janeiro, Lima, New York, New Orleans, Los Angeles, Panama, Mexico City, and many, many more. Even as a very young child, I was keenly aware of the vastness and diversity of our planet and its many species. We had a globe of the world which I spent hours looking at, creating stories about the various places. I loved the name San Francisco and vowed to go there one day. I actually liked to wear a fez hat Dad had brought from Egypt.

(One interesting result of Mum's global letter writing happened during The Beatles years. One of her pen pals was Gwen Marsh, who lived in West Pennant Hills, New South Wales, Australia. During our childhood, the two would exchange family photos. So it happened when The Beatles arrived in Adelaide during their Australian Tour—greeted at the airport by some 300,000 fans—George found, to his surprise, at one of their stops, photos of us Harrison kids in all the newspapers. Naturally, Gwen was very proud to have been a family friend since long before FAME hit us.

Mum's interest in letter writing came into play very conveniently when—in the early Beatles days—she and Dad began receiving at first hundreds and later thousands of fan letters per day in Liverpool. Their immediate impulse was to respond to all of these fans. Their attitude was this: since all these people admired their son and his pals, the least they could do was to "give back the love." And so it transpired they would spend their evenings sitting across the kitchen table from each other, Dad hand addressing the envelopes and Mum writing a short letter to each person. *(See photo on page 207.)*

While George visited me in Illinois, he'd given me a copy of the first issue of *The Beatles Book*, a monthly magazine devoted exclusively to Beatles news. Impressed with the publication, I'd written a letter to the editor to compliment him. I signed off as "Louise, Benton, Illinois." He published

Dear Johnny,

I have just read the first two issues of "The Beatles Book" and wanted to let you know how much I enjoyed them. They are especially interesting to me as George is my youngest brother. He and my "middle" brother Peter are visiting me at St. Louis. This has been a great occasion for me and my family as it is now eight years since I last saw my brothers. My son Gordon, 6 years, and daughter Leslie, 4 years, have not met their uncles before.

We are all great admirers of The Beatles and the children know most of their songs (just this morning Leslie announced "The world is treating me bad—misery").

Judging by the local teenage reaction to the records I have by "The Beatles" I am quite confident they could do very well here in the U.S.

By the way, who does the little pen sketches of the boys shown in the No. 2 issue? they are really good and I hope you will continue to use that idea.

Well that is all just now,

Cheerio from Louise,
Benton, Illinois 62812, U.S.A.

Johnny Dean writes:
Thanks for your letter Louise. John, Paul and Ringo tell me they want to visit America next year with George. The drawings you mention are done by Bob Gibson.

my letter in the magazine; subsequently, I too, was then deluged with Beatles mail—from all over the world—addressed only to Louise, Benton, Illinois. Funnily enough, it took the mail carriers there some weeks to figure out where to deliver all this mail! In response to my parents' urging, I also set out to reply to as many as possible and "give back the love.")

During my childhood, most of my—and my subsequent brothers'—clothing was either knitted or sewn by Mum. My favorite knitted outfit consisted of an outer coat, leggings, and a beret, all in a lovely plum color. Throughout my childhood, that outfit, as I grew out of it, was unraveled and made into a series of sweaters and other garments. **Frugal** could have been Mum's middle name!

At times Mum would take Harry and me to the large department stores such as Blacklers and Lewis', TJ Hughes, and various others. The trips were more for an excursion **to look** at stuff than **to buy**. I was constantly wandering off to explore. One day I discovered the escalator. I had lots of fun going up—I think at that time there were no downward escalators— and then I had to find either stairs or a lift/ elevator to come back down. I could always find Mum and Harry again, because—although there were no such things as cell phones, we had our own natural radar—Harry always trotted happily beside Mum, singing Irish folk songs. Whenever I was "lost," I would listen until I heard Harry singing "Danny Boy," or "The Rose of Tralee," then tracking the sound, find my way back to him and Mum. Fortunately there were no elephants in the store to attract my attention.

Blacklers was mostly famous for its large—about 12' tall—model parrot on a swing suspended from the ceiling. (Later, this was the store where Dad secured George his first job—as an electrical apprentice. After a short time, he left because— as he put it—"I kept blowing things up!" My younger grandson seems to have this trait. Although he is willing to help with any project, he steers clear of anything electrical! Other "Uncle George" traits he seems to have include a great compassion for those less fortunate. Last winter, for instance, he was really concerned about the many homeless veterans shivering in the cold and wanted to provide shelter for them. Unfortunately, we do not have the resources to follow his kind instincts. My other grandson, however, is a graduate of Full Sail, in Orlando, Florida, and is a sound engineer. He is not only great with sound, but in a recent tour of Asia had to rewire equipment in several theaters and has recently built his own computer. He is also my engineer on the audio version of this book and other spoken word projects of mine.)

Throughout our childhood, we never had the impression of being poor. In fact, once I started school at the Christmas after my fourth birthday, I was the envy of many of the other kids because, unlike their "store bought" clothes, mine—especially my homemade dresses with very full flared skirts—had so much more pizzaz. One day, my "show-off Leo" self was twirling around to show how wonderful my dress was when one of my classmates grabbed the skirt and tore it from the top of the dress. It was hand sewn, so was relatively easy to destroy. However, Mum just sewed it back together with tighter stitches and told me, "Stop showing off all the time!"

I suppose I was a pretty precocious, or even obnoxious, child. I had blonde curly hair, and due to my very outgoing Leo personality, my parents were constantly being told, "Oh, she's just like Shirley Temple. She should be in the movies." Knowing this opinion of me was expressed so often, convinced me that I was destined to be a movie star. I think the kindest assessment of me—by my teachers on an early report card—was that "Louise is quite a handful"—as if this was news to my parents!

One day when I first started school, we were given modeling clay and were told to make a model of what we would be when we grew up. We had to make a drawing and put the model on it. I made a model of me, in the spotlight, taking a bow. My best friend, Philomena, made a model of herself kneeling down praying, with God's light shining upon her. I was quite taken aback when our teacher thought we were both depicting ourselves becoming nuns at prayer. But I didn't argue; I was beginning to learn that **silence** could be beneficial at times.

Another recollection from my early school years was being cast as one of six ponies in a school play. We performed in the school hall for the parishioners just before Christmas. I don't recall the subject matter, but likely something religious. The ponies wore headdresses with a kind of eight-inch tall plume rising from the circlet on our heads. Having seen lots of horses nearby in stables in the Cobbles leading from the High Street to the Groves, I knew they shook their heads up and down a lot and whinnied, so in the interest of accuracy, I—as we were prancing around—shook my head also. However, in my enthusiasm, my plume fell down over my face. I paused for a moment, grinned sheepishly at the audience, adjusted the plume, and continued prancing. The audience howled with laughter, much to my satisfaction. Already I enjoyed causing laughter! So, as the play continued and my plume kept falling down, both I and the audience were having lots of fun. But, when the play was over, I was almost beheaded by the furious teacher producing the play! "Louise, you ruined the entire play; how dare you! You were supposed to be a pony in the background and you kept making people laugh, taking their minds from the real story!" So I guess, as much as I thought I was destined for showbiz, I didn't pass that particular audition? Mind you, although they did not know of the tongue lashing I had endured, many of the people in the audience patted me fondly on the head after the show, saying how much they enjoyed my "performance." I still remember how much fun I had despite the disapproval of my teacher!

Those first school years opened my eyes to much more than mere reading, writing, and arithmetic. Our Lady's was not far from a Church of England school, and I was soon to learn of the totally vicious hostility existing between the students of each of these schools. Students from our school were known as the Cattylics, and the others were the Proddydogs. These labels were apparently a sufficient reason for us to "hate" and try to destroy each other. These opposing factions would occasionally ambush each other, throwing stones and other missiles, so at times it was pretty dangerous simply going to school. Although we were all Christians, for some incomprehensible reason, we were encouraged by those "in authority" to behave with much hostility toward each other. It was drummed into us that Roman Catholicism was the "one true" religion. I can remember having a very long argument once that I was not a "Roman," I was an ENGLISH Catholic! As I progressed through life, I found that there are throughout the world literally dozens of "true" religions whose adherents are just as hatefully inclined to all the others. I also learned from Dad's non-organized religious point of view that so long as we are striving to reach our Creator—and doing so with kindness and compassion toward all other earthlings—then whichever path we choose will likely get us there. How very tolerant.

(I have been proud of my baby brother, who during his adult life entered into a very public spiritual quest. I am proud that he never asserted self-importantly, "I have found the only one true religion" He merely related *his belief* that within us, our life force known as a soul, is a drop of God. We all share a drop of that same force. It is up to each individual to either embrace or reject that drop of divinity within. At least those ideas shouldn't create yet another world war. Though unfortunately wars and hatred, fuelled by ignorance, just seem to be escalating in the 21st century.)

Mom and Dad, I realized much later in life, were quite an exceptional couple. Dad was a highly intelligent man, very likely of genius level. He was calm and thoughtful, had a very strong personal presence, a generally gentle demeanor, and a quiet sense of humor. Nowadays, I visualize him as the lighthouse standing firmly on the solid rocks, shining a bright light on our surroundings to help us better know how to avoid crashing on the treacherous rocks of life. He would smile and nod his head in approval when Mum, always ready for "a good laugh," was being particularly goofy. Whenever I came across problems I didn't understand, I would turn to Dad for answers.

One day when I was only about four or five, a teacher had yelled at me calling me a "sinner," so I asked Dad, "What is a sinner?" Now, Dad was not a Catholic, and for that matter did not have too much respect for most of the so-called "organized religions." (He would have loved Bill Maher.) He did, however, have respect for "The Creator" or "Supreme Being," but on that occasion he merely told me not to worry about it… "You are too little to know how to sin."

At school, I was getting a different message. I was being told I had to kneel down in church and pray to ask God to make me into a good girl. After several weeks of kneeling and ardently begging, "Please, God, make me into a good girl," I was dismayed to notice I wasn't growing wings and I didn't have one of those shiny round things glowing around my head, so it seemed I wasn't getting to be good yet. Frustrated, I again went to Dad. "How will I know when God turns me into a good girl?" I suppose I had read too many books where a fairy Godmother could zap you with a magic wand and change you into a princess or a frog, so I expected the "good girl" transformation to occur in a sparkling flash, complete with wings and a halo. That, after all, was how the good ones looked in the church's stained glass windows.

I will always remember Dad's "non-organized-religion-type" reply. He suppressed a chuckle, his eyes twinkling, and told me—though not perhaps in these exact words—"Well, Lou, if you try to be kind and helpful to everyone, don't ever do anything to harm or injure any other living being, then if you can do that—no matter what anyone says—you ARE being good." This may not have been what any priest would have told me, but I trusted Dad more than anyone else, so I've tried to follow this seemingly simple— but I realized much later on—all inclusive advice. This same advice he gave to all of us.

As I grew older, he added other advice originating from Shakespeare: *"This above all, to Thine own self be true,"* and he explained the concept that "one's own self," or the life force within the body, was actually a tiny spark or drop of God, or Our Creator. Whatever you do or think, God is within you and is aware of those thoughts and actions, so it is not possible to go behind God's back to do nasty things without God knowing. Pretty much the same as the teachings my brother's later Spiritual search came to acknowledge.

(Unfortunately, most people seem to think if they show up at some public place of worship and be sanctimonious for an hour a week, they can then do as many rotten things as they wish. I was horrified when a person who claimed to be "saved" told me, "Once you accept Jesus as your savior, anything you do afterwards is *forgiven* because Jesus died for our sins." What a crock! And, how convenient if you are so brainwashed that you are blindly locked into one tiny schism. You then excuse yourself and take no responsibility for any future wrong doing. I sometimes joke that if Jesus was here today, his theme song would be "Please Don't Let Me Be Misunderstood." How tragic that His kind and loving teachings have been so badly hijacked and misinterpreted. I prefer to believe most of my readers—as Beatle People—do not fall into this category; we tend to take responsibility for our actions and seek Love and Peace rather than Hate and Fear.)

Another incident during my early childhood years put the fear of DOG into me! Mum's oldest brother, Uncle Johnny, the only person we knew who ever owned a dog, had a black Labrador named Nero. This animal had one blue eye and one brown eye. When I was about two, I was in a room with Nero, who was lying on a couch near a doorway, his head resting on the arm of the couch. I can see the scene quite clearly even now. The door was covered with a heavy red velvet curtain to keep out drafts. Wandering over to look at Nero, I was fascinated at the sight of his two different colored eyes. This is all I consciously recall. I was later told that perhaps I had tried to touch his eyes because he bit me through my nose and lips. Mum had been in the next room and, on hearing me cry out, rushed in. When she saw my injured face, she lamented, "This is going to disfigure her for life!" Then another in my series of trips to the Children's Hospital took place. They must have had some pretty good surgeons, as apart from two tiny hollows on the tip of my nose, there is very little evidence of the incident. But afterwards, for the remainder of my childhood, I would take the long way home if it meant having to pass a dog. Fortunately, very few people could afford the expense of a dog, so there were not too many around.

Bathrooms were also in short supply in 1930s Liverpool. We had a flush toilet in a little room at the end of the backyard. However it was not until I was eighteen and on my Christmas holiday from college that we moved into a house (at Upton Green) complete with a bathroom. During my childhood, Saturday night was "bath night." We had a galvanized tub, about 3-1/2 feet long x 2 feet across. This hung on the wall in the backyard when not in use. On Saturday the fire would be stoked up all day. Mum usually also made homemade bread, which was cooked in the oven heated by the fire. We had a large iron kettle, which we heated to provide hot water for our baths. We had only cold water coming from the tap in the kitchen. Water for cooking, tea and baths had to be heated on the fire. (Eventually we bought a small two-ring gas stove for cooking—quite a luxury then. We did have gas light.)

I recall an incident one bath night when Harry was about three years old. I had finished my bath and it was his turn to get into the tub, but that night he was in a really grumpy mood and despite Mums entreaties, he refused to get ready for his bath. Finally Mum lost patience with him and yelled, "That's enough, you *will* have a bath." At that he said "all right!" and stepped into the tub of warm water fully dressed, shoes and socks, pant, hand knitted underwear and sweater. Every item of clothing, soaking wet, was stuck to him like glue. It took Mum a very long time to remove all his clothes and his shoes were ruined. But even as Mum struggled to peel his clothing from his wet body, I remember she started to chuckle, and although I had been standing beside the tub all apprehensive, I joined in the laughter too. Mum said to me, "I'll think twice before I get mad at HIM again; he certainly won that round." Subsequently Harry was always able to disperse Mum's ire by joking with her. I remember whenever she was upset with him about something, he would laughingly say, "Mum, don't go on and on, and on and on, and on and on, and on and on" until she would laugh back and hug him in forgiveness. Looking back, I realize affection and humor always saved the day!

During Dad's two-week paid vacation each year, before the war started, he and Mum would book a cottage in Anglesey, or some other Welsh seaside resort. Throughout the remainder of my childhood we mostly spent our vacation each year visiting North Wales; we have numerous photos of ourselves standing in front of ancient castles, or ruins. However, very many years later when we were all fully grown, and one of us had even become a Beatle, there was an interesting turn of events connected with one of our castle photos.

(As most of my readers know, George and Pattie bought and lived in a lovely "stately home" known as Friar Park in Henley on the Thames. But before they found their "dream home," they had spent many months exploring Britain looking for just the right one. After one such excursion, when George arrived back to visit Mum and Dad, he was telling them of the strange feeling of déjà-vu he had experienced when visiting one of their potential purchases. He told Mum and Dad "I was standing in front, before going inside, and I had this strange creepy feeling that I had been there before—it just seemed so *real*." Mum asked, "In North Wales, what was the name of the house?" and George replied "Gwyrich Castle." At that, Mum and Dad both started to laugh and Mum took out our family photo album; lo and behold, there in front of Gwyrich Castle stood Dad with his two young sons, Peter and approximately five-year-old George. At that George was able to join in the laughter and say, "Oh, so I wasn't going crazy; I really had been there before in this same life." *(See photo on page 199.)* But as Mum and Dad pointed out, it *was* a rather different life in one way; this time you were looking to *buy* the place rather than just be photographed in front of it!")

I think it was when I was seven that my Granddad French died in the springtime. That year we went to the Isle of Man, located in the Irish Sea to the northwest of Liverpool. Dad told me later that this particular trip was not so much a holiday/vacation as an opportunity for Mum to grieve the loss of her dad. This island was famous for the TT motorcycle races held there each year.

The cottage we rented that year was located at the far end of the Isle of Man at an area known as Langness Point. This was a very narrow peninsular with cliffs on one side, a meadow where livestock grazed, and gently sloping rocky terrain on the other side. There was a lighthouse near our cottage, and we became friends with the lighthouse keeper's family and spent much time there. We were allowed to climb the narrow stone spiral staircase, which was built out from the wall and wound all the way up to the beacon room. It had no handrail on the outer edge of the steps, so it was prudent to really hug the walls.

Our rented cottage was very remote! Except for the lighthouse, there were no other signs of habitation for many miles, and it was a long walk into the village. There was an outhouse some twenty feet away from the cottage, and it was very scary to have to go after dark. There was a covered deck around the cottage, and at one end was a large rain barrel, which was our source of drinking water. For us there was no such thing as radio or TV. In the evenings we would sit around the fireplace and tell stories. After Harry and I went to bed, it was very comforting to hear Dad reading aloud to Mum while she was busy knitting. One evening as we all sat inside laughing and joking, we were suddenly stunned to silence when we heard rather loud, slow-moving footsteps outside on the verandah. For several moments, we sat in apprehensive awe, wondering what "monster" or stray human was about to make itself known. Dad took the iron poker from the fireplace and quietly walked over to the door and—just as the footsteps stopped outside—flung the door open, with raised poker in his hand. The intruder thrust its curious head into the doorway and greeted us with a friendly MOOOOO! Dad gently shoo-ed "Betsy" back into the field, after making sure she had the refreshing drink she was searching for from the water barrel. Naturally, this was another wonderfully comic story to add to our series of family adventures, known thereafter as "The night of the MOO-nster!"

Another evening Mum had walked into the village to get some milk. By the time she was on her way back and getting close to our cottage, the sun had set, and it was quite dark. She could hear what sounded like a group of people talking in rather conspiratorial tones not too far away. The conversation seemed a bit hostile, and as she walked she was getting nearer. With no means at all to call Dad for help, she just kept on walking—and as she told us later—the Irish in her was hoping the chattering would just be ghosts! After a few hundred yards she found herself face to face with the talkative group. It was not a ghost, nor a Moo-nster, just a rusty wind driven sort of water pump, rattling and grinding in the light evening breezes. With a sigh of relief Mum continued to the cottage ready to give us a good laugh when she told of her scary adventure. Having a "good laugh" was one of Mum's favorite pastimes!

Back in the early 1930s, life was so very different! Before automation, there were lots of jobs that do not exist today. For instance, each week the rent man would stop by to collect the ten shilling weekly rent. An insurance man would come by to collect the life insurance fee. Being admittedly precocious, I wanted to know what insurance was all about. Mum told me she and Dad paid a shilling each a week for life insurance. Naturally enough, I wanted to know why they did not have it for me too. After all, I didn't want to die either. When Mum explained to me that life insurance did not stop you from dying, it just helped pay for your funeral, my logical young brain thought, "Why pay for life insurance if you still die?" If I had been aware of these words then, I would have called it a "R.I.P-Off."

(Looking at the extremely profitable multi-faceted insurance business now in the 21st century, maybe I was not too far wrong in my assessment?)

Other weekly pre-war visitors included the tea man, a salesman who came with a suitcase filled with packages of tea and some sweets/candies. Mum used to buy a bar of Kit-Kat for us to share. There was also the rag and bone man, who would pick up items which were not trash, but could be reused, which—in today's world—would be known as recycling.

Another weekly visitor was Iky (Isaac) Orlins. He collected money he had loaned for the only item my parents ever bought on what was known as hire-purchase: a Singer hand-operated sewing machine. After the Depression, Mum and Dad bought only the items they could pay for completely in cash. In this case, Mum knew she could make up for the seven pound price of the Singer by making more of our clothes herself—clothes my schoolmates could not easily rip apart. The way most people thought of hire-purchase was this: if you cannot afford to purchase, you pay much higher! Might be a good thought to keep in mind with today's almost mandatory credit system. During the months Iky collected his payment, he was trying to get Mum to let him adopt me. I guess he didn't know what he might be letting himself in for. Apparently, he and his wife were quite wealthy and were childless, but Mum told him NO! I guess for some strange reason she wanted to keep me.

I've spoken a lot about Dad and his calm wisdom. Mum, on the other hand, though quite bright, was much more of a firecracker—very vivacious, full of fun and laughter, but capable of the occasional flash of anger when we children were naughty. She would strike fear into Harry and I by saying, "Just wait until your Dad gets home and I tell him what you did!!!"

My visualization of Mom is the view of the night sky on "firework" night, November 5th, Guy Fawlkes Night in England. The excitement caused by the whizzing sounds, the beauty of the sparkles in the sky, spectators gasping in awe and delight—that is how it was to be around Mum. Whenever *she* arrived at an event, that's when the fun began. (More about this aspect of Mum when we come to the Royal Command Performances during Beatle days.)

In retrospect, despite Mum's threats of "telling Dad about our offences," we never suffered any physical harm from Dad. But, I can recall covering my face with my hands and begging, "Please, don't look at me with your eyes!" His punishment consisted of a look of stern disapproval from his usually friendly, good natured, but piercing brown eyes. To have him look at me with disapproval was the most terrible punishment I ever experienced.

My early childhood days were happy. We lived in an area known as The Groves located near the Picton Clock in Wavertree, known locally as "the clock tower." *(See photo on page 220.)* You could go from High Street up "the Cobbles," a short cobblestone street in which were located some stables and a smithy. You then arrived at Arnold Grove, Albert Grove, and Chestnut Grove. A short distance from there was Our Lady of Good Hope Catholic Church and its companion school. (I'm sure many readers have been on "The Beatles Tour" during visits to Liverpool.)

We lived at 12 Arnold Grove, and my maternal grandmother, "Nanny French," lived at 9 Albert Grove, along with some of my four uncles, who would come and go. (When it became virtually impossible for George to travel unnoticed as a Beatle, he sometimes booked his travels under the name Arnold Groves.) Our family spent a lot of time doing things together; for instance, our uncles would sometimes take Harry and I to Calderstones Park or Sefton Park and take us rowing on the lakes—a real treat. There were many really wonderful parks in Liverpool, and Mum would take us to them often. We also embarked on the ferry across the Mersey many times to go to New Brighton, Wallasey, Seacombe, and other points along the river where there were beaches.

Another rather important factor of our upbringing—also significant when you consider The Curse—was how we regarded Christmas. Yes, we knew about Baby Jesus and the Wise Men, etc. We also knew the story of the rich gentleman from somewhere in Eastern Europe, maybe Russia, known as St. Nicholas, who long ago took gifts to the children in his town each Christmas. We also knew that lots of fat old men dressed up in red, put on long white beards and masqueraded as Santa Claus at this time of year. However, we were never expected to believe the impossible dream that jolly old Santa, aided by non-winged animals such as reindeer, could circle the Earth in one night, stopping to climb down chimneys—most of which in winter would have fires burning in them—

and deposit just the appropriate toys by the fireplace. Mum and Dad did not insult our intelligence with this fabrication. Most of our schoolmates were expected to believe this myth, though, and I can recall how upset they became when at about the age of six or seven, they found out "There is no Santa Claus."

Permit me a comment here from the vantage point of my now senior years: How can our society expect children to grow up to be honest when their own parents persist in "pulling the beard over their eyes" for the first few years of their lives? Oh, I know most people think it is a harmless stunt, and the most important thing is to move a lot of merchandise at this time of year. Our money-driven culture, with its cleverly-crafted—though often idiotic—commercials, seduces the public into spending more than they have—for things they do not need—and does not rely at all on "truth-iness"—as Stephen Colbert says. I wonder if many parents realize how bitterly disillusioned a six year old can feel when he or she finds out Mum and Dad have been lying to him about this most wonderful day of his or her life?? I suppose it does prepare them for the way things really are! All I can say is that although there have been so many times—due to our expectation of honesty in others—George and I have been severely ripped-off, how thankful I still am to have been raised by parents who, despite the prevailing mindset, stuck to the credo *"This above all...."*

I've told about many events and social patterns that prevailed in Britain in the early '30s, and although I could fill another chapter, I do want to get to WWII; you may enjoy it as much as we did!

Chapter Three

WORLD WAR II WARRIOR

WE SAY NO, TO FEAR. YES, TO HUMOUR AND DEFIANCE!

Shortly after my eighth birthday, there was a BIG happening! It was called The Declaration of War. The first effect this had on my life was in connection with my mum's brothers. Uncle Johnny, the eldest, was in the Irish Guards; George, the next, was in The Merchant Navy; Jimmy was in the Coldstream Guards; and Eddy (who was only seven years my senior) joined the Guards when he became sixteen. All four survived the war, but were very much involved. *(See photo on page 194.)*

Uncle Jimmy was in the Evacuation from Dunkirk, and I recall him telling of his experience. His battalion arrived at one part of the beach when the volunteer flotilla of small civilian boats arrived to help rescue them. His battalion was ordered into the water and told to swim out to the boats and do their best to board. The seas were rough and visibility poor. When he arrived at a relatively large ship, he was able to cling with his fingertips onto a narrow rim on the edge. One of his buddies came up behind him and tried to hold on to his coat. The few on board were reaching down to help the multitude of men in the water. Jimmy says he could feel his grip on the rim loosening, and his only way to survive was to kick his buddy off his coat. This 6' 2", twenty-year-old guardsman had tears of anguish rolling down his face as he told this story to us. Yes! We agreed as we heard this and many other similar tales, it must be terrible to be a soldier in a war....

...but that was before the air raids began, and we learned the soldiers weren't the only ones allowed to participate in a war. We children could "play" too! In fact, before long we were all issued gas masks and taught how to use them; they had to accompany us at all times. (Now, whenever I am at an event when veterans are asked to identify themselves, I stand with them; as far as I am concerned, it was not necessary to have been issued with a uniform, a weapon or receive a paycheck in order to be considered as having participated—with your life at risk—in a war. It turns out war is the most equal opportunity employer on the planet; no one is left out!)

My second brother, Peter, was born on Harry's sixth birthday in 1940. He was just an infant when the gas masks came on the scene, and babies were given full body-sized protection. These contraptions were designed to envelope the child and were so large they had to be put into the pram/baby carriage to accompany the infant. At that time, the only method of getting around was either to walk or take public transport. There were no private cars, or petrol to run them, available during the war. I recall Mum saying, "Well, I'm not taking *that* thing with me everywhere, so I will just leave MY gas mask at home, too." Harry and I were so concerned about this that we made a pact that in the event of a gas attack, we would not wear our masks either and risk becoming "awfuls." We did not know the real word was "orphans;" we had heard there were kids with no parents, and "awful" sounded to us the correct term for having no Mum and Dad. *(See photo on page 211.)*

About thirty years later, when I recounted the story of our pact to a friend, it occurred to me then that had there been a gas attack when we were in school, Mum may well have been at home and quite able to use both their masks, so Harry and I only saw the worst case scenario, and in retrospect, we need not have been so worried.

As is always the case, the ever-vigilant entrepreneurs made a good profit by creating "gas mask cases," which were more attractive than the cardboard boxes in which the masks were issued. They were a sleek shape, came in a variety of colors, had a shoulder strap and were considered quite a fashion statement.

Prior to Peter's birth in 1940, there had been no air raids in Liverpool. In June, though, Harry and I both had a really bad bout with whooping cough. Because of the risk to the expected new sibling, Harry was shipped off to Auntie Kathleen across the Mersey, and I was sent to a children's convalescent home in Hoylake, a seaside town just up the coast from Liverpool. (This is the town in which John Lennon's first wife, Cynthia Powell, lived.) This was my first time away from Mum and Dad, and I was horribly homesick. I cried most of the time until a nurse allowed me to write a letter home. However, once she read it, she refused to let me send it. She would not allow me to let my parents know how unhappy I was. During my stay at the home, my worst experience was being forced to eat a bowl of rice pudding. I normally enjoyed the rice pudding Mum made, but this one was made with very sour milk. The matron of the home stood over me while I struggled in tears of protest to get this "tasty treat" down. Once I finished it, nature fortunately took its course, and with relief I promptly threw up.

Shortly after this incident, I received a letter telling me that my new brother had arrived on the twentieth of July. Harry then claimed the new baby as his "birthday present." Dad joked with Mum at the time, "For us to have two sons on the same day shows it is a big day in history." As history proved in 1969—July 20 did turn out to be a big day—the day a human first set foot on the moon!

Mum asked me to choose one of three names for my new brother, and I chose Peter. I had to stay at this convalescent "home" for several more weeks because, unbeknownst to me at the time, Peter had been born with his intestines protruding into the umbilical cord. He had been rushed to Children's Hospital and, at a mere three hours old, underwent a successful operation. This particular procedure, called **exomphalos**, had never been performed successfully before in Britain. Peter was eleven and a half pounds at birth so had a much better chance of surviving. Finally, to my great relief, when he was about a month old I was able to go to my *real* home.

We were all so happy, but before long, the War came to Liverpool in the form of nightly air raids. At first, they were short and mostly directed at the docks. There were eleven miles of docks along the River Mersey, filled with lots of wartime activity. After about seven or eight months of air raids, Mum noticed an interesting phenomenon. The air raid sirens had two different tones: the "alert/warning" had a rising and falling tone, but the "all clear" was just one sustained tone. Mum noticed that each evening as soon as the warning sounded, Peter went off to sleep, but on the occasional night when we had no raid, he fussed and cried a lot before going to sleep. We were of course amused that this little fellow must have thought the sirens were singing his lullaby!

In reflecting on the events of the 21st century so far, I find the most interesting factor of my WWII experience to be the lack of fear! It could be that our leaders, including the royal family and Winston Churchill, were *not* wimps and did not encourage their countrymen and women, or children, to cower in fear. Oh, no! Even during the worst, sometimes eleven-hour raids over Liverpool, sitting on a mattress under the stairs, I felt only defiance.

Early in the war, all citizens were instructed to observe what was known as "Blackout"; in other words, all homes had to secure the windows with plywood and tar paper coverings in order that no chink of light might be visible to any enemy aircraft flying above. In fact, we were only allowed candlelight during the raids. Even traffic, like the bus Dad drove, had to have coverings over the headlights so that they could not be seen from above. This was just prior to the development of radar; at that time, as long as there were no lights visible from above, it was difficult for the enemy bombers to know just exactly where a high density population was located. Happily, most Brits are very "law abiding people," so this disguise of cities was pretty effective. Unlike the mindset I have experienced in the United States (i.e. the laws don't apply to me), we Brits do tend to understand that sensible laws should be obeyed and often save lives. Also, the life saved could be one's own!!

Though it became especially evident during The Beatles Era, Liverpudlians have long been known for their wit and humor. During the air raids, humour was a very real part of our defense. WE called the Germans "Jerrys," and co-incidentally, the commode—which in those days was usually kept conveniently under the bed in case of nocturnal bathroom trips—was also called The Gerry. One of our family favorite air raid funnies went like this:

Nanny French had become quite deaf and could not hear the air raid sirens, so since she lived nearby, we usually had her come to our house during the raid. *(See photo on page 193.)* One night, Uncle Johnny was home on leave and staying with Nanny at her own home. She was already in bed that night when the sirens wailed. Uncle Johnny called to her, "Mother, here's the Jerry!" and she calmly replied, "OK, just put it under the bed." Johnny, anxious to get his mother to come downstairs, then called "No mother, it's the other Gerry, the Germans." She then replied nonchalantly, "No problem, they can hide under the bed too!"

Another air raid funny, went like this: Fred and Joyce, a couple in our neighborhood, both worked shifts in the munitions factories. Joyce was known to be overly flirtatious. A few days earlier, they had suffered a direct hit on their house, resulting in a large hole in the roof. During the war, repairs were not possible, so the hole remained. On the night of this story, a raid was in progress and the couple was at home. At one point, Fred went into the kitchen to make a cuppa' (tea), leaving Joyce sitting in one of their fireside chairs. As luck would have it, during his absence, a landmine attached to a parachute, silently drifted down from the bomber above through the hole in the roof and nestled into Fred's vacant chair. The landmine itself was a six foot metal canister, and the parachute draped itself around the bomb, which was ticking loudly. Joyce was sitting staring in horror when Fred returned with the tea. Seeing the large form in his chair, he asked in anger, "Who's that you've snuck in here behind my back?" Joyce whispered apologetically, "But it's only a landmine, Luv!" Moments later, as the ticking increased in frequency, they both understood the situation and rushed out to find an air raid warden. As I recall, that landmine was dismantled and—apart from Fred's suspicions—caused no harm.

Another comedy of errors took place the night an active landmine exploded nearby. The landmine fell beyond the wall that separated the Groves from a more affluent area, but the blast also badly shook most of our homes. The middle wall in our home between the front room and the kitchen, where we were all sheltering under the stairs, was damaged, and the door between was crushed. An air raid warden was checking out all the homes for casualties. Since the blast had smashed most of the windows in our street, he could thrust his tin-hatted head through the openings and call out to those inside. When he came to our house, he did the same, only to find that he had crashed his head through the only intact pane of glass in the street! Naturally, we all had a good laugh at this mishap. We considered this episode another funny story to add to the continuous "hilarity" of the war.

We also had comic songs to make fun of our enemy: *We're goin'ta hang out our washing on the Siegfried line; have you any dirty washing mother dear? We're going to hang out our washing, if the Siegfried line's still there!!* The Siegfried Line was a series of defensive posts along the borders of Germany. We also had a song called "Run, Rabbit, Run," and it rhymed with Hun, but I don't recall the words to that one!

Apart from the physical damage caused by their bombs, our enemy also attempted to scare us with other ploys. For instance, for a period of time they had some kind of attachment which caused the bombs to make a "screaming noise" as they plummeted to the ground. We kids soon found this to be another big joke. We would run out into the backyard and yell up to the bombers—not that they could hear us of course—"If you want to *scare us,* you'll have to do better than making scary noises. We're not scared of you lot!"

(I recently spoke—mainly about The Beatles—to a 3rd grade class, but when I mentioned our defiant attitude and lack of fear during WWII, they were really interested and asked dozens more questions about it. This surprised me, but it later occurred to me that maybe American kids would be equally fearless and defiant had their leaders not been such knuckleheads after 9-11, creating all kinds of excessive security, thus giving the terrorists such a clear advantage over us.)

Of course, on the serious side of things, we did all visit the local town hall each day to read the "casualty lists" to find out who had lost their lives the night before. Even then, though, we would joke, "I'm not on the list today, so I'll just have to go in to work–or school—anyway!" There were times when a classmate would not show up, and we would say a prayer for his/her soul, but again we found a whimsical solace in the fact that the departed child didn't have to go to school anymore, or sit through any more air raids. There were no big 'boo-hoos' from us.

As the war progressed, most beaches in Britain were closed to the public, thus, we lost on our few sunny days our favorite form of relaxation. Rolls of barbed wire were strung out along the beaches to make it difficult for our enemies to land, should they attempt to invade. During this time, many enemy aircraft were shot down and vessels sunk. Oil and tar would wash up along the coasts, thus making the beaches unfit for us kids to enjoy. Sandbags were used extensively to help barricade buildings from bomb blasts. One day, some of my classmates and I found a sandbag that had been split open. This was, to us, like finding Long John Silver's treasure! We pulled and tugged the damaged bag to the "Wasteground," a vacant lot next to our school. Then we emptied the sand out and had our very own—rather tiny—beach! We spent hours with our little buckets and spades making sandcastles, and then we "dropped bombs" onto them so we could start all over again. We found this vastly entertaining. Back then, we did not have exploding video games to amuse us—we were much better off. We, on a daily basis, found no expense was spared to provide us with The Real Thing!

Early on in the war, we were all issued ration books. From what I recall, each person was allowed two ounces of butter per week, four ounces of margarine, two ounces of bacon, two shillings' worth of meat, a one-pound pot of jam/jelly per month, one can of fruit per month, one pound of sugar per month, and so on—I do not recall the amounts of all the other items, but literally every category of food was rationed at one time, including potatoes, bread, and milk.

With five or six ration books to our family, we usually took our meat ration in the form of a leg of lamb, which would be our Sunday dinner. I would go to the butcher's shop to pick up our ration. In those days, the entire animal carcass would be hanging inside the store, and the butcher would cut off the amount to which your ration entitled you. I recall one occasion when I was watching the butcher weigh the cut of lamb. There was a lot of commotion across the street where there had been a direct hit on a bomb shelter the night before. My attention was drawn to the scene. The air raid wardens were recovering body parts and stacking them on the sidewalk in an effort to reassemble bodies for identification. I looked back at the meat on the scales, and it struck me that this was the body part of yet another creature. For months afterward, I could not tolerate the idea of eating meat.

Eggs were like gold. We would get an "allocation" of one egg per person about every six weeks. The egg shortage was mainly due to the severe bombing; the stressed hens were not producing many, and as most foods were in really short supply, priority was given to feeding the troops. Mum would bake homemade bread each week, and it was a big day when the egg allocation came around. Tea Time on **that** Sunday featured homemade bread—spread with our butter ration— and the "piece de resistance," a soft-boiled egg each. What luxury! Wow! What a feast!

A grassroots movement became popular as the war progressed. Most working class city homes did not have enough land on which to grow vegetable gardens, therefore many families rented a small lot about 20' x 60' on the outskirts of town. These plots were known as allotments; several of my uncles had them. These small gardens were a tremendous help. They provided fresh vegetables, potatoes, carrots, peas, lettuce, tomatoes, cucumbers, radishes, etc. to supplement our meager rations. Many folks also kept hens, and I can assure you, those people were very popular! This custom became a very vital part of our survival. A slogan "Dig for Victory" became well known and the plots became known as "victory gardens." Apple trees were native to Britain, so we did have those. Also, a variety of small berries grew wild in the hedgerows, but it was possible to transplant them and help them thrive. So blueberries, blackberries, raspberries, gooseberries and also strawberries—the latter did not come from the hedges, but grew on the ground—could be added to our diet. More exotic items, for instance oranges or other citrus fruits, we saw only at Christmas, and only then if the shipping convoys from either the United States or the Mediterranean arrived safely after crossing the U-Boat infested oceans and seas. We were aware of the odds, so it was a grand Christmas morning if we kids each had both an apple *and* an orange in the foot of our hand knitted socks, which had been hung with great hopes at the fireside the night before. Bananas did not reach our country until my brother Peter was about seven years old. That was when he actually saw a banana for the first time. This may not seem a "big deal," but it indicates the difference between then and now!

For the richer folks there was the black market. They would pay the larger families for the use of some of their ration books, thereby getting more to eat. The larger and inevitably poorer families could not afford their full amount of allowable rations in any case. We were okay; Dad had a steady job and, until 1943, just three children.

The everyday Brits were busy conserving materials to be reused, such as empty tin food cans, which we collected to be made into artificial limbs for injured troops. We also dropped off our kitchen waste, such as potato peelings and cabbage stalks, to be used as pig food. It was quite a long walk to both of these collection sites, but knowing it was the correct way to behave, we collected with great enthusiasm.

Another memory from those air-raid days I actually recounted a few years ago at a Michael Moore rally at the University of Arkansas. The rally was part of a presidential campaign, but focused on "lets not get into another war type theme." I was invited by Michael to speak, and I told of the following wartime incident:

"At the height of the raids, we kids had been talking in the school yard one day. We were all "full of fire" as to how we would tear to shreds any "Gerries" who showed their faces in Liverpool. That night during the bombing, I started up with some of our kid bravado rhetoric. Mum quieted me down, and to my surprise, said, "You know how Uncle Jimmy and Johnny used to take you out to the parks and take you rowing on the lakes?" "Yes," I replied somewhat doubtfully, wondering what this had to do with the bombs still falling around us.

"Well," she continued, "those Gerries in the planes up there probably have nieces and nephews and they probably would much rather be taking them to the park than flying up there being shot at and having to drop bombs on people they don't even know. It is not the soldiers or airmen who start wars; they are just the ones who get wounded and killed. It is the rich owners of the bomb factories and their friends who decide to create wars because they can make a lot of money from selling bombs and guns and bullets; they are the ones you should want to 'tear limb from limb'" (quoting my tirade).

Naturally this "out of left-field point of view" had never occurred to me before and certainly was not a mainstream idea, but all those years later at an anti-war rally, it was the perfect story to relate.

I know the common wisdom takes the view that "troops fight wars," but in my experience the so-called civilians are just as involved. We spent months in a classroom with no roof; when it rained (rather often in Britain) we wore our raincoats, and our teacher would hold an umbrella over her head. I learned the "real truth" that no matter how many wars are fought, how many are maimed, and how much blood is shed; there is *never* a definitive winner (except perhaps a cynical billionaire in a bunker somewhere). The hate and fear keeps festering and eventually spreads to another generation and another part of the world.

This brings me to tell you about an item I have treasured for many years. It was given to me by my Dad—a copy of a speech by Alexander the Great in (note the date): 324 BC. This oath has been quoted by Ptolemy (from Alexander's diary), Plutarch and Eratosthenes. The following version of the pledge is taken from an online source—the Ready to Go Ebooks website—which acknowledges that "over the centuries wording has been changed, but the main points are still there." According to history, 9,000 people were present at this speech.

I insert it here to let my readers see for themselves just how far our so-called 'civilization' has regressed in the past couple of thousand years! War, hate and greed have never solved our problems, but perhaps we can one day Imagine... Love and Peace?

The Pledge of Alexander the Great, 324 BC

It is my wish now that wars are coming to an end, that you should all be happy in peace.

From now on, let all mortals live as one people, in fellowship, for the good of all. See the whole world as your homeland, with laws common to all, where the best will govern regardless of their race. Unlike the narrow minded, I make no distinction between Greeks and Barbarians.

*The origin of citizens, or the race into which they were born, is of no concern to me. I have only **one** criterion by which to distinguish their virtue.*

For me, any good foreigner is a Greek, and any bad Greek is worse than a barbarian. If disputes ever occur among you, you will not resort to weapons, but will solve them in peace. If need be, I shall arbitrate between you.

See God not as an autocratic despot, but as the common father of all, and thus your conduct will be like the lives of brothers within the same family.

I on my part, see you all as equal, whether you are white or dark-skinned. And I should like you not simply to be subjects of my Commonwealth, but members of it, partners of it.

To the best of my ability, I shall strive to do what I have promised.

Keep as a symbol of love this oath, which we have taken tonight with our libations.

What a pity this wise person lived only into his early thirties.

Comment: My experiences in WWII, and observations regarding the present day, ongoing international conflicts, lead me to offer these thoughts for your consideration.

From what we know of history from Roman times on down, the "wealthy ruling class" have often been thoughtless, self-centered, and greedy. Today there are many good and decent super rich folks who are offering to make the correct decisions but it seems that in our present century, some of the rich, are much worse, and much more powerful than in the past. Unfortunately, the corporate interests—at present—have the upper hand. They run a vast foxy media propaganda machine, feeding the simpler folks amongst us with outrageous "facts," and doing it in such a crafty way that many good-hearted, decent people are being horribly misled and urged to vote against their own best interests. Thus, for the first time in many years, they are destroying the effectiveness of democracy because the power is not with the people anymore. I would urge all thinking Beatle people to gather your information carefully before making important decisions. If you understand the message of love and peace, which The Beatles brought to the planet, seek out those who also think in terms of compassion, kindness, tolerance, fairness and harmony. If you do this, I believe you will not go far wrong in making correct decisions. It has been my experience in life that if enough good folks "come together," "we can work it out"!

Now, in the 21st century, I am somewhat encouraged to witness the resurgence of "little people with big hearts." For example: the Wisconsin and other state protests—also, the

Keep Money Out and the Occupy Wall Street movements, resisting the control of the powerful and greedy "suits." We, the people, are starting to push back. However, the hundreds of millions being poured into politics is quite obscene. Also, the concerted efforts to curtail the voting privileges of major segments of our population—in another era I believe would be considered close to treason.

But, should my worst fears become reality, we will have all the more reason to Come Together for the sake of "we the people." I think you all know where The Beatles fit in to this scenario.

If this is published I guess we shall know that there is at least one company with integrity.

Chapter Four

EVACUATION TO WALES

*T*he war became routine to us. We would check the casualty lists posted at the Wavertree Town Hall each morning to see if we had lost any friends overnight. Then off to school we went to sit in "air-conditioned" discomfort. Of course, no one had invented air-conditioning at that time, but we had it anyway: A large part of the roof had been blown off, so, as I mentioned briefly in Chapter Three, on rainy days our teacher would hold an umbrella over her head, and we kids would put on our macs/raincoats. Just to explain—whenever bomb damage occurred, there were no resources to repair anything. In most cases, we salvaged whatever was possible, but in the case of complete destruction, the site would just be left to become a rather dangerous, though perhaps exciting, playground. So until several years after the War ended—when building materials and manpower once again became available—the visible destruction from the raids just remained.

As the war progressed there was a brief spell when we had classes at a nearby convent, the Cenacle in Lance Lane. Meanwhile, many of our surviving schoolmates were "evacuated" into remote parts of the countryside where little or no bombing took place. Mum resisted this concept. She firmly believed that we were much safer under their care than with any of the families who took in evacuees. But after a devastating series of raids in Liverpool, an announcement was made that evacuation of all school children was to be made compulsory. Mum and Dad discussed this at length and came to the conclusion that Harry and I would have a better chance of being assigned a good home if we went with the next smaller batch of evacuees, rather than in the event of compulsory evacuation for *all* school age children. And so it was that with our jute backpacks, nametags, and all our worldly goods, the two of us set off by train to Wales. This happened, I think, early in 1942 when I was ten and Harry would have been seven.

We were familiar with North Wales, particularly Caernarvon, because we'd been there during Dad's annual two week paid holiday a couple of times. We also took a vacation to the Isle of Man on one occasion. Unlike most of the other evacuees who'd never ventured far from their own backyards, Harry and I were pretty experienced at travelling. After a long train journey to Lampeter, we went by bus to a tiny village named Cilcennin. This village was so remote it only had once a week bus service to the nearest town, Aberaeron. The German bombers would never find us there!

Harry was assigned to the James family, who had two teenage sons. Since his name was Harold **James** Harrison, he felt right at home and became very much their youngest son. I went to live with a childless couple in their mid-thirties, and I knew them as Mr. and Mrs. Jones. They were kind to me, and I'd lots of freedom to roam around the countryside when not at school. The school in the village was about four miles from their home, so I walked there and back each day, staying at school for lunch and munching blueberries from the hedges along the way back and forth.

Although the concept of evacuation was to provide safety for children, I found there were far more alarming factors in the country, than anything the Germans could think up! For instance, on my four-mile walk to school each day, I had to pass the next farm, some quarter of a mile from the Joneses'. This farmer owned about eight cows and a bull, some pigs, and a flock of geese. The geese were protected by a fearsome gander. This gander would block my path each morning and confront me, hissing loudly. Sometimes, I'd to push my way through a nearby hedge into a field to avoid this very scary creature. The Joneses, with a smaller farm, had two cows, three pigs, and a lot of hens. It became my task to collect the eggs from underneath the sitting hens each morning. I quickly learned how to do this without being pecked at! I had become quite fond of their pigs, and although I don't remember their names, all the animals did have Welsh names. It became my task to bring the pigs and the cows in from the field at night into the barn.

During my explorations about a mile from the Jones' farm, I discovered a river; it was about 20' wide, and though not very deep, was fast flowing. At one point a tree had fallen cross the river; the trunk was about 16" in diameter, and this I found made a great 'bridge'. Thus I was able to cross the river and continue exploring. Returning to my bridge a couple of hours later, there had been quite a downpour of rain, and I found the trunk of my wonderful bridge to be very slippery. So, instead of bravely walking like a "high wire performer" as I had earlier, I found myself crawling across the tree, holding on for "dear life" and quite apprehensive of the now much faster flowing waters some twenty feet beneath my perch. It amazes me now when I think back that I was undaunted by that experience and made frequent trips over my bridge afterwards. There were no other children within miles, so all of my adventures were solo; after my precarious first return trip I didn't tell Mr. and Mrs. Jones about my bridge, so there was no one to tell me no. I probably wouldn't have given up my bridge anyway.

There were two other experiences that, in comparison, made the air raids seem like the proverbial stroll in the park. One day, Mrs. Jones told me we were to have a new, plentiful supply of ham and bacon. This sounded like pretty good news because I knew these things to be in very short supply back in Liverpool.

However, what happened next was so horrifying to me that I can still hear the screams. A man came and took one of the pigs, tied her up by her feet, and plunged a kind of spike into her neck. The poor creature struggled and screamed. (Recounting this some seventy years later, I am still moved to tears.) I ran away to the nearby river and returned a couple of hours later. By then, the butcher had finished his gruesome job and slabs of meat were neatly laid out in the kitchen. I was then given the task of helping to salt the flesh. I was given one of her ears with which to apply the salt. I then had to rub salt into the still warm animal to preserve it for eating. Tears streaming down my face, and with her screams still ringing in my ears, I obediently rubbed salt for hours into the cut up pieces of my poor dead playmate.

Naturally, my city life had not prepared me for the realities of how the neat little slices of bacon or ham get into the packages. Nor was I prepared for the realities of my next horror. However, this was not quite so traumatic: no life was taken! The farm of gander fame also had a bull. Very few farms had both cows and bulls, and I had been taught by the Jones' that the cows were the ones you milked. They had four-pronged udders, whereas the bulls had one dangling appendage. This information was important because it was okay to cross a field containing cows, but not to go into a field with a single bull because it was likely to attack you. One day, Mrs. Jones and I led one of our cows—let's call her Sally—to the next farm, where, apparently, she was to be "serviced." The bull was led over to Sally, and the next thing he started to climb on her back, and she tried to get away; however, both animals were held with ropes. I think these country folks possibly had some perverse pleasure at having me witness these events, but in any case, the next thing I knew, a huge, wet, pink column appeared from the part between the bull's back legs, and at that point I fled. "These Welsh people have some very strange tribal rituals" was the thought that went through my city-bred mind.

Several months later, in order that I would have the company of another child, the Joneses had invited a niece of theirs from Swansea in South Wales to come and stay. Myra was several years older than I.

Myra's presence was to introduce me to yet another new and scary experience in life. Before we set out on our evacuation journey from Liverpool, all children were given a thorough physical exam, including an inspection of our hair. Now Mum had been in the habit of regularly combing our hair with a fine-toothed comb to check for "dandruff?" That is what I was told, and I wasn't aware of any other reason to inspect one's hair. The inspection done before our journey revealed that Harry and I, plus two children from another family, were the only ones with no lice. All the other kids had to go to a "cleansing station" to be de-loused. This was a total revelation to me, so you can imagine my horror when Myra, with whom I had to share a bed, would frequently scratch her head vigorously. I piled an extra pillow between our heads, but the little critters were undaunted, and the next thing I knew, I was having severe itching, too. In my next letter home, I told Mum the terrible news, and she promptly sent a bar of Durbak medicated soap with which to shampoo my hair. Myra was sent home and I spent the next few weeks working to rid my hair of this infestation.

The local Welsh kids, being farm raised and more knowledgeable about the "facts of life," liked to tease us city folk. I vividly recall being the victim of one of their pranks. During recess, I was surrounded by a large group of locals. I was cornered and told I had to answer a question. I could foretell nothing good was to come of this, but said, "Go ahead." They asked, "Has your mother ever been pregnant?" There was a lot of "wink, wink, nudge, nudge' kind of laughter going on. Thinking this must be a pretty bad crime, I answered indignantly, "Of course not!" This reply had the locals rolling on the floor with laughter. For them, it was most certainly a "gotcha" moment. But, hey! I had survived a couple of years of air raids, so I could certainly survive a bit of ridicule. The meaning of that word was revealed to me during the next year!

The Welsh are known for their poets and singers, (Dylan Thomas, a particularly famous Welsh poet, was the inspiration for Robert Zimmerman our '60s poet/songwriter who changed his name to Bob Dylan), so it was that during my evacuation time. Mrs. Jones began teaching me some Welsh songs. It was the practice in that village to give a welcome home concert to any local soldier who came home on leave. Anyone with a modicum of talent would perform. Mrs.

Jones urged me to try, and at my singing debut—for all my earlier eagerness to be a "star"—I was so scared that only the front row could hear me. Subsequently, Mrs. Jones taught me how to sing a popular Welsh folk song in their language. I learnt phonetically—just as I had learned to read—so do not know how to spell the words, but the song was about goats, and it sounded like "oyc gaver etta."

At the next concert, with the confidence Mrs. Jones had instilled in me *and* singing in their native tongue, I sang loud and clear. To my surprise, I became quite the little "heroine evacuee" in the village. I continued to learn songs in Welsh and sing them. Naturally, I wrote many long letters to, and received many from, Mum during this time. I visited with the James family and Harry a few times, but on learning that their only toilet facility was to make use of the cow barn, I was reluctant to visit again. The Jones home did have an outhouse some 10' down the kitchen/vegetable garden, so was much more civilized.

About a month after the disaster involving lice, Mum arrived to rescue me. Harry was content with the James family, so he stayed on till New Year 1943. Once I returned to Liverpool, by my reckoning now an experienced worldly child, my relationship with Mum became more of best buddies. She was, after all, the youngest Mum of any of my peers, being a mere twenty when I was born. It was more the general custom back then for young women to be in their mid to late twenties before becoming mothers for the first time. So it was that she confided in me the news that another sibling was due at the beginning of February. Mum was really happy and looking forward without apprehension to the fourth, and as both she and Dad affirmed, their *last* child! Their own initial accidental headlong plunge into parenthood had caused them to understand and adopt the concept of sensible family planning, especially living in a city and in an era when many families produced literally dozens of offspring without any thought as to how they would provide for them.

Always effervescent, Mum loved to play the homemade radio Uncle Johnny had constructed. On Sunday mornings, we would listen to Radio India, broadcast by the BBC, and Mum would dance around the kitchen, making the kind of sinuous arm movements she had seen dancers in Indian movies perform. I'm quite confident that the sound of a sitar was familiar to the youngest Harrison even before he was born, and certainly during his infancy when Radio India remained a favorite in our household.

Once I arrived back in Liverpool, the priority became the Junior City Scholarship, which each year awarded full high school tuition to about 100 students who passed a rather rigorous exam. This exam was also known as the Eleven Plus, for students between the ages of nine and eleven. Since I was now eleven, time for me was running out. In time for Christmas that year in 1942, Harry arrived back home from Wales to find young Peter, not so much of a birthday present now, a handful of sheer determination to do things his way.

Chapter Five

HE HAS ARRIVED,
AND TO PROVE IT, HE IS HERE!

*A*t the end of Chapter Four, back in Liverpool after months in Wales, I was preparing to take the scholarship examination for high school. However, another event took place that year which was more fun and held more significance in my life. Mum had told me another sibling would arrive at the beginning of February. For quite some time I'd been aware that I was the only girl at school without any sisters. So now I felt there was a chance of the "longed for" sister. I don't understand why I wanted a sister, except that I suppose I thought if everyone else had at least one, I was somehow deprived. How silly of me!

Due to my total innocence of the reproduction process, I was unaware a baby had been ordered, until Mum told me; however, all the neighbors apparently had prior knowledge. From the first day of February, when I was heading to school, the "nosy neighbors," as Mum jokingly called them, would ask me "Has the baby arrived yet?" This went on for weeks, and always I had to tell them "No." I was getting to the point that I thought these people were nuts; obviously, there was some mistake and no baby had been ordered. I resigned myself to continued sisterlessness!

To explain a little of how very different things were then with regard to a child's knowledge of reproduction, let me say that I'd progressed from the myth that babies were delivered by stork, or found underneath a gooseberry bush. My knowledge had advanced to the point that I was aware that babies had to be "ordered in advance" and were delivered by our local trusted midwife, Nurse Ryand. She always made deliveries carrying a bulging black bag, likely I thought, containing the baby.

Also back in those days, women always wore flowing garments to conceal the unattractive swollen abdomen. Since a pregnancy proceeds very gradually, I certainly didn't notice any change in Mum's appearance—she was still Mum—so no clues for me there! Then, late on the evening of the 24th of February, Dad went to bring Nurse Ryand, from her home to ours. I was allowed to stay up quite late that night, and there was an atmosphere of suppressed excitement. It was then I knew Nurse Ryand was there to deliver the new baby. At around 11:30 p.m., I was sent off to bed. I was pretty tired anyway. The baby arrived at ten minutes past midnight on the 25th.

Next morning when I woke up, Mum called me into her bedroom. There were only two bedrooms in the house. Harry, Peter, and I slept in one and Mum and Dad in the "front" bedroom. Both bedrooms had fireplaces, and this particular morning there was a fire crackling in the grate in the front bedroom. Looking forward to finally meeting my "sister," I eagerly ran into the room. Dad called me to the bed, and Mum allowed me to hold the new infant. I considered myself very grown-up. I had experienced quite a lot of variations living in this world, so at eleven I thought of myself as quite mature.

Liverpool was home to lots of Irish Catholic families. Many of the men were in the habit of spending most of their weekly earnings at the local pub on Fridays. They would arrive home quite drunk and demand their "marital rights" with their cowering wives. This resulted in an abundant amount of babies arriving very frequently. I was accustomed to seeing many of what I regarded as pathetic creatures, all wrinkled and red. I could not understand why anyone would want so many of these noisy, smelly, horrid little things, especially when mostly they were left unattended when pub time rolled around.

But that morning, when I held my eight-hour-old new brother, I was so thrilled to find, in the context of the knife scene in the *Crocodile Dundee* movie "This is a Baby!" In one of his songs, George used the phrase "when I stepped out of the womb," but he did actually arrive the usual way, "head first." He weighed in at ten and a half pounds at birth, and due to the extra three weeks he had waited to make his entrance, his face was smooth and pink; he had a thick tuft of blonde hair, his eyelashes were long and curved, his fingernails were fully grown, he was...absolutely perfect. He opened his eyes, and when he looked at me with those gorgeous big brown eyes, for the first time in my life I experienced real unconditional love. All thought of sisters vanished—what in the world could ever be better than this!

Later that day, Dad went to register the birth. To backtrack a moment, I had been named Louise for my mother, and Harold James had been named Harold for Dad and James for an uncle. In Peter Henry's case, I had chosen the name Peter, and Henry was for our paternal grandfather. There had not yet been any discussion about a name for the current child. In those days, too, there was no poking around before birth to discover if it was a boy or girl, and I of course had been hoping for a sister.

So when Dad returned from the Registrar's office, Mum asked, "What did you name him?"

"George," said Dad.

Mum asked, "Why George?"

Dad's now-famous response was, "If it's good enough for the king, it should be good enough for him!"

I certainly agreed with this, especially after having seen so many of the other pitiful, scrawny, smelly creatures assigned to other people. I knew this child, like Harry, Peter, and I, would never have to sit on the sidewalk outside a pub waiting for drunken parents to emerge. He would be cared for and protected by intelligent and loving, responsible parents and his siblings.

Incidentally, only Harry and Peter had "middle" names; George and I had just one first name (regardless of what some so-called Beatle Books may tell you)!

Whilst on the subject of Beatle myths, shall we clear up another? I was speaking recently to a DJ in Baltimore, preparing to do an interview on George's birthday. The subject came up regarding the report that George had been convinced by some "enlightened being" that he was born on the 24th, not the 25th. In clearing up this misinformation, I explained to the DJ—and now to all my readers—that George was, in fact, born at ten minutes past midnight on the 25th of February 1943, Greenwich Mean Time in Liverpool. As most of us know, a day starts at the International Date Line, which runs jaggedly from north to south through the Pacific Ocean. The day then progresses to the west, across Asia, Europe, the Atlantic, and America, which is the reason why New Year festivities take place in California hours after they do in New York!! So maybe the argument was, that if George had been born at a different location perhaps to the west, at exactly the same moment, he would have been born on the 24th. But sorry to the folks who were taken in by the invented story. I have in Mum's own handwriting, in answer to a question from a fan club president, "At what time on the 25th was George born?" Mum's reply, as I have always known, "Ten minutes past midnight." And, the location *was* Liverpool, England. Also Mum was conscious for all our births. No anesthetic. Okay? Case closed. My major reason for writing my memoir is simply to correct the many Beatle-related fantasies concocted during their career. The other reason is to answer questions people have about me and also to make clear that my participation in The Beatles Saga began long before they became "Rich and Famous." Truth be known, I loved and was protective of my kid brother before he even had teeth, let alone money!)

However, one of Mum's brothers, Uncle George, was particularly pleased with the name of the new baby. He was so delighted he gave Dad a ten shilling note to start a bank account for the newest Harrison. So, in a way, George did start out comparatively rich!

Uncle Johnny visited the next day, bringing some boiled ham to make a sandwich for Mum. (Boiled ham was an almost unheard of luxury in those days.) We were all gathered around Mum, who was still in bed and nursing the baby, as she breast-fed all of us. The sandwich was then presented with great ceremony. Lo and behold, this day-old baby reached out, grabbed the sandwich, and pulled it toward his mouth. Wow! What a surprise! We were all stunned by this precocious infant, and I do not remember who made this comment, but someone solemnly said, "It's pretty obvious this one has been here before!" Maybe this remark was a preview to his future? Either that or he had a weakness for boiled ham!!

Despite the war, we had a happy Christmas and New Year season of 1943. Harry had returned from his evacuation in Wales. Peter, at two and a half, was thriving after the trauma of his birth and the immediate surgery. Our family was reunited, and completed in February with the arrival of the newest and final Harrison. Yes, even in those days it was possible to make a decision on how many, or how few, children you would choose to care for.

The next few months, I was working hard at all the exams and other preparations in order to—hopefully—win a scholarship to attend high school. When Peter had been a baby, Mum had taught me how to help him learn to talk, and I would sit with him for long periods of time, saying over and over 'ma, ma, ma' and 'ba, ba, ba' and "da, da, da' until the baby, intently watching my lips, would start to copy and speak. It was very satisfying to assist a helpless little being to become a real person, able to talk, eventually walk, and communicate as an individual, developing his own unique personality.

As soon as this new brother could respond to these lessons, I enjoyed being able to also aid his development. One of my very grown-up tasks, usually on a Sunday afternoon, was to take my brothers out for a long walk, usually about three miles, around the suburbs of Liverpool while Mum spent the afternoon preparing Sunday dinner. When Peter had been an infant—due to the trauma of his immediate surgery— he tended to frequently cry in distress. I found when I took him for walks, that if I kept walking the pram/baby carriage under areas where there were lots of trees, he would relax and enjoy looking at the foliage. So, I resorted to this strategy with the new baby also. When we were walking through an area devoid of trees, I would find a leafy branch and hold it over the baby carriage simulating the trees coverage. On the way home, we would usually be pretty hungry, so I devised a "magic" custom—if we rubbed the middle button on our coats, the dinner would be ready as soon as we arrived home. This worked out well!

On the rare occasions when Mum and Dad went to a movie, one of our uncles would stay with us. There was never a time when any Harrison children had to wait for a parent to come home from the pub. My parents strongly disapproved of the "pub-mentality." They would be concerned at seeing children sitting on the curb outside the many pubs waiting for the parent, or sometimes both parents, to stagger out at 10:00 p.m.

The only time we had alcohol in our home was at Christmas when one bottle of Port wine and one bottle of hard cider would be our Christmas cheer! We kids would be allowed to fill one of Mum's sewing thimbles with wine, and after drinking the awful stuff, we would stagger around—pretending to be drunk—copying what we had sometimes observed of our neighbors' occasional drunken behavior. Christmas was also the day when we would move into the front room, which was furnished with the art-deco furniture brought back from the States when Dad was "at sea." We would light a fire in the fireplace, and sitting around the leaping flames, Dad, and sometimes Mum, would tell us ghost stories. Being a seaman, Dad's favorite tale was the story of the sailing ship the *Marie Celeste*. This story later became known on TV documentaries as one of the Bermuda Triangle mysteries. Dad told the tale from the perspective of one of the sailors who boarded the abandoned vessel, although I now realize that *that aspect* of the tale was to add drama and make it more authentic. How better to tell a "ghost" story than to be in it?

Mum's own family ghost story took place in County Wexford in southern Ireland at their family home or estate. The story as was told to us went like this:

A family member met his death (I do not know how) near the front entrance to the home. There was a long driveway from the house to the road. Each year, on the anniversary of his death, a horse-drawn carriage could be heard coming up the driveway, pausing a moment at the front entrance, then taking off again down the driveway. Apparently, when my Granddad French was a twelve-year-old boy, just before he moved to Liverpool, he actually heard the horse and carriage. He was familiar with the legend and apprehensive, so he took refuge under the kitchen table. It appears from the frequent retelling of this event that throughout the years, adult family members would—on the appropriate evening—stand watch in order to view the horse and carriage. Everyone heard the sounds each time, but no one ever witnessed any physical evidence of either coach or horses. Curious! I'm aware that stories of ghostly or supernatural phenomena are given far more credibility amongst the Celtic races.

Little did we know that our latest arrival would become a worldwide phenomenon, causing our entire family—willing or not—to live a rather public life on the world stage. Throughout this book, I have referred to Mum and Dad's philosophy, which clearly influenced our decisions and reactions throughout life. George is widely known for his spiritual quest, but in order to better understand the man he became, you may care to know how and by whom those early seeds were sewn.

By the time I started grade school, Dad had left Cunard/ White Star and was employed for the remainder of his working life by the Liverpool Corporation Passenger Transport, or LCPT. His hat badge was #982. He started out as a bus conductor. The duties of a conductor consisted of collecting the fares from the passengers. He also rang a bell on the platform at the rear entrance to the bus to signal to the driver, who was obviously "up front" in a separate drivers cab—when passengers needed to get on or off at the designated bus stops. And, he made sure the smokers all went upstairs to the upper deck.

(Incidentally, in The Beatles song where Paul sings, *"Woke up, fell out of bed, dragged a comb across my head...made the bus in seconds flat. Found my way upstairs and had a smoke...,"* he was referring to the rule that cigarette smoking was only allowed *upstairs* on those double decker buses. So, for those who "heard" otherwise, this song had no hidden drug references. Likewise, "Lucy in the Sky with Diamonds" was actually about a picture John and Cynthia's son, Julian, had drawn in school and *not* about LSD.)

After a year or two, Dad took his driving test to obtain a license to drive those Big Green Double Decker Buses. I remember when he took the exam and his satisfaction at being able to progress to a better-paying position. Yes, all of four pounds, ten shillings a week!

However, this wasn't the only way Dad progressed. He also became treasurer of the Liverpool branch of the National Transport and General Workers Union.

Unionization of workers was relatively new and not highly accepted in Britain during my younger years. I recall during the war a coalman would deliver a hundredweight bag of coal each week at a cost of two shillings and sixpence, known as a half crown. However, once the miners formed a union, they were constantly going "on strike" for more pay, which resulted in ever higher prices for our weekly bag of coal. Of course, I should note here, the formation of unions was at that time an urgent necessity to counteract the ill treatment of workers. Throughout most industry, safety measures did not exist and, if anything, even speaking of safety was considered "petty complaints." Many other general abuses existed such as: very long hours for very little pay, no vacations, no medical care at all, and no rest breaks during the shift. In fact, company owners offered very little consideration for the well being of the men and children workers at that time.

But with regard to Unions—like so many other worthy causes—our species somehow manages to take them "over the top." When Dad became a union official, his membership was around 6,000 men. Every so often, some hot head would want to call a "one-day" strike for more pay. Dad would painstakingly visit the six depots throughout the city to talk sense into his seething throngs. He would explain to them that even if they should force a penny or two an hour raise, it would take them several weeks to make up the money lost by the one day strike—to say nothing of the disapproval they would earn from all the citizens unable to get to their jobs on the day of the strike. Usually, he managed to call off these 'lightning' strikes.

Quite suddenly, one of Dad's close friends, Bob Meacham, went off to the Far East—I think Ceylon. He returned after a year, and to the amazement of all, became manager of the union at a salary of nine pounds a week, plus the use of a company car! The average driver's pay was by then five pounds a week. Dad one day asked, "Hey, Bob, how did you manage to do this?" Bob's unexpected reply was this: "Harry, it's the chance of a lifetime! You could do it, too. All you have to do is—and I can recommend you because you have great influence with the lads at work—just come and join the party." "What party?" asked Dad warily. Bob replied, "Why, the Communist party of course! At the rate they are going, they will bring England to its knees in no time!"

Dad was furious. Since the time I had returned from evacuation, he had discussed world affairs with me, keeping me informed of trends in world politics. He spoke to me of Bob's betrayal with much sadness that his friend would sell out for the sake of a bit more money. What hurt Dad the most was that Bob understood *him* so poorly that he actually thought Dad might sell out also.

After that incident, Dad understood the cynical plan behind the workers being encouraged to keep striking for more pay—if they kept it up, they would eventually, as he put it, "Price themselves out of the market." We already had seen how coal prices had increased due to the miners' constant strikes, making it less affordable for the average family. As treasurer of the union, he fought constantly to protect the men from their own misguided attempts to bring down the bosses. He fully understood that for all to prosper, there had to be mutual respect and co-operation between management and labor, that goods and services had to be priced within the reach of the general public, and the workers making up the public also had to be able to afford those goods. A careful balance had to prevail. (What a pity he was not in "office" during the past 10 years.)

Mum told me with great pride of an incident on the day of the transport workers' annual company picnic. The parade of buses had arrived back at the depot at Smithdown Road from their happy outing in North Wales. Across the road, at a clearing that had been a former bomb site, was a man giving a speech, perched on a wooden box. A large crowd had gathered. Dad wandered over to see and hear what was going on. He found that the speaker was urging the crowd to "Join the Communist Party." To Mum's astonishment, her very calm, 5' 7" husband took hold of this man by his tie, lifted him from his box, and—looking at him with those fierce brown eyes—told him in no uncertain terms to vanish! The man quickly picked up his soapbox and scurried away to the jeers of Dad's co-workers. Naturally, Dad's workmates were impressed by his courageous actions. He was a naturally calm and confident leader and at that moment gained even more respect from his men.

His intelligent response to this and other events did not go unnoticed by the administration at LCPT located at Hatton Garden headquarters. Dad was called in, and quite by chance the conversation turned to the schedules or timetables for the several hundred buses travelling about thirty different routes throughout Liverpool. Dad commented that the travelling public would be better served if the scheduling was rearranged.

His suggestion was this: by synchronizing schedules where routes intersected, it would be possible to decrease the "wait time" to around five minutes so that passengers needing to transfer to another route, could cut down the time it took to get to work. This idea made a lot of sense (naturally, it was Dad's idea) and appealed to the administrators. However, they had no one on their staff capable of working out such a complex mathematical timetable. The result was, "Great idea, Harry. Go ahead and implement it—work out the schedules."

For the next few months, night after night, Dad would sit at the kitchen table pouring over reams of papers, working out timetables for each route so that they intersected in a way more convenient for the public. Although he was never offered any extra pay for this efficient and monumental accomplishment, somehow word did leak out throughout the world of transport systems. One day Dad was approached—I guess it must have been by mail, as few people had phones in those days—by the government of the Anglo-Egyptian Sudan. They wanted Dad to move to Khartoum and take charge of creating a public transport system for that city. Naturally, I—with my spirit of adventure—was ecstatic. Dad, who had travelled the world extensively, was also happy to have an opportunity to put his considerable and virtually untapped abilities to use. Alas! Mum did not have the same spirit of adventure. The idea of living in Africa caused her to stereotypically remark flatly, "I'm not going to go and live up in a tree!" Regrettably for me and Dad, *that* was the end of *that!*

(I really do still miss Dad. After Mum died in 1970 on Ringo's 30th birthday, Dad often travelled with George. Being there to support his son with his own great strength of character and calm intelligence was an unseen rock on which George was able to rely throughout many tough times. In a way I AM thankful Dad is not here today to witness that many of his concerns have come full circle. All those years ago, he recognized that the union movement, whose initial goal had been to champion the downtrodden, was— due to outside forces—beginning to turn into an institution propelled by an ideology more in tune with Greed than Need. Dad could see the imbalance coming, when goods and services would become more costly than their intrinsic value, thus leading to higher costs to the consumer and fewer profits for the producer. The end result has been the exportation of well-paying jobs to areas of the world where *much* less pay is accepted. This situation was a partial cause of the dire economic hardships we are now experiencing. If he was here today seeing manufacturing companies closed and many of the good jobs shipped overseas—not one to gloat—he would likely sadly say, "I tried to warn you, but you were not ready to listen!")

Earlier I mentioned that at this time I was working toward winning the Junior City Scholarship in order to be able to go to high school. Most kids those days left school at fourteen and found a job. It cost quite a lot to send a child to high school, not to mention the loss of their potential income. But, Dad was determined to give me the opportunity to reach my potential. So, although they could not afford the fees to send me to high school, they did all they could to encourage me to succeed.

My parents were aware that I was pretty bright, but was way behind in my education due to the war. They opted to take me out of the Catholic school and send me to one with a very high standard for education and a good reputation. It was a public school operated by the Liverpool City Council and was located at Lawrence Road. It was quite some distance from Arnold Grove, but I had by then been accustomed to a four mile walk to school each day in Wales. Once I moved to this new school I found education to be far more interesting and challenging. The teachers were dynamic, and discipline, as in all British schools then, was firm and fair. My class teacher was Miss Pritchard, and the Head Mistress was Mrs. Edwards. I became really eager to get to school each day.

Without the distraction of the ever present, dreary catechism stuff *(ironically the way we had been taught prayers and catechism was to memorize and be able to recite them. We just learnt what we thought were the words; for instance, in the "Hail Mary" there is a phrase, "blessed art thou amongst women" which we all recited as "blessed are now a monk swimming." Very devout?)*, at public school I was able to concentrate on subjects that required our comprehension or understanding rather than mere recitation, thus more worthy of attention. Learning was so much fun I did not realize how hard we worked. Before very long I became one of the top three in a class of 52 students. At home my parents and kid brothers cheered me along.

Prior to being accepted to compete for the Junior City Scholarship, participants at each school had to qualify by reaching a specific score on a review test. After the review test, results were read out to the assembly. WOW! I scored 170 out of 200, our school's highest score.

The next week we were given an IQ test. None of us understood what IQ meant and were not too concerned. This test turned out to be a really fun test, asking all kinds of questions that were more like puzzles and not about "which year a certain treaty was signed"—that dull stuff that most tests were all about. A few weeks later, we got the results. No one told us what high score was possible in this test, and so far as I was concerned, it was just a fun test and not about any of the "important" things we had to learn. I was told my score was 168, and my best friend's was 112.

In our innocence, we concluded that IQ must have something to do with our date of birth. In England we write the day, the month, and then the year. My birthday is 16/8/31, and my friend's is 11/2/31, so 168 and 112 were to us obviously something to do with our birthdays, Duh! We were not terribly curious about it and it did not occur to us to see if this theory matched any other birthdays, since 168 was lower than my score in the review test, it was not too impressive, we thought, and soon forgotten.

(After I arrived in the United States back in 1963, I had become accustomed to the American way of writing my birth date 8/16/31, so had forgotten the 16/8/31. It happened that while watching *"The Bob Newhart Show"* one night, I found out what the mysterious IQ meant. The episode was about Bob's wife, Emily, being inducted into Mensa. He was upset because she qualified to join Mensa, but he did not. I do not recall what their numbers were, but I suddenly recalled 16/8/31 and my mysterious 168—at that moment I discovered to my surprise that my IQ was okay. Fortunately, I also remembered Dad's admonition that I could not take personal credit for innate abilities or gifts; thus, I have since attempted to "use it wisely." Mind you, although a high IQ may be perceived as a benefit, I find it is often also a handicap that causes one to be somewhat isolated. I have recently been watching the TV series *Bones* (which recounts the experiences of a forensic anthropologist). Although I have nowhere near *her* smarts, I can relate to her puzzlement toward mainstream ideology. I, for instance, have never been able to understand the significance to our species as a whole, or why there is so much fascination in, watching a bunch of people running up and down a field or chunk of ice, chasing a ball or puck and attempting to propel it into a specific aperture. This includes many team ball games. Neither can I understand why anyone would find entertainment in observing other people being beaten, punched or kicked, or willingly undergoing traumatic or embarrassing situations.

I know there was a time in our collective history when certain cultures used team sporting events as a means to settle territorial disputes, but as far as I am aware this is no longer the case. Another ancient custom that would bear reviving was when two warring factions would have their leaders face off in some form of combat. The dispute would be settled depending on which leader won. What a novel idea! Think of the expense this would have saved after 9/11. Just Dubya versus Bin Laden. Maybe the entire world economy would not have been devastated? The main purpose these days seems to focus more on financial gain for sports team owners and players and organizers of expensive and polluting events like "fireworks displays."

And, of course, there's the "reely big shew" every four years—the Olympics! Yes, the Olympics challenge athletes to get the best performance from their bodies, but do we do anything to encourage getting the best performance from our brains? Seriously—do these events actually advance the well-being of humanity as a species? Or, are they simply a cynical modern version of the Roman Empire's "Opiate of the Masses?" In other words, are they simply ways to deflect our collective consciousness away from the really important issues in order that, the *"Emperors"* can play their games without being bothered by the voices of the people. My dear readers, please, as my brother has also urged, "don't allow yourselves to be manipulated or brainwashed—*think!*")

The next event in my young life was the city-wide scholarship exam itself. When the results were announced, my parents were told in confidence that—lo and behold—my scores were significantly higher than any other student's in Liverpool. They were also told I was offered an opportunity to enter yet another scholarship contest. If I should succeed, this would help greatly with the expenses involved in higher education. It would cover such things as books, transport, uniforms etc.

At this stage, my dad had another serious talk with me. He explained that he and Mum were very happy with my achievement. But, I should regard these accomplishments, not with personal pride, but with thanks for having had these abilities bestowed on me. He told me I could no more take credit for being smart than I could for having green eyes. These were gifts I had inherited, and I had a responsibility not to waste them.

My scores on the Eleven Plus attracted the attention of La Sagesse, one of the three schools my dad had advised me to select as my preferences. The governors of this school were those who had invited me to take a second scholarship exam. My parents told me that this scholarship would cover the cost of my uniforms, books, and transportation to and from school. This gave me quite an incentive to try to win. After all, this scholarship would remove a large financial burden from Mum and Dad and give my parents the freedom to allow me to pursue my education.

In Britain, education is quite different. Schools do not provide special buses. Students find their own way to school on public transport, and can choose to go to any of the schools available in their city. Most high schools have their own uniform; therefore, it is obvious which school you attend. Behavior reflects the school image and is therefore important. As a bus driver, my dad was well aware which schools had the best-behaved students. Apparently the students at La Sagesse behaved impeccably.

So it was, that I entered, and won, the scholarship to La Sagesse, which was a Convent School in Grassendale, located far across Liverpool from Wavertree, and near the River Mersey. That year was the first time this school had been more or less forced—due to the war—to take scholarship children.

In the past, all their students had been daughters of very wealthy or prominent people, such as earls, ambassadors and others.

I think it may make sense to add here some of the ways Mum also influenced her children, including her youngest son. The experience during the Great Depression led her to abide thereafter by most of these life lessons:

1. Only purchase items you absolutely *need* and can afford to pay for fully. Debt is easy to get *into*, but very difficult to get *out* of.

2. Look after your own family and their needs as a *first* priority. If you have anything left over, put most into savings. Whenever there is anything extra, you should share with needy friends. I can recall Mum baking homemade bread each week. On one occasion, when she was in the hospital to have an abscess removed from her left upper arm muscle, she made friends with two very old ladies living on their old age pensions who were also in the same ward. Mum's compassionate nature led her to bake two extra loaves each week to take to each of these old ladies. They were seventy-three years old. In those days I considered them very ancient. One of these old ladies told Mum a story, which was passed on to us as a life lesson. As a young girl, this lady had been working at a farm in Ireland. One day she had to take a basket of fresh eggs into the village market. As she neared the village, a tramp/homeless person was walking toward her. Nervously, she avoided looking at him. When he drew near, he said to her softly, "Lassie, I know you have no money to give me, but you could have given me a **SMILE!**" This story has been such an important factor in my life. Many times I can be in a situation when a nearby person looks extremely "grouchy." I find giving this person a friendly smile almost always results in an answering smile. Sometimes all we need is just a tiny symbol of friendship?

3. She told another old lady story. This lady lived in a village named Churchdown, spread over several acres

at the base of a hill. The local church had been built, with much effort, on the top of the hill. The villagers going to church from various locations eventually wore several pathways up the hill. The lesson from this story (one we really need to consider today) is this: It does not matter which path you take, as long as your goal is to reach the place where you believe you can connect with our Creator/Supreme Being/God.

These are some of the lessons Mum brought to our lives. I am very proud that when George started his much publicized spiritual quest, he never came out—as so many misguided folks do—and stated:

"I have found the one and only true religion."

No, he was intelligent enough to understand that with so much diversity on this planet, we each have to find our own path, and as long as our goal is pure, we can reach and connect with our Maker.

I am thankful to have been so fortunate with regard to the biological family into which I was born. I do not expect my readers to agree with all my views. Naturally, you too have the freedom to choose your own. But these tenets have worked for me, and trying to be gracious, kind, and compassionate is what our parents taught. I just hope I have not disappointed them.

Earlier in this chapter I said that learning more about our parents would afford you a better insight into the highly respected man George became. His kindness, compassion, and spiritual leanings were taking root long before he became a Beatle. I know because—unlike most other people who have attempted to interpret my kid brother—**I was there before his beginning, shared the same parents, experienced the same upbringing, was supportive of his efforts to become a successful musician, and last spoke with him two weeks before he left this planet.** Therefore, what could I possibly know?

Chapter Six

"Louise, We'll Have Nun of That!"

A s previously mentioned, I was not really concerned with conditions such as poor and rich. My parents were decent, compassionate, and lots of fun; therefore, we had many good friends and a very enjoyable life, despite outside challenges, *i.e.* the war, which we took in our stride.

In my earlier years attending Our Lady of Good Hope Catholic School, which was located close to a Protestant school, I found it rather puzzling that the kids from each school called each other Cattylics and Proddydogs. They would ambush each other, throw stones, and otherwise try to make the others' lives miserable. Why should there be such violence just because we went to different churches? I assumed that these juvenile behaviors would be left behind in the high schools, which at that time in Britain were mostly all-girl or all-boy institutions, unlike the co-educational grade schools. *(See photo on page 200.)*

On arriving with great anticipation at high school, I thought, *"La Sagesse, no less. One of the most respected high schools in all Liverpool. WOW! How great is that?"* This school was operated by an order of nuns known as Les Filles de la Sagesse, or the daughter of wisdom. Their motto was Deus Seul or "For God Alone." It was the custom to write DS in the margin at the top of every page we wrote. The order was founded by a monk, Louis de Montfort, who was elevated to sainthood during the time I attended this school.

Then, came the rude awakening.

We Harrison children had learned from our parents to be confident of our abilities or talents, to use them well, and not to become conceited by forgetting that everything we are, and can possibly accomplish, depends on the strength of our connection to our Creator. Although seldom the center of attention, I was secure in the loving support from my family.

Now, I was entering a new dimension. Here they *did* have rich and poor. The rich were adored, coddled and somewhat revered. The poor, however, were considered disgusting-ugh- and to be avoided lest one became tainted by association. Being rich was the ultimate virtue. As time progressed, I became more and more disillusioned by the obsequious way the nuns fawned upon the rich.

(A whimsical thought just occurred to me. Could it be that the 21st century GOP, the Grover Norquist gang, and the members of the public who elected them, had been educated by similar nuns?)

The other girls in my class liked me well enough, especially when they found I always had my homework done and received good grades. Next thing I knew, many of my classmates were asking me to let them copy my work to turn in. Somehow this did not seem the correct thing to do, but being an obliging sort of child, I let them copy my homework. I did, however, ask them to change a word here and there so it would not look exactly like mine.

As the term wore on, I formed a friendship with three other students, Sheila Higgins, Maureen Treanor, and Cecelia Carney. Except for Cecelia, who we called Toozie and who lived in Hunts Cross, they all lived nearby in Grassendale in rather grand homes compared to mine. Sheila's father was an airline pilot; Maureen's was a successful businessman. Cecelia later became a Nun. We thought of ourselves as the Three Musketeers and d'Artagnan. I—being the ringleader type—was of course d'Artagnan! I would go to their homes after school ended at 4:00 p.m., for homework and other activities, often not arriving at my home on the other side of Liverpool until maybe six or 7:00 p.m. I do not think I was ever reprimanded for my late arrival, as my parents were happy that I had found new friends. Also, back in those days, there was no need to be concerned regarding the safety of children wandering freely around the city—as would be the case in the 21st century. WWII was ongoing, but the nightly air raids were no longer hitting Liverpool. Another girl I really admired for her sweet and gentle demeanor was Patricia Harvey. I heard some years ago that she died when she was only forty-five. (Perhaps an example of "the good die young." I am still here in my eighties if that tells you anything?) Although not one of the musketeers, she was far too gentle for our rambunctious activities—she was always at the fringe, following and watching us with a sort of restrained envy, as though she wished she had the daring spirit to be part of our group. Whenever we were "in trouble" with Iggy, the headmistress, she would try to find a way to explain our behavior to exonerate us. What a dear ally and supporter she was! There was a kind of beauty and purity about her, we all sensed. We accepted her as part of, yet "apart from" our behavior.

In about our third year, one of our activities which Patricia, very sensibly, would have no part in at all, was this: Around the outskirts of the school grounds was a wooded area about 25' wide, featuring a pathway which both the nuns and students used to walk on in order to recite the rosary. I guess we were about fourteen when, someone happened to acquire a package of cigarettes. Naturally, we daring ones decided to use our private "forest" to learn to smoke. So it was that we would saunter through the woods, choking, hacking, gagging, having dizzy spells and sometimes throwing up, all with the idea that we were being "grown-up." I, fortunately, was never able to master the art of inhaling, so never became addicted to that particular legal weed, or for that matter any other weed!

My first personal encounter with the snobbery of the nuns was when the mother of one of my Musketeer pals happened to visit the school for some reason. Quite by chance, I overheard the nun tell this lady, "I am really concerned about Maureen. You must be careful; she has become quite friendly with one of those awful scholarship children that we have been forced to take in." She added with a shudder, "Her father is a bus driver!" It took a few minutes for the significance of this to hit me! "Wow, she must be talking about ME? Why would anyone need to be careful of me? I did not have access to any bombs, and I was pretty happy about winning the scholarship. Wasn't that a good thing?"

I did not mention this incident to anyone, and certainly not to Mum and Dad. After all, it was Dad who had chosen this particular school as the best option in Liverpool in his desire to help me realize my potential. For the first time in my life, I held back information from them. I've never been ashamed of my background, but at that time I did start to become secretive about where I lived. Fortunately, Wavertree was too far across the city for any of my pals to be likely to venture there, so I was pretty safe from any of my friends discovering just how "un-grand" my home was compared to theirs.

(Once again I'm going to jump way into the future to tell of a really hilarious story with regard to "my secret humble home." In about 1986, some dear friends of mine from Sarasota, Florida, returned from a lengthy trip around the world. On their return, they visited me to tell of their experiences and brought photos to show me. They were both so excited, and the first thing they told me was this: "The highlight of the whole trip was the day we toured Liverpool and went to see your former home in Arnold Grove. Thousands visit every week, and the poor lady who lives there now can't stand Beatle Fans." Rather ironic, isn't it? The modest little home that caused me such anxiety is now considered by many people to be the highlight of a world tour. As George said in one of his songs, "It's all up to what you value!")

My first term at La Sagesse continued, and I seemed to be constantly "in trouble" and sent to the Head Mistress, Sister Ignatius, for discipline. But regardless of the negative side, these were many more positive aspects to my high school experience. The faculty included both nuns and lay people, all women of course, were highly qualified, and we received an excellent education. Just about every subject became an exciting adventure. Our math teacher, Sister Margaret-Marie, helped us understand the logic behind math and geometry, though I didn't catch on to algebra too well. Sister San Christophe, our geography teacher, had been a ballet dancer who, before becoming a nun, had suffered a severe injury that caused her to walk with a distinctive limp. She simplified geography in such a way that we learned there were a number of climatic patterns worldwide. For instance, "the northwest European type climate" is similar to the climate of the northwest United States due to their similar location with regard to the land mass. Also, that the center of any large land mass experiences much greater differences between summer high temperatures and winter lows than a location on any coast, which would have the moderating effects of the seas or oceans. She taught about the geological makeup of the continents and many other things that made it so that, when asked, for instance, "What was the main export of any particular country?" the knowledge we had would enable us to make an educated response. We learnt the annual mean average high and low temperatures and rainfall of areas all over the world, and it was possible to be able to accurately state the name of the city when she gave us a high, low and mean annual rainfall. This knowledge has been invaluable to me considering all the different areas of the planet I have lived so far. From the lessons she taught I have had a very good idea what to expect wherever I have been. That is of course regarding geographic matters–not politics or people. Most days Sister would give us short tests of about ten questions just to make sure we were paying attention. These tests would be graded on a score of ten. One day she gave us twelve questions, and it happened I correctly answered eleven of them. She was amused when she gave us our scores and I had eleven out of ten. She chuckled about it saying, "It's a good thing this is not a test that goes toward the end of term results, otherwise I would have a hard time explaining to Mother Superior how I am grading,"

Our biology and science teacher, Miss Marrott again, with her well-equipped lab, did a wonderful job of helping us understand how our bodies functioned, as well as how our planet functioned. Our knowledge of those subjects today is more advanced, but considering it was the late '40s, I have to admit the basics I learned then make it easy to keep up with and understand new discoveries as they become available.

By the time I reached high school I was already a voracious reader, but my choice of reading materials was not always "nun-sanctioned." Mrs. Jillian was our English teacher for both language and literature and she certainly helped me gain a decent command of our rather complicated language. Although I have commented on the mendacity of those nuns, I *do* have to give sincere great thanks for the really high quality of education I was fortunate to receive at both the high school and, later, the college convent schools. Thank you ladies!

At home we were pretty happy. By this time, the war was just an everyday slight inconvenience. We four kids had lots of fun, and I was often designated to take my brothers either to one of the many parks in Liverpool or sometimes to a movie.

On the topic of movies, throughout my early years, Mum enjoyed the basic slapstick humor of the times. I recall sitting beside her at a Three Stooges movie. Mum and the rest of the audience were roaring with laughter at the antics, but I was sitting frowning, concerned about their eyes being poked out, etc. I can recall Mum saying to me, "Laugh, why don't you laugh?" and I sullenly replied, "But, Mum, it's *not funny!*" Another popular comedy act was Laurel and Hardy. Most of their movies I did enjoy, especially the story where they ran into a series of problems whilst delivering a piano to an upstairs apartment.

(Looking back from the perspective of the 21st century, I realize Laurel and Hardy were, in fact, the forerunners of a whole genre of humor. The idea consisted of two men—one very much the alpha male, usually somewhat self-assured and bombastic—and the other a knucklehead, very much the "follower" and usually turning out to be the "loser" in most interactions. We can cite Jackie Gleason and Art Carney, Fred Flintstone and Barney Rubble, Yogi Bear and Booboo, Archie Bunker and Meathead—though Meathead did fight back somewhat. Throughout the decades, there have been many more such Odd Couples like Walter Matthau and Jack Lemmon. More recently, we have Charlie Harper and brother, Alan. This entire concept seems to create unlimited situations for humor.)

When we were living at our Upton Green address, one humorous situation developed as an aftermath from taking my brothers to see the Gene Kelly version of The Three Musketeers. Throughout the movie, there were tremendous gymnastic fencing scenes. When we arrived home, the two younger boys—Pip and Geo, as I called them—went up to their bedroom. Impressed by the athletic prowess of the actors, they were attempting to reenact the movie. Mum and I were in the living room. Suddenly, there was a tremendous crash, followed by complete silence. Mum and I anxiously dashed up the stairs. When we opened the bedroom door, we discovered the wreckage of what had been a folding bed. Apparently, one Musketeer had leapt from his perch on top of the dresser onto the bed, causing it to collapse with that horrific thud. The two were standing looking very sheepish as we entered the room. Once she realized the boys were unhurt, Mum—in her usual way—burst into laughter, and after setting the bed back on its feet, brought the boys down to comfort them with biscuits (cookies) and milk.

Harry and I sometimes had a bit of a sibling scuffle ourselves. On one occasion I had caused Harry a nosebleed. He in return had given me a black eye. Well, the nosebleed stopped in a matter of minutes, but my eye blossomed from blue to yellow to red and then purple for several days, becoming ever more like a rainbow as the week went by.

This incident happened just prior to the end of term at school, and we all gathered in the gym for the reading of our grades. The mother superior, along with the entire faculty, took the stage. In England, the first level in high school is known as Form Three. Then we have Lower Fourth, Upper Fourth, Lower Fifth, and Upper Fifth. Graduation usually occurs in the Sixth Form. The reading of the grades began with the youngest—Form Three—my class. Mother Superior, known as Bonne Mere, solemnly stepped to the podium. All was silent.

"Here are the grades for the Third Form." She continued, "First in class—Louise Harrison—with 75%." She paused then with a twinkle and added "and a black eye!" The entire student body, along with some special guests, roared with laughter. As a self-confessed ham, I've always enjoyed causing laughter, but this time I was quite humiliated. After the assembly, we all returned to our classrooms. I was congratulated with "pats on the back," which in most cases were more like punches. At that point, I decided being number one was a goal I would strive to avoid in future.

(It has been interesting to observe throughout my lengthy time on Earth just how significant, and how very different, one's role in life plays out, for those endowed or inflicted with "number one-ness." In almost all social-animal behaviors, and in most fields of endeavor, eventually a leader, or leaders, will emerge. As the common saying goes, "the cream will rise to the top." If this should be an individual's fate, it seems there is no way to avoid the responsibilities inherent in this leadership factor. Take for instance the example with which I am most familiar—The Beatles. No matter how they tried to "lay-low," "hide," "disguise themselves," and in other ways disappear, they could *not* escape the prominent role they were destined to play. Even now that Ringo is in his seventies and has asked to be allowed to retire in peace, many are indignant that he should wish to live out his remaining years in quiet, near anonymity. "How dare he forsake us!" many tell me. So as I learned that December day in my first year in high school—being #1 is not always beneficial; a great deal of accountability comes with the territory! The other big drawback is the envy, resentment and often sabotage, many number one-beings have to endure. Take for a vivid example the way the "Greedy Old Plutocrats" treat President Obama!)

It was around this time in my high school years that I had another of my long talks with Dad; I asked him if he could explain the reasons behind some of my school experiences. In church and school, the official theme was that we were all God's children, all equally loved by Him, and capable of gaining absolution for our "sins." However, the atmosphere in which I spent my school days gave a far different message. As one of the very few scholarship children, I was looked down upon and considered not worthy of mixing with the upper crust. Most of the other students came from very affluent families, some daughters of nobility, ambassadors and consuls; the nuns almost worshipped the very wealthiest.

Dad's own father had been quite a prominent architect and builder in Liverpool but, when he was killed in the first year of WWI, the family fell on harder times. There were no programs then to help the families of those whose lives were lost in "whatever the latest war was about." So, as a youngster he himself experienced the difference between comparative affluence and harder times. Later in his working life, which started at sixteen, Dad's own experiences as a first class steward on board the Cunard cruise ships also taught him a great deal about the discrepancies between rich and poor. I asked his opinion on the situation in which I found myself. His response is possibly a little surprising, though I believe he was teaching me an important life lesson. (I'm pretty sure George learned this, also.) He actually was rather sympathetic toward the handicap of being wealthy. He told me that our lack of great wealth was beneficial inasmuch as we would never be targeted or befriended for the purpose of getting close to our *money!* The friendships we enjoyed rested on our value as decent human beings with compassion and a huge sense of fun. We would never need to be suspicious that any of our friends would harbor gold-digging motives!

But he explained, having sincere friends was more of a problem for the rich. He had sympathy for those who were targeted and manipulated by the unscrupulous. A scenario, abundantly evident throughout the lengthy history of "so called" mankind, went like this: *"Fortune hunters would insert and ingratiate themselves into rich families; subsequently, they would invent ways to discredit the biological family of the rich person in order to get a stranglehold on the wealth."* So, we grew up confident in our own strengths and abilities and knowing that kindness to others was important. So, we had "no worries" as to the likelihood that any of us might become wealthy victims, loved for our money (poor George). Our tendency was to have a degree of compassion for the "vulnerable wealthy" souls.

Although I was able to get solid and comforting answers like this from Dad about the weirdness of life in general, I had big doubts about my mother's fervent desire for me to become a teacher. For many years she had told me about the teacher who had been her mentor and because of her encouragement. Mum had always wanted to become a teacher. Unfortunately Mum herself had no opportunities to do so, but now felt I had the potential to fulfill her dreams. Inside I was in turmoil. I had no desire to become a teacher; in fact, back then I really did not have any particular goals (except to be Shirley Temple). World War II came to an end in 1945 and we celebrated with a street party. *(See photo on page 197.)*

The next few years at high school were relatively uneventful except for the death of Sheila's father. One evening—when on the approach to what is now John Lennon Airport—the plane he was piloting crashed into the River Mersey not far from our school. In fact, the next day when my classmates and I went for our lunchtime walk in organized lines of two-by-two (which was known as a crocodile), we passed the scene of the crash. Shortly after this, the famous Danny Kaye, whose movies we all loved, came to Liverpool. As a sort of condolence, Sheila was invited to the Empire Theatre to see Danny, and I was able to go with her. Even under these circumstances, to be able to enjoy the show by this hilarious comedian helped lift our spirits.

One popular project sponsored by the City of Liverpool Corporation was to arrange transport once every couple of months to take high school students throughout the city to a special performance by the Liverpool Philharmonic Orchestra. The orchestra's conductor, Sir Malcolm Sargent, would give a wonderful verbal interpretation of the various symphonic pieces they would play. For a while, I had a bit of a crush on the first violinist named Manoug Parikian. He was from the Middle East and nowadays would likely be profiled as a terrorist! He was the first—and I think only—person for whom I ever stood in line to obtain an autograph. Whenever I could afford it, I would attend the performances at the Philharmonic.

In Britain the annual summer school holiday/vacation was just five weeks—the last week in July and all of August. Therefore, since my birthday is in August, my age was always in sync with the beginning of each new school year. By the time I reached seventeen, I had passed all the exams necessary to enter college. But, in Britain at that time, one had to be eighteen in order to register with a college. So, I had to wait another year at La Sagesse before I could actually attend the college at which I had been accepted, St. Mary's College. This college, again a convent, was in Newcastle on Tyne, approximately 400 miles to the northeast of Liverpool, close to Scotland.

During that final year in Sixth Form, we mostly spent time studying theology, apologetics, and philosophy. The priest who conducted these lectures, Father Young, was a friend of Sister Ignatious, and many times during his talks she would sit at the back of the room. I found his topics to be of great interest. Most importantly, he encouraged us to *think!* by examining the things we were told, doing research, having discussions and—with that additional knowledge—reaching a sensible conclusion rather than just being "taken in" by everything we were told. I am so thankful that I was exposed to more than one teacher who believed in helping us use our own abilities and resources to reach valid conclusions, rather than become victims of the general propaganda which is so invasive in our society. (What a pity more people had not learned to think! If they had, we would not be so vulnerable and so brainwashed by the unscrupulous in our present day media. We seem to spend so much time, energy and money ensuring our bodies can achieve athletic perfection. It seems strange why do we not also try to enhance the performance of our minds? GOOD QUESTION. Responsible minds would be able to detect corruption, and that would not make the corruptors happy, would it? Therefore for their own protection those in "control" do not encourage the masses to think and examine—no just watch Fox News and trot along as directed.)

Back at school, as usual, my "enquiring mind" caused me to get into trouble. (I haven't changed much.) We were having a discussion regarding the theological juxtapositions regarding free will and predestination or fate, the general belief being that to God, all is in the present. I asked question after question, trying to get my brain to accept this concept, but Father Young kept giving answers that seemed to make things more confusing. So, wanting to properly understand, I kept asking more questions. After the fourth question, Father Young said, contrary to his usual methods, "It is a mystery. You just have to accept it." I, in my eagerness to get to the truth (if there is such a thing), replied: "But, Father, if there really are mysteries, why didn't you say it was a mystery three questions earlier?" Sister Ignatious exploded, "Louise, you arrogant child, how dare you!"

LOUISE! We'll have *nun* of that!

Having had a lot of experience with Iggy, as we students called her, I decided from that point forward to resort to silence whenever she was present. I instinctively sensed Father Young could not be as forthright as usual in front of her. On one occasion, I happened to have a public library book at school with me. The book *Captain from Castile* was by Samuel Shellebarger. It dealt quite thoroughly with the Spanish Inquisition. Finding the story to be fascinating and revealing, I had lent the book to one of my pals. Unfortunately, her mother called the school to complain. I was thoroughly reprimanded for daring to read such "terrible lies." When I thought more about the subject matter in the book, I could understand why any "good Catholic" would go berserk regarding the revelations in that book. The Spanish Inquisition was *not*, I suppose, one of their finest hours/ centuries! (That book was later made into a movie starring Tyrone Power.)

I should mention here that back in my teen years in Britain, racial equality was the norm. The so called "n" word was commonly used, but merely as a descriptive and not derogatory term. We learned in our geography classes that skin color was entirely due to the location on the planet your forebears originated. We were taught that due to the relative positions of the Sun and the Earth, the parts of the earth nearer the poles received less intense sunlight than regions near to the equator. Since the energy from the sun is important to life, as our species evolved (and *yes* even our nuns believed in evolution), the populations where the sun was less intense had pale skins to better absorb the energy; conversely, those populations where the sun was most intense had a dark pigment in their skin to protect from the more intense suns rays. We did not know as much about radiation and ozone as now, but we did understand that skin color had nothing to do with either superiority or inferiority. Those traits are purely individual.

Although racial equality was normal in Britain at that time, we were still a long way from the notion of equality for women. True single women could become nurses or teachers, and a few women were becoming secretaries, but the overwhelming mindset still had all women in the category of "would-be wives." We were expected to "find ourselves a man who would marry and care for us for the rest of our lives—so long as we promised to *love, honor and obey,* till death do us part. Thus we became dependent, bodily servants for the rest of our lives. Of course there were still many good marriages, as in the case of my own parents, but the point IS: at that time, apart from nursing and teaching there was very little alternative for a woman, except to "find a husband." In view of these factors, I understood that though I was not keen on becoming a teacher, it was for me the best choice.

Would you now like to hear how much more enlightened I became at St. Mary's Teacher Training College, which again was a convent? Despite my reluctance, I did go ahead and attend a teachers' college. Once again, my tuition, travel expenses, and board at college were all covered by scholarships. This time though, there were quite a few other interlopers who, having no money, had no right to be amongst those who did. It occurs to me that when nuns take the vow of poverty, it somehow scares them whenever they have to deal with those to whom poverty was not by vow/choice. Since I personally had never thought of our family as poor, I was indignant at the snobbery shown by just about every nun I ever met.

This college was another new experience. We all lived in. Our upstairs rooms were divided into houses with about forty students in each house. I was in one called St. Bede. I suppose the reason for the four houses was to invite competitiveness. We each had our own very nice little bedroom, furnished with a single bed, a dresser, a table and chair, and a small lamp. The bathrooms were grouped at the end of the corridor. We had schedules as to when we might take a bath.

Downstairs was a chapel, huge dining room, library, and common room. In the mornings we were expected to attend Mass at 7:30 a.m. each day. I did not go every day. But, I did complete what is known as nine first Fridays, when you attend mass on nine consecutive first Fridays of the month. This effort is supposed to get one a guaranteed spot in heaven, but I am not going to hold my breath or brag that I am "saved!"

After classes, we had dinner at 7:00 p.m. and lights-out at ten. No one was allowed off the convent grounds after 8:00 p.m. unless one had a special pass. After dinner most nights, we would retire to our rooms to study or work on papers. Usually, students would first gather in a large group in a common area near the bathrooms and chat. For the first couple of weeks, I hung out at the edge of the crowd, but eventually I found the conversations to be so girly, crass and generally vapid that I would go straight to my room, thus gaining the reputation of a "swat or egghead." But, being alone gave me more time to think about more significant concerns. I was by this time in my convent school life accustomed to this treatment, so it did not bother me anymore.

So, here I was eighteen and at college, doing quite well in my studies.

The work load was very heavy and each three-week period we were given a major project. We had to produce a dissertation on a selected subject. Usually there were several books on the chosen topic we had to read, then we had to write approximately thirteen hand written legal size pages outlining our conclusions about the subject. We had a deadline of 11:00 a.m. on the 3rd Sunday to turn in our papers. Although I accomplished all of the reading ahead of time, I discovered a disturbing facet to my personality. No matter how much I tried, I could never start the actual writing of the dissertation until about 9:00 a.m. or about two hours before the paper was due to be turned in. It seemed I needed to be in an urgent situation before I could "kick myself in the pants" to act. I started silently calling myself "last minute Lou." I've never figured out the cause of my procrastinations, except perhaps some deep seated concern about the problems I caused by arriving here on Earth a little too soon. Since working on this memoir I now understand one has to be in a creative mood in order to be able to create!!

One college project I really enjoyed was when we had to come up with a "child study." I was happy to select my two young brothers, Peter and George, as the subjects...naturally I knew more about them than any other children. However, I apparently missed the point of the exercise, as my study just told how much fun they were instead of digging into and understanding the psychology behind their behavior. I recall telling of incidents when the two were playing—one that still stands out. Peter was three years older than George, and when they were about three and six, they were playing in our kitchen with a couple of toy trains (they had no tracks). At one point Peter called out very importantly, "I'll be the engineer." Young George replied very agreeably, "Okay, and I'll be the engine over 'ere." I can still remember the slight confusion on Peter's face at this unexpected and off the wall reply. I, of course, was chuckling heartedly, as I still am right now! As my two young brothers grew, there were many more endearing moments. I recall when Peter in his teens saved up to buy his first sport bike. He came to me and said, "Lou, come and look, just see the balance." He held the bike up suspended on two fingers and smiled proudly. Although we did not have many material "goodies," those we worked for were highly prized. These were the stories I included in my "child study" long before the rest of the world was interested in that particular child.

(I must make it clear right now; yes this book is mostly of interest because of the subsequent fame of my kid brother, however, as many of you reading this already know, I have been very open about all the parts of his Beatle life which I shared, but, I have always been protective and respectful of the moments in his childhood that were private. Although there are many cherished moments like those I have just revealed, please be satisfied with this little glimpse of a very dear soul, and allow me the discretion of stopping now and *not* making a mockery of my relationship by "telling all." He never behaved in a way I would be ashamed to tell about, but I think you will agree he deserves the small amount of privacy I can still protect. I love you, little brothers—all three little brothers!)

And so the hard work at college carried on. With the scholarship conditions, the agreement was for me to teach a minimum of two years before doing anything else after receiving my teaching certificate. To an outsider, things appeared okay. But inside me, the stress of wanting to please Mum and live her "teaching dream" manifested itself in a series of abscesses appearing in various places all over my face.

Unlike high school, at college the head mistress, Mother Ward, had a soft spot for me. When I first met her, she used to tease me with a little rhyme because of a curl I had on my forehead. It went like this:

There was a little girl, and she had a little curl
Right in the middle of her forehead.
When she was good she was very, very good.
But when she was bad, she was horrid!

During our first term, we each had two weeks of teaching practice at a local area school. Somehow, my turn to do this did not happen until close to the Christmas holidays. At that time, Mother Ward selected me as the student to teach a class in English literature before the entire student body, the college staff, and the National Teaching Inspectors. The Inspectors (or Examiners) toured the country, grading the performance of each college. At the time, no one spoke of the importance of this situation. However, I was to teach a class in poetry. A lengthy ballad called "The Ballad of Inch Cape Rock" was selected. Briefly, the poem told the story of the crew at a lighthouse who had not been heard from for a number of weeks. Therefore, a search party was sent to investigate. The rescuers thoroughly searched the tiny Island, as well as the lighthouse, and finding no living beings anywhere, were leaving Inch Cape Rock in their little boat. However, once the boat pushed off, they noticed three large black crows watching them from an outcropping. Pretty spooky!

It was a lot like the *Marie Celeste* story that Dad had told to us at Christmas times. So, I naturally enough entered into the spirit of the storytelling and put the right amount of suspense and drama into my voice. Not only was Mother Ward gratified, but the Inspectors/Examiners gave the college very high marks. But, the potential best outcome for me, which I discovered at a later date, was this: Father Agnelus Andrews, the official BBC priest in Britain, had also been in the audience. He was so impressed with the reading of the ballad that he told Mother Ward he would personally give me a letter of introduction to the BBC in London should I wish to pursue a career in radio. At that time, the BBC did dozens of plays on radio. An actors' most important asset was to be able to convey the effect of story with only the voice. Not until the fateful abscesses did Mother Ward reveal this news to me.

As I said earlier, Mother Ward did like me, and when she noticed the eruptions on my face, she asked me about them. I told her why I was so stressed. My parents had made great sacrifices in order to give me the benefit of an excellent education, but I told her I really did *not* want to be a teacher.

She responded with this surprising comment, "You know, Louise, out of 200 students each year, I consider only about two or three to be really good teaching material. This year you are one of the three!" I thanked her for her kind words, but admitted I REALLY did not want to teach; I was just doing this to please my mum. That was when Mother Ward revealed to me the offer Father Agnelus Andrews had made to introduce me to the BBC.

At that moment, I knew for certain that a career in radio was what I really wanted to do.

But things are never quite as easy as one would wish. I guess it's the challenges that cause us to either grow or wither. Mother Ward, however, did put things into motion so that I could leave college without any penalties. One month into my second year, I was to take the train back from Newcastle on Tyne to Liverpool. Mother Ward and I had both written to Mum and Dad to explain, but I knew this decision was to be very hard on them. Mum met me at Lime Street Station in Liverpool. I still had eruptions all over my face, but when I saw Mum, her face looked grey. I was horrified and ashamed of myself to see that she looked like an old, old lady, although at that time she was just 39.

When we are young, we tend not to understand quite how much we hurt our parents, but that was one moment when I knew how I had disappointed her; unfortunately, much worse disappointment was to come. What a pity it takes so long to gain a little wisdom as we go through life! Despite her disappointment, Mum hugged me, and I was still excited at the thought of my promising career—performing in plays on radio. I felt as soon as my parents understood how much better this new radio career would be for me, they would be able to be happy and proud of me again, but I reckoned without Dad's protectiveness toward his only daughter.

For weeks after my return, I begged, pleaded, cajoled, and did everything in my power to convince my Dad to let me go to London to start the career I felt was a perfect fit, both for my personality and my God-given gifts. He was firm in his resolve—as he always had been. One of his sayings was to "have the courage of your convictions." Well, he sure had HIS, and although I had mine, I had to give in.

His worst fear, I learned, was the so called "white slave traffic." I understand this practice is just as prevalent today. I was so very naïve and innocent I suppose I would have been easy target. So, I guess he did have a very valid point, but back then it was really frustrating. Obviously, I had to get a job, and the next good offer was as a reporter for the *Liverpool Echo*. Again, Dad said "No!" He didn't want me digging around for news stories that could put me into dangerous situations. So, I finally settled on the not so exciting, but very safe job as a chair-side assistant to a dentist. Little did we know, the biggest danger to me was lurking at the bus stop where I caught the bus to my safe job each day!

Chapter Seven

I NEVER MET A HORMONE
I COULD TRUST!

*T*his chapter is the most difficult one of all. Most of my life, I've kept these details to myself, primarily because I was terribly ashamed of the pain I inflicted on my parents. I'm telling this story for two reasons: 1) it happened, and 2) to hopefully prevent at least one young person from making the same mistake. The second reason stems from a conversation I had with George during the '70s. His latest album, *Extra Texture*, had some really insightful lyrics, but it wasn't selling quite as well as usual. I recall saying to George, "It's such a pity more people are not getting to hear the messages in these songs." His reply to me provides the reason I am revealing the most shameful part of my life. He said, "Well, Lou, as long as even **one** person understands, it is worth doing!"

I hope at least one person will understand what I am about to tell.

Much more is known in the 21st century about our biology. We humans when we enter our teen years are at our most vulnerable. We have little experience of life, but tend to think we "know it all." We are full of enthusiasm about our potential future, and dismiss as archaic the advice of our parents and teachers. At that most vulnerable time, we are afflicted with one of the most dangerous and powerful forces we ever have to confront. Unfortunately, when I was a teen we had yet to scientifically discover what we now know about....

Hormones!

Once in their power, our ability to make reasonable/cognitive decisions is, for too many years, paralyzed. Once we fall prey to these treacherous hormones, few of us escape before really messing up our lives. In days past, many young people from prestigious families were disinherited due to the unsuitable and potentially destructive choices made under these influences. We have seen more recently, men holding responsible positions in government and business lose their families and the respect of the public because they too fell under the control of these sneaky hormones. They then jettison everything worthwhile in their lives due to the often erroneous conviction that some new hormonal attraction is *true love.*

It matters not how much we love and respect our parents. It matters not how intelligent we may be. It matters not how great a sense of responsibility we may have. It matters not how great a potential we may have to make a significant, positive contribution to society. For a few crucial years, all that DOES seem to matter is the influence and lack of mercy of our hormones.

Our most noble instincts fade into a murky mist when our sneaky hormones take over. I know from my own experience how we can be totally betrayed and powerless in the face of the overwhelming urges these hormones inflict upon us. Eventually, many of us realize we've badly messed up our lives due to the hypnotic and total control of these nasty, confusing hormones. For most of our early years we find them impossible to resist. How I wish when I was at that stage in my life someone could have explained all this to me—but in those days we weren't aware that these dangers, which we know about now, were hiding just beneath the surface of our consciousnesses. They hold us just as captive as any other addiction such as tobacco, alcohol or more potent drugs.

I sincerely hope and pray that these paragraphs will help one or two youngsters from falling into the same trap. Please, if you are in your teens or early twenties, still young and vulnerable, pay attention! The misery you could endure is worth avoiding! If you are parents of vulnerable teens, please have them read this. It is meant with great compassion, and hopefully to be of assistance to the young people who have still to confront and struggle with these forces.

Bottom line: No relationship is worth losing your values over—no matter what your hormones whisper to you. If it seems wrong, it usually IS and will surely lead to misery.

So here goes! At the end of the last chapter, the danger lurking at my bus stop was in the form of a rather handsome, Gregory Peck-ish, much older man. A dozen or so people were usually waiting at each bus stop, and as is the case with Liverpudlians, we all chatted to each other. For several weeks, we nodded "Good Morning" to each other before taking the bus to my very safe job as a dental assistant in downtown Liverpool. I was in the habit of taking this same bus in the opposite direction to Hale most evenings to visit my former high school pal Sylvia Wilkinson. She lived in a lovely modern thatched home. They had a TV set, quite a luxury in 1950, and I was invited to watch those early TV shows because our family was a long way financially from owning such an innovation—but Sylvia, like most of the students at my school, had been in a much higher income bracket.

Anyhow, I usually caught the last bus home from her house and would see this same man from the bus stop, striding along the road going home. So, one morning after making the usual casual greeting, I said, "I thought I saw you walking last night when I was on the bus coming from my friend's house in Hale." He smiled and replied, "Yes, I go to play darts with my buddies at the Child of Hale Pub." And that was all.

Several days later, he asked me if I would like to meet him after work in the city to go for a drink. I was nineteen-plus, and in Britain old enough to legally drink or go into a pub. Apart from the times when I accompanied my parents to their social club at Finch Lane where Mum and Dad taught and ran dances, I had not yet done so. My first reaction was a question. He seemed so much older than me, thirty-one, that I asked, "Are you married?" He said, "Yes," and pointing across the road from the bus stop said, "that is where I live with my wife and kids." In my innocent mind—and having parents who always went everywhere together—I came to the conclusion that this man who went to the pub alone probably did not have a babysitter. Babysitters were quite a new idea at that time. I thought if I got to know him and his family, I could offer to babysit in order that he could take his wife with him. With this strategy in mind, I agreed to meet him at a pub named The Grapes on the corner of Lime Street in the city, quite near where I worked. It was 31 March and—appropriately—the day before April Fools' Day!

Naturally, I did not think of this as a "date"; he was way too old. I had been on quite a few dates with boys I met at the many dance halls popular in Liverpool. Some had kissed me goodnight. One, to my horror, actually tried to put his hand between my legs, and I could not imagine why anyone would wish to touch an excretory part of my body. That weirdo was quickly dumped!

So I met this man. I found he was an engineer, and we had a great conversation. He was so much more knowledgeable and intelligent than the boys I usually spoke with. He told me of his stern Victorian-type father, and when I asked if he would like for me to babysit in order for him to take his wife out, he explained to me how his marriage came about:

During WWII, he volunteered and became a corporal in a tank battalion. Stationed in Bournemouth, prior to overseas deployment, he went on a date with a girl, Dora, who was working as a companion to a rich old lady. Apparently, the lady became angry when Dora arrived home late from her date with him and dismissed her from her job. The next day, he received his orders to be shipped to France in seven days—into the thick of the war. That afternoon, a tearful Dora came to the army station. She told him he had caused her to lose her job, so, very much the considerate gentleman, he suggested to her that they get married before he left for France. That way, she would have his army pay and—like most young soldiers at the time—he did not have great hopes of survival. But he did survive, and he found himself married to a girl for whom he had no strong attachment. Life went on, and they eventually had three children.

I could well understand this situation, and back then divorce was not the easy option it is today. But, at least I had my answer: he did not need a babysitter. We took the bus home to Speke, and he walked me from the bus stop to my family's new three bedroom home at Upton Green. We shook hands and said goodnight. Unfortunately, and to some degree, fortunately, this was not the END it should have been. Due to our work schedule and constant proximity, we often sat together on the bus and had interesting conversations; thus, we became friends. As time went on, we began to meet for the occasional drink, and eventually the walk home from the bus to Upton Green ended with a kiss.

I now encountered those *"fiendish thingys,"* namely hormones!

Before long I was madly in love. And I know now why they use the word madly! I had to tell Mum and Dad about him, and they invited him to our home to discuss the situation. Despite the fact he was only eight years younger than Mum, both parents liked him as a person, but begged us to stop seeing each other. We did try, but it was impossible since we took the same bus every day. I believed he did genuinely love me, and as naïve and inexperienced as I was—at 20 still a virgin—I thought this was the *real* thing, too.

He admitted to his wife that he had finally met someone he really loved and suggested they file for a divorce, but divorce was such a rarity then that she did not agree. (I did not know until many years later that he had been quite a womanizer during his loveless marriage and had fathered two illegitimate children by two different women. So, his wife had no reason to believe this affair was any different from the other frequent times he had strayed.)

Early in 1952, he suggested that the only way his wife would agree to a divorce was for him to move out and for us to go away together. He found that there were a great many employment opportunities for him, and perhaps me, in Gloucestershire.

The aviation industry had several major companies in that area. First, there was Rotol, which was Rolls Royce/ Bristol Aircraft. There was also G.A.C., Gloucester Aircraft Co.; this company was involved in building the first delta-winged, or swept-winged aircraft. Another company, Dowty Engineering, invented the hydraulic suspension landing gear now used on almost all planes. Hawker-Siddeley, yet another aircraft company, built the Hawker fighter plane. Gordon resigned his job with Pilkington Glass and applied for a design position with Rotol. On his acceptance, he persuaded me to go with him to Gloucester. Naturally, my hormones agreed! I did not really enjoy being a dental assistant anyway. All those rotting teeth!

Swearing my brothers to secrecy, I had them help me pack my trunk, the one I had used to go to college, and carry it downstairs when Mum and Dad were out. I think we took a taxi to the railway station and bought our tickets to Gloucester. My parents had started a savings bond account for each of us when we were quite small, and in 1952 my account could be cashed in for about six pounds, enough for both of our rail tickets. As I recall, there was enough left over to buy a wedding ring for appearances. It was a few months until my 21st birthday, when I could legally make my own decisions, so I needed my location to be unknown to my parents for that period of time.

When we arrived in Gloucester, he went to his job, and I found an apartment for us. Although this was 1952 and the war had ended in the mid-'40s, we still had ration books, bearing our legal names. The idea of two unmarried people living together was not widely accepted, so for lots of reasons, mostly shame and embarrassment, I legally changed my name to his, and used the wedding ring.

I quickly found a job in the accounting department at G.A.C., but after a month, he told me of an opening at Rotol, so I took another position in the computing office there. Of course, there were no mechanical or electronic computers then, but my job consisted of working out very complex mathematical formulas for the Society of British Aircraft Constructors (SBAC). I had to compute things such as how many pounds of thrust it took to lift a plane weighing x amount of pounds, to x altitude, at x speed. The result was plotted as a curve on a graph. I am quite sure I could not attempt such complicated math now, but back then I had taken calculus at college and had been very well educated, so I found these calculations really interesting.

We were both making—for those days—pretty good pay. Each week, he continued to send his wife the same housekeeping allowance as when he was still with her. We made sure she did not suffer financially due to our affair. After several months, we moved from the apartment in Gloucester to a 20-foot by 8-foot camper in Twigworth at a campground more convenient to our work. Soon after this move, I turned twenty-one. Greatly relieved to be able to contact my parents once more, I wrote to Mum and Dad to let them know where I was, and to apologize for the heartache I had caused them. I told them about my challenging job, the camper and how beautiful the surrounding countryside was.

A week later, I received a package and a letter from home. One did not make phone calls in those days. I opened the package to find a wonderful variety of clippings from the plants in Mum's little garden. She wanted me to be able to make my own little patch of ground attractive, too. I understood for the first time in my life the real meaning of unconditional love. I shed so many tears that week, thankful for the forgiveness. The utter sadness I felt was for another reason. I also understood I had been fooled by those seductive hormones into thinking what I was feeling was actual love. But, a few weeks into living with him I discovered I most certainly was *not* in love.

He was a heavy smoker and had emphysema. Like most men in those days, he used large, white cotton handkerchiefs that I had to boil and hand wash/rinse each week. I found this chore to be so disgusting—all that mucus! Oh no, this was not love! But I felt so awful about how I had hurt my parents after the sacrifices they had made for my education that my guilt caused me to make an even worse mistake and decide that in the words of the proverb, I had made my bed and would just have to lie in it. So, I made no attempt to leave. A year or so later his divorce was processed, and I was of legal age to marry. In 1954, Mum and George came to

Gloucestershire to the town of Cheltenham and were present at our wedding on July 3rd—the day before America's Independence Day! Although I was in my early twenties, I'd already faced enough challenges to know that even the most attractive rose garden hid many, many thorns. Assessing the whole picture, I knew I was not "in love," and it seemed life on Earth was far from perfect. We had caused a lot of misery to other people, and I didn't think I could back out then.

Shortly after my twenty-first birthday, he received a check from the pension fund at his previous job at Pilkingtons. This money he used to buy us both new 3-speed bicycles. We then had the freedom of being able to ride anywhere we wished without having to wait for a bus. We were living at Twigworth then and the distance from my work was about eight miles each way and about twelve miles round trip to his job. I soon developed very strong leg muscles!!

Both our jobs paid well, and we did in fact enjoy our work. I still enjoyed my husband's friendship and his intelligence. He had absolute integrity regarding his engineering designs. His reputation as a skilled mechanical design engineer was spreading within the industry. He was lured to Dowty Company; I moved to Hawker-Siddeley to an even better job. But, my route to work there took me up and over a very steep hill. Even my 3-speed bike could not make the grade, so I had to walk to the top of the hill—it was called Churchdown—however, once I made it to the top, I could just 'free-wheel' the remaining four miles to the gate of the factory. Wheee!

The whole "in love" concept was shattered for me. Not wanting to hurt his feelings, I didn't admit this to him. He was, for reasons I did not know at the time, a very skilled lover. In fact, many years later when I read the Karma Sutra, I discovered that humans had for many centuries been engaged in acts I thought we had invented! I came to the conclusion that things could have been a lot worse, so I accepted my fate.

Meanwhile, yet another engineering company approached him. This was Cable Belt Company in Inverness, Scotland. This company had designed a long-distance conveyor belt to move coal and other minerals from the working face in a mine to the shaft. These belts could cover very long distances, two to three miles in many cases, using only one drive unit. However, most mines had lots of twists and turns, and the belt, using their existing design with the same drive unit, could not go around corners. My husband was brought in to devise a way to get the belts around the corners. Within a few months, he had solved this problem and, using a series of strategically placed and timed pulleys, created the first long-distance "round the bend" conveyor belt for the mining industry. It could go anywhere underground powered by only one drive unit. This invention was a major advantage for the whole industry. Once he had solved the problem, he grew a little restless, and he started to talk about immigrating to Australia or Canada. Being my father's daughter, I had no problem with the idea of exploring more of our planet.

It wasn't until way into the future that I recognized a certain pattern to my life. It seemed in retrospect, in each new place, once I'd started to make friends with other workmates or neighbors and was developing a social life, *that* was the time my husband would get restless and start looking for another job. To the best of my knowledge he was always well respected by his bosses. His eagerness to move was not prompted by anyone's dissatisfaction with his work. He just would say he had "itchy feet."

I was very much indoctrinated, then, by the concept that a woman always has to follow wherever her husband decided to go. Times have changed!

I had enjoyed my work in Gloucestershire at the aircraft companies, but I also found I really enjoyed living in Inverness, Scotland. I suppose my teachers in high school were correct: "Louise is very adaptable."

During our time in Scotland, Mum and George had visited. We made a trip from Inverness to Ben Nevis, the highest point in the British Isles, around the famous Loch Ness. Though we looked diligently, we did not see Nessie! *(See photo on page 196.)* We also took a trip to the Isle of Skye. Before getting to Skye, Mum, George and I were in the railway station in Inverness waiting for the train. We were all thirsty and decided to buy something to drink. We asked young George to go ask the price of apple juice. When they told him it was a shilling, he turned to Mom and me in horror and called to us, "They want a shilling, and it isn't even alcoholic!" Naturally we had quite a chuckle at his reaction.

Cable Belt Company had also helped us find a very nice little home, which we set about furnishing. I went for six weeks training in Aberdeen in order to work as a telephone operator for the GPO. We were actually considered Civil Servants as the telephone company was government operated, as was the BBC. But, once again as I was finding my niche at a really enjoyable job, and before we were finished furnishing the house, we were again following those "itchy feet." This time we went to Canada!

My Uncle Eddy had moved to Canada a few years earlier and, due to his earlier business knowledge, had an excellent position with Smith Transport in Toronto. During WWII in the Guards, Eddy was stationed in Cortina in Northern Italy. He took an advanced business course and also actually learned to type. This was *not* considered a manly task in those days. However, with these skills he became the right hand man to the town major, commanding the troops in that part of Italy. This business experience proved very valuable throughout Eddy's life, causing him to gain success in various high profile positions. In Toronto he was the night supervisor for all the shipping in and out of Smith's Toronto terminal. I had always kept in touch with Eddy by mail, and when we started thinking about moving overseas, he immediately encouraged us to choose Canada. Throughout my childhood Uncle Eddy had always been my big brother. Just seven or eight years my senior, we attended the same grade school. When I was just a beginner, Eddy was already almost 6' tall, their head boy and football captain. Each day he would come to my house in the next street, hoist me onto his shoulders, and carry me off to school. Eddy had married an Italian girl, Mimi, whilst stationed in Cortina. When the war was over, he became a mounted police officer in Liverpool. *(See photo on page 195.)*

About the time we were thinking about Immigration, Eddy was well established in Toronto. He and Mimi had two sons, George and Gregory. Eddy sent us some *Toronto Star* newspapers with the want ads so that my husband could get a feel for the available opportunities.

One possible position was as Chief Mechanical Design Engineer with a gold mining company, Kerr-Addison, in Virginiatown, Ontario. An application was sent and he was quickly accepted and offered a salary, which was approximately ten times what he was earning in Britain. We took care of all the paperwork, and soon he was booked on the Cunard vessel the *Saxonia* to sail out of Liverpool. I was to follow a month later on the *Ivernia*. We sold all of our very new furniture.

For that month, I moved back to Liverpool, with Mum and Dad and my brothers. Just prior to my husband's leaving, George was stricken with a severe illness, nephritis, causing a stay in hospital. In Britain, visiting hours at hospitals were few and far between. The general idea was that during an illness a patient's contact with the outside world should be restricted as much as possible. It made a lot of sense, but we could visit George only for one hour on Sunday. Mum and Dad, my husband and I, and a couple of George's schoolmates showed up. We all surrounded his bed, and I recall being quite amazed at his diplomatic and mature way of handling this situation. He was thirteen at the time, and although there were three distinctly separate groups around him, he made sure he greeted each of us with an appropriate conversation. He juggled the situation in such a way that at no time did anyone feel left out. At the time, I thought he certainly had a skillful way of handling a variety of people all at the same time. A day or two later he was out of hospital.

I was able to spend the next month with my entire family once more. We made the most of our short time together and visited all the favorite places we had enjoyed when we were much younger.

Too soon it was the day for me to sail. My husband sent money from his first paycheck for my passage. He also sent upkeep money to his ex-wife each month for quite some time into the future, as I recall. The morning of my departure, I went through my luggage and the contents of my handbag to make sure I rid myself of anything unnecessary. I burned a few items in the fireplace. However, when I arrived to board the *Ivernia*, I could not find my ticket, and—to my great embarrassment—realized it had been amongst the items I had burned. Maybe fate was trying to tell me not to go? Dad went with me to the Cunard offices close to where the ship was anchored at the Pier Head. He had them reissue my ticket. I boarded, and whilst the ship was preparing to move, I watched my Dad from the deck, waving to him for what I was afraid may have been the last time I would ever see him.

The adventurous part of me was looking forward with great anticipation to the experiences of yet another culture and country. I wondered if the adjustment would be as unsettling as the wartime evacuation from a bustling vibrant city like Liverpool to a remote village in Wales. As we moved toward the mouth of the River Mersey, I was both excited and distraught, tears running down my face as my Dad, waving from the dock, gradually became invisible.

Chapter Eight
I'M OFF TO SEA...

*T*he voyage across the Atlantic took six or seven days. Weather in the North Atlantic was fair and I enjoyed my first ocean voyage. The final destination was Toronto, but the destination for quite a number on board was our first stop, Quebec City. Friends I'd made on board went ashore with me there. We toured the city and visited Chateau Frontenac on the cliffs above the St. Lawrence River. The next day we arrived in Toronto. Uncle Eddy met me and escorted me to the train station. I then took the long rail trip to Kirkland Lake, Ontario, some 400 miles north of Toronto.

We had our own really nice home when I arrived in Virginiatown. The Kerr-Addison Gold Mine—was at that time the largest gold producer in the world, refining as many as seven bullion bars per week. The company provided homes for all of its employees at a very nominal monthly rent. The type of home was fitted to the status of the job. Since my husband was Chief Mechanical Design Engineer, we qualified for one of the better homes. The floors throughout the home were all natural birch hardwood. There was a large L-shaped living room and a spacious kitchen on the ground floor, three bedrooms and a full bathroom upstairs. A wood furnace in the basement heated the home. The wood we used was discarded pit props from the mine provided to employees at low cost. There was also a covered porch along one side of the house. Each home had about a quarter of an acre yard. A few miners grew vegetables, but actually very few!

Naturally, he was really pleased to be able to provide such a lovely home. He had already bought bedroom items and a dining set, but waited for my arrival so I could choose the rest of our furnishings. The local all-purpose store was Lockie Lockes. You can imagine how thrilled I was to be able to choose a houseful of furniture and meet the many friends my husband had made in the previous month.

Most of the miners' homes were within easy walking distance and closer to the mine than ours. Although our home was, compared to homes in Britain, fairly plush, the very top administration had much fancier homes on a nearby hilltop even further from the actual mine offices. Of necessity, most of the senior staff all had cars, so before long, we too had to acquire our own auto. We had not been accustomed in Britain to making use of a credit system, but my husband soon discovered Household Finance Company and like a kid in a candy store fell enthusiastically into the pit of debt! He bought a Chevy to use for his one mile walk to the offices at the mine. I, however, had to walk about two miles into the small town center to buy groceries, Men mostly regarded "women drivers" as very scary! So, for "lots of reasons," we ladies were *not* encouraged to learn how to drive.

The common practice was to set up an account with the local grocery store, which was taken care of each month on payday. Money was still sent monthly to the ex-wife. I think most of our furniture was bought on credit, but considering the higher income we had, compared to back in Britain, I found it difficult to understand why all the use of credit. Mum and Dad had, except for the Singer sewing machine, only bought those goods they could afford to pay for completely.

Soon after buying the Chevy, we took the 400-mile trip south to Richmond Hill, in the northern suburbs of Toronto, to visit Uncle Eddy and his family. Eddy took us on Highway 401 to Niagara Falls for the day. I must admit viewing the falls up close is far more impressive than any movies or photos I had seen. We took The Maid of the Mists boat trip right up to the swirling cauldron at the base of the Falls.

(I recently was to recall that trip very vividly when, together with many Sarasota citizens, we witnessed Nik Wallenda's historic walk across those same falls on a 2" high wire. Many of those present have a close association with the circus and the Wallenda family, and I can tell you there was great outpouring of family pride in his achievement, to say nothing of my own great feeling of relief when he safely dismounted from the high wire in Canada! More recently he successfully crossed the Grand Canyon. If I was part of his family I think I might be inclined to say, "Enough is enough!" But then I never walked on a high wire.)

Our Niagara trip was about nine months prior to the birth of my son, who was born in Kirkland Lake, Ontario, on April 12, 1957. My daughter was born at the same hospital September 29, 1959. A story circulating in Virginiatown claimed that the pinkish-colored acrid smoke issuing forth from the smelter wherein the gold was refined contained a chemical ingredient favorable to fertility. This was likely a ploy to forestall any complaints about the smoke, which, depending on the direction and speed of the wind would sometimes swirl around close to the ground and inhibit breathing. People were unaware of pollution then. I don't know if there is any validity to this fertility claim, but it certainly worked for me!

During this time, I was adjusting to more culture shock! People on this side of the pond seemed very "spoilt." After the austerity of my life, I was horrified to find one wife complaining dramatically that her dishwasher had broken down. Although I made no comment, my somewhat sarcastic thoughts went like this: "My goodness! Having to wash dishes in your sink, with your hands? Oh! Poor, mistreated, overworked person!" Others complained because the phones were "party-lines," which meant that sometimes when you tried to use the phone, the other party may be using it. Until that point in my life, the only time a phone was needed was maybe once a year in a dire emergency when you would have to go to the nearest public phone booth located quite some distance away. I still keep my phone conversations short and to the point.

During my first pregnancy, my husband and I would occasionally go to the local movie house, and I found the smell of popcorn to be quite stomach churning! I experienced severe morning sickness for the first three to four months, so the doctor prescribed a new miracle morning sickness drug. I filled the prescription and was appalled at the cost—six dollars for each pill. But, I was suffering badly. I took the pills for two days with no relief at all, so, considering the cost, returned the pills to the pharmacy. They refunded my money. This turned out to be the most remarkably fortunate thing I ever did. Just a few short years later, the public learned "thalidomide" was the cause of babies being born with stumps instead of arms and legs. What a lucky break that those same pills did not curtail my nausea!

Life in general was pleasant. Our social life tended to be restricted to visits with others on the same occupational level of the husband. Mostly for safety and "chain of command" reasons, the bosses were not encouraged, on a personal level, to mix socially with the miners and laborers. But there were social outlets that were available to all. My husband had volunteered and served in the British Army throughout WWII, so wherever we lived he was always invited to become a member of the Legion.

(During his service in France as a tank commander, he had endured—as did most troops—many traumatic and really gruesome experiences. In retrospect, I'm beginning to understand that much of his often irrational and sometimes cruel behavior was a result of what we now recognize as post-traumatic stress. In those days it was simply known as "shell shock" and not considered a serious "disability." I was aware that on occasions when people were setting off fireworks, he would shake violently and be unable to function normally.)

On Saturday nights, the Legion club usually held a dance. Once I had children, I and other mothers would take turns babysitting and thus give others an opportunity for a night of dancing. Thinking back, I see how well the wives co-operated and stuck together in a supportive way. Especially when you consider every wife was from "someplace else" on the planet, it made sense too, because society still treated women as second class citizens. (Has it really changed?)

At the working surface underground the temperature was very cold, or was it very hot? Women were not allowed underground; in fact, we were strictly taboo, so I never knew from experience which it was, too hot or too cold, but I recall being told that the temperatures are quite different way down at as deep as 6,000 feet. On returning to the surface after their eight-hour shifts, the men would shower, then go home briefly for supper. Most men sought the company of their workmates, rather than spend the evening with wives and kids. They would spend their off duty hours at the bars, either in Virginiatown itself, to the west in Larder Lake some seven miles away, or to the east at Rouyn/Noranda about twenty miles away over the Ontario border in Quebec province.

On the relatively rare occasions whenever I was able to go out, I preferred either the Legion or the Club in Rouyn/Noranda because both places had dancing. I enjoyed dancing because during my teen years, Mum and Dad had taught dancing on Monday nights at the Transport General Workers' Club at Finch Lane in Liverpool. Then on Saturday nights they would emcee dances for all the members. Once I left college they would often take me with them to the Saturday night dances, and I was one of their most enthusiastic students.

At that time in Canada, in order to buy alcohol for home consumption, one had to go to an officially licensed store, which only operated a few hours a week. The nearest one was seven miles away in Larder Lake, so most men found it simpler to take advantage of the camaraderie of the local bars. But, my husband also found that many Canadians made "home brew." So, he diligently went about collecting and sterilizing six cases of beer bottles. He then bought a five gallon stone crock and a bottle-capping gadget. Every few weeks he would make his batch of brew.

One sadly, funny incident occurred when we had a party. My husband had recommended and hired a former colleague from Inverness, Don Tyrrell, an excellent engineer, who at that time lived next door to us. He was a Baptist and did not drink, so during the party he happily played bartender and poured the beer for all our guests. Next day, most attendees had really bad abdominal problems. I was okay, as I didn't drink the nasty stuff, and my husband had poured his own drinks. We traced this situation back to our Baptist friend. He didn't know that home brew has sediment lying in the bottom of the bottle. When pouring the brew, one needs to be careful to pour very slowly in order to keep the sediment from getting **out** of the bottle and into the glass. My husband had not thought to impart this important factor to our tee-total volunteer bartender—with disastrous results.

I was gradually becoming aware that my husband was seldom without alcohol. Maybe if I'd known there was such a thing as alcoholism when I first met him, I might have realized his nightly trips to the Child of Hale to "play darts" had less to do with darts and more to do with the fact that alcohol was served. I'd been aware of the "once a week drunks" who lived in the Groves, but they only had enough money to pay for booze *before* they handed over what was left of the weekly pay envelope to their wives. The most notable "drunk" in the Groves was a very huge Irishman known as Morgan the Almighty. He would yell and curse all the way home on a Friday night, and no one ever stood in his way. His wife, Lily, was a good friend of my Mum's, and she would usually take refuge at our house on Friday nights. Mum and Dad did not believe in "wasting" their hard earned money on anything as frivolous and unnecessary as booze. As I mentioned earlier, Christmas day was the only time alcohol was even brought into the house. So, my only experience of alcohol problems was limited to the Fridays night "drunks"— boy, was I naive?!

Considering the number of times Gordon went out drinking at night, it was rather ironic that he was arrested for DUI on the one occasion we had gone grocery shopping to Noranda in Quebec province. That evening he had just one scotch, followed by the usual beer "chaser," but we were stopped by Quebec police, and more or less railroaded. He was very indignant and that led to him being arrested, put in jail and subsequently having a six-month driving suspension. This in turn led to my sudden promotion from a passenger to an actual driver of a vehicle. I took my drivers course and passed my test in time to be able to take my then ten-month-old son along to bring his father home from fourteen days in jail. Whilst he was in jail, he was introduced to the novels of Ayn Rand and soon became a fervent disciple. He had been raised in a very wealthy family, so her views were "right up his street." This was early 1958. He introduced these books to me also so I also read *Atlas Shrugged*, *The Fountainhead*, *We the Living*, and *The Virtue of Selfishness*. Then for a while we went around saying mysteriously, "Who is John Galt?" But to me, it was a bit too similar to the way the nuns pandered to the wealthy during my school years.

Although his attraction to alcohol was eventually to become a serious problem for me, I have to admit that he never allowed his addiction to interfere with his work in any way. He never ever drank when he was working. He felt his responsibility to the workers very strongly. When we arrived at Kerr-Addison in 1956, the underground shaft descended some 6,000 feet. Soon after we arrived, new stopes were discovered at a much greater depth underground. Stopes are the cigar-shaped geological formations containing pyrites from which gold is extracted. He designed and oversaw the construction and sinking of an additional 2,000 feet of shaft, bringing the total depth to 8,000 feet. The stresses and pressures of the ever-shifting rock—in addition to the many different types of rock he had to penetrate—made this task enormously challenging. He had to be absolutely accurate with all his calculations. Each day he tested the batch of concrete mix that was to line the shaft. He made sure it was the correct consistency to withstand the pressures of each different type of rock he was boring through. Before the calculations could be made, he had to find out what kind of rock the next few hundred feet of shaft would reveal. For example, talc was very soft and granite very hard. He was aware that the lives of his crew depended on the accuracy of every calculation he made. His engineering integrity was absolute. No matter what else happened between us, I cannot ever fault him for his devotion to his work ethic. He came home from the mine at 4:00 p.m., had supper, jumped into the Chevy, and went off to the various bars in the area. Regrettably, when he arrived home from these prolonged drinking bouts, a different, nastier version of him would emerge, soon to be known as Mr. Hyde.

I realize now it was mostly our intellectual compatibility that enabled me to tolerate my life with him, as well as the conversations we had about engineering. He would involve me in discussions about the daily decisions and challenges he faced in his work. I grew to be very knowledgeable in engineering matters, understanding the principles behind hydraulics, stress, and torque, etc. Also, we spoke of world politics and other topics, conversations I'd previously held with Dad. His views were ultra conservative (except when it came to buying things on credit), and as my upbringing was, to say the least, "fiscally conservative," if not downright frugal, I tended to lean that way too.

During our time in Virginiatown, he worked closely with many others, including the mine captains. One of these captains turned out to have also been a German tank commander during WWII. Coincidentally, both men had been involved in a longish battle in a certain small town in northern France. When they, purely by chance, discovered this, they further discovered that they, in opposing armies, had been chasing and trying to destroy each other in this small town for several days. They each recalled the challenges and the streets and landmarks involved in the pursuit. So it was, that many years later, working as colleagues, they looked back and realized that they both had been "victims" of a system which placed decent men in combat against each other, men who had no quarrel with each other and who in the right circumstances, could work together in harmony. This was the beginning of a kind of epiphany for myself and my husband that, by golly, Mum was right when she said, "It is not the men fighting the war who start it, but those who manufacture the weapons and make lots of money from the suffering of others."

This was when I first began to clearly understand how "we the people" are horribly manipulated by those we elect to "serve us?" I will list what have now become my firmly held convictions on that subject.

1. Wars are seldom fought for a legitimate cause. Territorial disputes arise, although it has never been clear just what entity authorizes any human or group of humans to actually have "ownership" of any piece of Earth's surface. Our Creator made this planet without boundaries or fences, or "For Sale" signs.
2. Most often, religion is used as the excuse for wars since THAT is one sure way to arouse passions.
3. Wars are seldom definitively WON, nor does war resolve the root causes, as unfortunately the same scenarios are repeated over and over throughout history.
4. Mr. and Mrs. Everyman are seldom interested in fighting with people they don't know over matters they are neither concerned about nor understand.
5. The only ones deluded enough to believe they are winners are the cynical and greedy instigators, those who manufacture the various weapons we use to crush and kill each other. As long as they can claim their "pot of gold," they are prepared to completely disregard the suffering and human misery they cause. Unfortunately, there are many who have not yet learned that "money can't buy you love!" Could it be they do not have the capacity to understand love and compassion, in which case they are lost and lonely, albeit money-rich souls.

We remained in Canada until my daughter was two. Once the extension of the shaft was complete, my husband again became restless and began to search for a new challenge. At that time Cerro De Pasco Mining Company—producers of copper, lead, and zinc, located in La Oroya, Peru—was looking for a Chief Design Engineer. He applied for the position, and we were both flown to New York to be interviewed. This was my first flight. The plane was a four-prop Constellation, and as luck would have it, while I was watching with interest the whirring of the propellers, the one just outside my window stopped. Uh-oh! But we made it safely into New York on the three remaining props.

We were approved for the position. On my daughter's second birthday, we flew first class to Miami; then on to Panama, where we deplaned for a short time; and finally on to Lima, Peru. For most of the trip, the children were allowed to sleep in the overhead bunks provided in first class. My children each received a certificate from the airline to certify and confirm their first crossing of the equator. I don't know if this is still done. We stayed for a couple of days at the Hotel Bolivar in Lima, and I recall my son made quite a lot of friends amongst the pre-teenage boys on the staff because he was playing in the corridor with a friction-driven car. Quite a crowd gathered, and they all took turns playing with the car and sending it back and forth until a senior member of the staff came along, and in a very friendly way, dispersed them.

We were greeted by officials from the Cerro de Pasco Company, and were thoroughly briefed on the differences we would experience living at an altitude of 12,000 feet. The next day, our little family set off on the Central Peruvian Railway—possibly the most hair raising train ride on the planet—from Lima to La Oroya. Once there, we were accommodated at the company Hotel Junin, where we were to stay until our own home was ready.

My husband proved, on our first evening, he was not a man to allow the dire warnings to interfere with his addictions, one of which was smoking. We were in the lobby being assigned our room when he decided to light a cigarette. He promptly fell to the ground unconscious. Most of the people greeting us, to my surprise, just burst out laughing.

"This happens all the time to those arrogant ones who disregard the warnings about how the lack of oxygen in the air at this altitude can affect you," I was told. At that stage of my relationship with him, I was getting to be less than sympathetic to his often obnoxious behavior, so leaving him on the floor, I was assured by those in the lobby he would "come-to" in a few minutes. I took the children and—accompanied by a bellboy with our luggage—went to our room to unpack. Then we went off to the dining room for a meal. Before long, I was joined by a very embarrassed husband. Apparently, when he "came-to," the other company employees in the lobby just told him what a fool he was for disregarding the lengthy familiarization we had undergone in Lima. So, for the first time at a new job, he was not hailed as a conquering hero.

It was now 1961. Since leaving Britain I had written long and detailed letters home telling of my travels and experiences. My youngest brother George, from the time he became an uncle at the birth of my son, had begun to write to me. Having a similar adventurous nature, he wanted to know more about the world I was discovering. Now having adventures of his own, he wrote to me of the band he was in and how they had toured Scotland. When I lived in Inverness, he and Mum had visited me there, so during this tour he sent me a postcard of the hotel he and his band had stayed at in Inverness. He marked their room on the postcard with an X.

(I wonder which collector now owns that?)

Shortly afterwards a Liverpool agent booked them into a series of clubs in Hamburg. It was during this "era" he wrote to me with great eagerness and enthusiasm that his band had been approached by none other than Bert Kampfert. He was a famous German record producer, and was recording Tony Sheridan, a relatively well-known singer at that time who had somewhat of an Elvis sound. He selected George and his band mates to be the "back-up" band. The lads were ecstatic at, what they were sure, was the beginning of their trip to the toppermost of the poppermost. But sadly, nothing came of this at the time except that it did lead to the eventual meeting of Brian and "his boys."

I recall George explained just what this process would mean. Taking the concept that making a record was a totally revolutionary **new** invention, he joked, "Now we can sing a song, and even when we are no longer actually singing, people will still be able to hear us!!" That was his rather typical whimsical humor!

Naturally our whole family was pleased at this potential big step forward for them. Another comical happening in relation to this recording—apparently when the discs came on the market—the German word to translate, beat boys or Beatles, turned out to be a German word for one's—"naughty bits"—as the Monty Pythons say. Naturally back in Liverpool the word got out about their recording and their Cavern fans went searching for copies. They knew one cut was the folk song "My Bonnie"; the search for this led many Cavern fans into the nearby NEMS Department Store in Whitechapel, where the young son of the owner had been appointed to run the record department. Enter Brian Epstein! In his own bio, "A Cellarfull of Noise," Brian recounts how he had been somewhat of a disappointment to his successful businessman father, and eager to show how well he could run the record department, he undertook a search to find this "in demand" recording. On finding it, he ordered a couple of hundred copies, which to his total gratification sold out very quickly. This story is so well known I will say no more. The newly released 50th anniversary Beatles first Kampfert recordings are now available. Listening to these songs for the first time fifty years later was quite an interesting experience for me and I'm sure will be something all Beatle people will enjoy.

This was all happening in Britain, meanwhile in Peru....

(Readers, just hang in there! I've covered a lot of ground in these past eighty years, and as events unfolded all over the planet, this became my theme: "Be Here Now"—i.e.: "I'm always *here*, and it's always *now*." You also may find when you have experienced eighty Earth years, *time* need not be feared, nor followed too closely.)

Once we settled into the hotel in La Oroya, it was the custom to hire a maid—everyone did—to provide work for the Quechua Tribe, who lived locally. Our maid was Nellie, and we paid the going rate of fourteen dollars a month! Unfortunately, she was about the same size as me, and I started missing shoes and items of clothing. The other wives informed me that anything not tied down was considered fair game for the maids. Well I had plenty, and they not so much, so it was okay.

Whenever I went into the street with my two blonde, blue-eyed toddlers, I would be surrounded by the native peoples, who would exclaim, "Que linda! How beautiful!" *(See photo on page 200.)* They believed it was good luck to be able to touch the hair of such children. Their tribe believed in blonde, blue-eyed gods or goddesses.

One of the cultural differences I found to be really charming was "laundry day." Dozens of families would gather at the riverside and, pounding the clothes in the water on the rocks, would get them clean. Then they would spread the garments out on the riverbank to dry. While the clothes dried, they would picnic and sing and dance together. I thought, *"How much more fun this is than simply putting things into a washing machine!"*

One of the less charming cultural differences was this: Due to the lack of sanitation in the workers' housing—one toilet to about thirty homes—the custom of the native population was to relieve themselves whenever and wherever they happened to be when the urge came. So, it was prudent to "watch your step" when walking around the streets. Although not involving humans, but for a similar reason, New York made laws that folks had to take a pooper scoopers when they walked their dogs. Peru, however, did not know about pooper scoopers!

Cerro de Pasco Company arranged mandatory Spanish classes three afternoons per week. Actually, my children picked up the new language much quicker than we adults and were soon, much to my amusement, ordering in the dining room *"Mozo! Dos coca-colas, y helados, por favor!"*

During our stay in Peru, I made a few trips by bus with my children to places like Huancayo, Arequipa, Huanuco, Iquitos, and other places whose names I can't recall. One place was far into the interior and at low altitude in the jungle. That trip in particular I recall because one of the tires on the bus had a blowout on a precipitous road. When all the passengers came off the bus so it could be repaired, we were able to see that all the tires were as smooth as inner tubes, absolutely no tread whatsoever! But, the Cechua natives were not alarmed; they took the pause while the tire was replaced as an excuse for a sing along. Babies were usually carried in a papoose or sort of backpack, but whilst on the bus they mostly sat on their mothers' knees. I was interested to see that they had rather strange looking "pacifiers," or "teething rings." When I asked about them, I was told that the babies were given dried bats to munch on. They were certainly hard enough to promote teething, but did not seem very tasty to my rather different cultural views.

The altitude and lack of oxygen in La Oroya made it difficult to walk at our normal pace, and we found the food provided at the hotel to cause both my children to have constant stomach problems. The company did provide medical care, and we had to make use of this frequently. They had a policy to send employees to the coast every six months in order to breathe sea level oxygen. They owned a spacious private home in Lima, and at the end of our first six months, I remember our family taking the train down to the coast. No matter whether journeying up or down, the Central Peruvian Railway is itself quite a spectacular engineering feat, with dangerous gradients and switchback turns. At one of the turns, they would back the engine onto a turntable in order to change places from front to back to make it around the bend. However, the most remarkable experience was how we felt as we neared Lima. Approaching sea level and able to breathe more and more oxygen, we felt extremely invigorated. It was such a great feeling! I would love to be able to repeat that trip! Maybe I will put it on my "bucket list."

(Give this factor some thought for a moment! Those of us who live most of our lives at sea level don't appreciate how valuable mere invisible oxygen is to our well-being, do we? Nor do we seem to be aware how our industrial activities are reducing the presence of that precious necessity of life.)

When we arrived back in La Oroya after our two-week vacation, our promised home was still not available; we and many employees' families were still living in the hotel. There was one bathroom between each two hotel rooms, so we all had to share with another family. The food was still making the children ill. My husband wrote a letter to the company complaining that they were not fulfilling his contract, which had included our own private home. At that point, he became quite a hero to the many other families still waiting to move into "the promised home."

Shortly after writing that letter, he came down with typhoid fever, and while he was in hospital, the company terminated his employment *for health reasons*. He received a very generous severance pay and first-class flights back to Toronto. All our furniture, which was still in crates, was to be returned to Toronto also. He was given a glowing letter of recommendation. However, other long-term employees told us that "troublemakers" were not tolerated—his termination was due more to his letter of complaint than health! I, however, was relieved to return to Canada, as the children had lost weight and become quite sickly during their stay in Peru.

Naturally, we wrote to Uncle Eddy. It seems throughout my life it was often Uncle Eddy to the rescue. He was still living in Toronto holding a very responsible job. He found us a furnished apartment near his, and we moved in. For the first time since I had met my husband, he did not have a job waiting for his arrival. However, he did have a remarkable resume, and he was very quickly "snapped up" by United States Steel Corporation operating out of Gagnon, Quebec. This time, he was assured there would be a house ready within a month of our arrival.

As I recall, we had left our '57 Chevy with Uncle Eddy when we moved to Peru, and he gave it back to us. We drove from Toronto to Sept-Isles, near Port Cartier, toward the mouth of the St. Lawrence River. There were no roads inland from the St. Lawrence to Gagnon, so we and our car had to be shipped by rail. Once we arrived in French-speaking

Quebec, yet another language to learn, we found there were only thirty miles of paved roads to and from the mine and the town.

At first we stayed at L'Auberge du Lac, a beautiful resort hotel. Once again, my children adapted to the language and became favorites of the staff. They would go to the spacious lobby to play with their friction cars or coloring books, etc., and I would sit and read. One day, my son was coloring nearby, but I noticed my daughter had disappeared from my view. I knew it was pretty safe, but nevertheless, I went looking for her. I discovered her sitting in the bar holding a lively conversation with the hotel manager, her chin resting on her hand and a soft drink on the table. The manager jumped up, smiling, and said, "She was thirsty; I hope you don't mind. I should have checked with you first; I thought we would be back in just a moment, but she is so much more interesting to talk to than most of the adults I know!" She was quite a vivacious and sophisticated conversationalist at the ripe old age of two and a half! After all she had flown across the equator twice, could speak two languages reasonably well, and had already spent time in both Ontario and Peru.

At our previous Canadian location in Ontario, 400 miles north of Toronto, the coldest winter temperatures would get to 30° below zero. When it rose to 20° above zero, I could shovel snow in my shirtsleeves. But in Gagnon, we were just inside the Arctic Circle, and the temperatures would drop to 60° below zero, often with a strong wind—this was a really bitter shock to our bodily thermostats after living for six months just south of the equator.

Within a week or so, our house was ready, and our crates had arrived from Peru. So, toward the end of 1962, we settled into yet another way of life. My son enrolled in pre-school and would walk, with the other children, along the main (only) road from our house to the school. One day when he was in a group walking home, a classmate caught sight of her mother coming to meet her on the other side of the road. Excited, she ran to her mother. It was winter and the roads icy. Tragically, a huge 40-ton truck laden with iron ore was approaching at the same moment. My son witnessed the truck hitting his classmate, splattering her head all over the road. It was a horrific incident for all concerned, but my five-year-old son kept reliving the scene for months after and would be terrified whenever the monster trucks passed him on his way to and from school.

Once again, we did not remain in one place—this time Gagnon—for very long. We received an offer from one of the applications my husband had filled in when we first arrived in Toronto from Peru. It required us to apply to become permanent residents of the United States. The company was Freeman Coal Company in West Frankfort, Illinois.

Before we could leave Gagnon we had to go through the immigration process, and while we were still there, Mum sent me a 45 RPM single disc called "Love, Love Me Do." It was the first recording made by my kid brother's band after they contracted with George Martin in England. Martin was known only for his comedy albums with various BBC stars. I had one of his albums in my small collection; they were good, and like all Brits, we enjoyed having a laugh, especially at ourselves! I liked this new recording and thought it "is certainly different." After the relatively "non-results" of their Kampfert encounter, I for one, was not holding my breath waiting for big things to happen. However, this teaming with George Martin and the appearance of Brian Epstein was to make quite an impact on my entire future life and, dare I suggest, the lives of many others.

Once immigration was completed we were ready for the next adventure! It is a good thing I was accustomed as a child to hearing Mum announce each day as a new adventure. I did not realize then how true that would be almost all my life! At that time, the coal industry in the Midwest had finished gathering all the surface coal in the strip mining process and was ready to change to long-wall, or underground, mining. With his proven expertise sinking shafts, the immigration process had been very speedy.

For the next part of my story, you may want to revisit Chapter Zero!

I left that part of my story with my kid brother wowing an audience at a VFW Club in the small southern Illinois town of Eldorado. My husband and I and our two children settled into our home in Benton, just six miles from the main mine office. There were three or four mines in the Freeman Coal group, and his work often took him into the mines, resulting in the need to use a weekly dry-cleaning service. That was how I met Gabe, leader of the Four Vests. (Again, see Chapter Zero.)

Soon after settling into our home in Benton, my husband decided we needed to get a pup for the children. We found a beautiful six-week-old German shepherd with an excellent pedigree. My husband was big on such details. In the evenings he would take her out on a leash to obedience train her. Sheba soon became a well-behaved and obedient animal, and soon it was deemed okay for me to take her with me when I walked up to the town square with the children. I had a stroller for my daughter. We lived only about a half mile from the square, and there were a number of stores on East Main. The first time the children and I took Sheba along, we had quite a shock when suddenly she dashed in front of the stroller and into the door of Jim Southern's. At that moment, I knew exactly where she had been receiving her training! You may have guessed correctly! Jim Southern was a local bar, famous in the area for Italian beef sandwiches.

As I explained in chapter Zero, in a town of just 6,000 and in 1963, it was quite acceptable to take children into most of the clubs and bars. Let's face it, they were merely family gathering places, with nothing going on except eating, drinking, and playing pool or darts. Most bar owners, in order to preserve their liquor licenses, were very cautious not to allow over consumption, so we were able to go out fairly often and get to know the local folks. We joined the Boneyard Bocce Ball Club, the local Legion and the Rotary Club. At this stage, my husband's drinking was, I thought, mostly social, with just an occasional private incident late at night when "Mr. Hyde" would emerge. The next morning he would be apologetic and return to his intelligent and charming "Dr. Jekyll" other self.

Meanwhile, back in the UK, my kid brother's band was making ever larger waves. Each new single issued was immediately #1. Mum was concerned about Brian seeking my help with his other acts, too. My husband was concerned that I was becoming more and more involved in my quest to get radio play for Beatles music in the States. Copies of letters written to me that year, 1963, from many of the eventual major players in The Beatles Story are included in this book. *(See letters throughout Chapter 0.)*

Chapter Nine

BEATLEMANIA!

*I*n Chapter Zero, I told how George, in September of 1963, became the first Beatle to give a short live performance in the United States. On his way home from Illinois, he and Peter stopped briefly in New York to see the play *Stop the World, I Want to Get Off* starring Anthony Newly. They went backstage to meet the star. It seems ironic now that this was the name of the play George was to see before the onset of Beatlemania in the United States. Surely he could relate to *that title* in the coming months and years?

Once home in England, he resumed the former hectic pace of TV appearances and concerts, from which he had enjoyed a short rest. He wrote letters to me often, relating his adventures and telling of the band's famous London Palladium show. They needed motorcycle police escorts to get safely through the massive throngs that followed their every move. He would tell these stories then add, "Big Head" to show his bemusement rather than conceit at these demonstrations of affection by the fans. Mum also wrote frequently during those years, and I am preparing to produce a "companion" to this memoir, comprised of many of her letters telling the early Beatle story as it happened, and in her own words.

(I no longer have any of the early letters George wrote because in the late '80s, when I was staying with George at Friar Park prior to my second divorce, I returned all of his letters. I was aware that any scrap of paper a Beatle had touched was being sold for large sums all over the place so I did not wish his letters to "fall into the wrong hands." I recall him coming to me the next morning after he reread the letters and telling me, "I had forgotten how much fun it had been during those early days. Thanks so much for letting me have a chance to relive them." That morning we reread some of the letters including the one regarding his experience at the royal command performance. Then I told him of the phone conversation I had with Mum relating her and Dad's experience at the reception after that performance, an incident he hadn't known about. Here's what happened:

Apparently the very stately royal reception was in progress when Mum and Dad arrived. A very "regal orchestra" was playing very "regal music" and the guests were having a very "regal time." Mum told me she and Dad looked at all the bored faces and thought "we need to fix this." So, when the music stopped for a moment, Mum went to the orchestra leader and, using her vast experience as a dance emcee, she listed a lot of good dance music and asked him if he knew these songs. Well, he was delighted, and his band promptly swung into action. As was their custom at their own dances, Mum and Dad took to the floor, and after one turn around the ballroom, parted and each took another partner, soon getting the whole room participating. But, as I was able to tell George that morning...the sequel happened the following year when they were again at a royal party. On that occasion Dad tells that as soon as Mum entered the room, the band leader rushed over to her and said, "Oh Mrs. Harrison, what shall we play tonight? We've never enjoyed ourselves so much at a royal event as we did the last time you were here." When George and I had *that* conversation in the '80s, it was wonderful for us to be able to realize that though our parents are no longer with us in person, they had such a capacity to bring joy to others that our memories of them are all such happy ones. *(See photo on page 210.)*

I wasn't sure if he kept the letters or destroyed them. Considering his reaction to rereading them, I rather think he would have kept them. With the recent publication of the companion book to the Scorcese documentary, the letter he wrote to me regarding his potential visit to Illinois with Ringo in 1963 was obviously preserved.)

Between his US visit to me and his return in February '64, for the *Ed Sullivan Show,* George sent me a press clipping of himself on stage in Sweden being hugged by a fan who had jumped up onto the stage. I continued my campaign to get US airplay for the lads. Our dad always told us, "Don't ever give up," and I for one heeded his admonition.

Around about this time, too, my letters to and from the various players in The Beatles saga were being replaced by phone calls. I was in touch with Brown Meggs of Capitol Records and Vito Samela. Vito was the one to call me when "I Want to Hold Your Hand" became the first Beatles record to reach #1 in the United States, becoming a million seller in only nine days. When I was told *that* news, the Boys were in Paris, and I called the hotel to let them know. At that stage of their career, in view of my activities, they felt it important that I be kept informed as to how to reach them at all times. During that conversation with George, he told me—due to all the mania going on—he would not be allowed to travel to Illinois to visit me again, as he had intended. Instead, he suggested that I come to New York to stay with him. He said he would reserve a room for me and we could meet at the airport. A day or two later, though, he called and said, "We've been told that the media has booked every helicopter in New York City to cover our arrival, so it might be better if you just meet me at the Plaza Hotel. It seems it might be a little difficult for us to hook up at the airport!" *(See the itinerary on pages 162-165.)*

That could perhaps qualify as the understatement of the century.

I expect you have seen video shots of the scenes when The Beatles landed in New York that day.

I then contacted Nancy Hutchins, our reliable babysitter, to come stay at my home for a week. I packed all my best suits and dresses and made reservations to fly into New York on the afternoon of February 7, 1964.

Flying, in 1964, was still a pleasurable experience! I arrived at the Plaza Hotel mid-afternoon and checked in. George had booked me a room on the sixth floor. The receptionist gave me a verbal message from my brother, telling me he was in the Presidential Suite, and for me to join him once I had freshened up from the journey. So, I took the elevator to the sixth floor and duly deposited my suitcases in my room. The elevator was manually operated by a staff member. (Automation has certainly put a lot of people out of a job, hasn't it?) Eager to see my brother and meet—for the first time—his bandmates, I dashed back to the elevator and told the operator which floor I needed.

Stepping out, I looked to see which direction to go toward the suite number I'd been given. I then proceeded down the corridor only to find a huge throng of noisy people crowded around a long table that blocked the corridor. Knowing from the room numbers that my destination was beyond this crowd, I just tried to quietly slip behind them along the wall.

Next thing I knew, a huge Pinkerton agent slapped me on the shoulder, saying in a very sarcastic tone of voice, "And just where do you think *you* are going, sister?" My first naïve thought was, "At least he knows I am a sister!" Pointing in the direction of my destination, I told him nicely and politely, "Well, I am just going down there to visit my brother." For some strange reason, this remark caused the crowd much amusement. The Pinkerton man joined in the jeering laughter and said, "Do you have *any* idea how many times *that* has been tried today?"

Let's face it, the last time I had seen my brother was in Illinois, and no one had any idea who or what he might be elsewhere, so I was totally unprepared for this turn of events. Innocently, I protested, "He left a message at the front desk for me to come up." Since it was a verbal message, I had no proof. However, I am a Harrison, after all, so I persisted. "Don't ever give up." But, my identification was in my married name; thus, I had no ID in the name of Harrison.

Fortunately, I remembered having a Polaroid photo which had been taken during George's visit to Illinois. He had bought the camera as a gift. The photo was of me, Peter,

1.28.11   LW.

From: Brown Meggs
        Capitol Records, Inc.   *EMI.*
        Sperry Rand Bldg.   Revised: 2-4-64
        1290 Avenue of the Americas   212.786-   5ᵀᴴ Ave
        Plaza 7-7470   8906

                    AMERICAN ITINERARY: THE BEATLES

Friday, Feb. 7   Beatles arrive Kennedy International Airport
                    at 1:40 P.M. from London via Pan American
                    Flight #101 (International Arrivals Bldg.).

                    Beatles party (8) will consist of:

                    The Beatles (Messrs. George Harrison, John Lennon,
                    Paul McCartney, Ringo Starr); Mrs. John Lennon;
                    Mr. Brian Epstein (personal manager); 2 road
                    managers.

                    Capitol Records will officially greet the Beatles
                    in the International Arrivals Building and conduct
                    them into the airport press facility for an arrival
                    press conference.

                    Accredited photographers and cameramen only will
                    be admitted to the field proper to cover The
                    Beatles' deplaning. No other press will be per-
                    mitted access to The Beatles until the group has
                    been escorted through Immigration & Customs and
                    into the press room.

                    Special Note:

                    British press arriving with The Beatles will be
                    directed to the airport press facility, where they
                    may attend the arrival press conference, following
                    Immigration & Customs processing.

                    Following the press conference, Capitol will trans-
                    port The Beatles from JFK International to The
                    Plaza via special limousines. Limousine seating
                    will be assigned in advance; and no changes in this
                    arrangement will be permitted at the field. (Re-
                    sponsibility: Fred Martin, Capitol PR Director.)

                    Capitol will arrange for pre-registration of The
                    Beatles at The Plaza. Upon arrival at the hotel,
                    The Beatles will be escorted directly to their
                    rooms.

                    No provisions can be made by Capitol for the trans-
                    porting of press personnel to or from the airport.

Saturday, Feb. 8   Beatles rehearse for Ed Sullivan Show.

                    (Responsibility for entire day: CBS-TV.)

and George, who was holding my daughter in his arms. This
photo went the rounds of all the people in the crowd, most of
whom, I later learned, were members of radio and the press.
They all agreed; the girl in the photo was me, and one of
the boys "looked a lot like one of them there Beatles!" An
enlargement of this Polaroid that was missing for 50 years
magically appeared when I was preparing photos for this

```
AMERICAN ITINERARY:   THE BEATLES -- Page 2          Revised:  2-4-64


Sunday, Feb. 9        Beatles prepare for and appear on Sullivan Show.

                      Photographers (still cameras only, without flash)
                      will be permitted to cover the dress rehearsal at
                      Studio 50, Broadway near 53rd St., from approx.
                      2:30 to 3:30 PM.  Clearance must be obtained in
                      advance from Mike Harris, CBS.


Monday, Feb. 10       Beatles devote entire day to press conferences,
                      press interviews by appointment, and disc-jockey
                      reception.  All functions to be held at The Plaza.

                      Responsibility for coordination and administration
                      of all press functions:  Fred Martin, Capitol PR
                      Director.


Tuesday, Feb. 11      Beatles travel to Washington, D.C., for first
                      American concert at Coliseum (contact:  Mr. Harry
                      Lynn, LI 7-5800, Washington, D.C.).  Responsibility
                      for all travel arrangements, etc.:  Norman Weiss,
                      Jerry Perenchio, General Artist Corp.


Wednesday, Feb. 12    Beatles return to New York for two concerts at
                      Carnegie Hall (7:00 PM & 9:30 PM), to be recorded
                      by Capitol Records.
                      Concert promotion:  Sid Bernstein/Walter Heiman
                      (OXford 5-8630).

                      Concert press relations:  Merrick/Shefrin
                      (PLaza 2-4111).


Thursday, Feb. 13     Beatles fly to Miami, Florida.  Hotel:  Deauville.
                      Responsibility for all travel arrangements, etc.:
                      C.B.S.


Friday, Feb. 14       Plans indefinite.


Saturday, Feb. 15     Beatles prepare for Ed Sullivan Show (CBS-TV) from
                      Deauville.


Sunday, Feb. 16       Beatles appear on Sullivan Show.


Monday, Feb. 17       Beatles return to New York en route to London.
                      CBS responsible for travel arrangements from Miami
                      to New York.


                                 ###
```

book in March 2014. It is reproduced on the back cover of this book.

My identity being more or less established, someone was dispatched to the suite to tell George his sister was outside. He then came out of the room, and I was allowed to pass. We met halfway down the corridor, and he spun me around in a big hug. Well, you never saw a bunch of people change

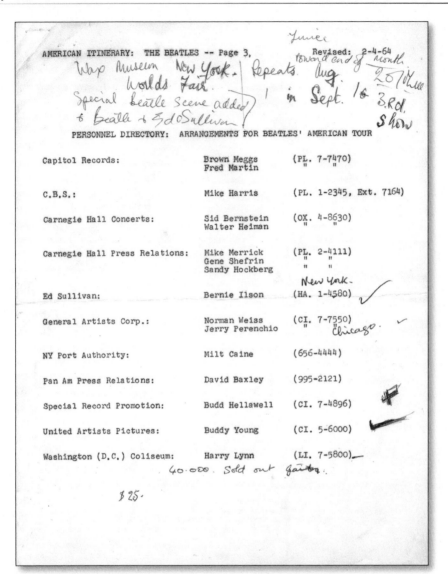

AMERICAN ITINERARY: THE BEATLES -- Page 3,   *June* *toward end of month.* Revised: 2-4-64

Wax Museum New York. Repeats Aug. 20th thru
Worlds Fair. *in Sept. 1 & 3.Rd.*
Special beatle Scene added) *show*
to beatle & EdoSullivan)

PERSONNEL DIRECTORY: ARRANGEMENTS FOR BEATLES' AMERICAN TOUR

Capitol Records:	Brown Meggs Fred Martin	(PL. 7-7470) " "
C.B.S.:	Mike Harris	(PL. 1-2345, Ext. 7164)
Carnegie Hall Concerts:	Sid Bernstein Walter Heiman	(OX. 4-8630) " "
Carnegie Hall Press Relations:	Mike Merrick Gene Shefrin Sandy Hockberg	(PL. 2-4111) " " " "
Ed Sullivan:	Bernie Ilson	*New York.* (HA. 1-4580) ✓
General Artists Corp.:	Norman Weiss Jerry Perenchio	(CI. 7-7550) " *Chicago.* ✓
NY Port Authority:	Milt Caine	(656-4444)
Pan Am Press Relations:	David Baxley	(995-2121)
Special Record Promotion:	Budd Hellawell	(CI. 7-4896)
United Artists Pictures:	Buddy Young	(CI. 5-6000)
Washington (D.C.) Coliseum:	Harry Lynn	(LI. 7-5800)

40.000. Sold out garden.

$ 25.

their tunes so fast. Instantly, the jeers turned to cheers! Then George and I entered the suite, and I met my three new brothers! With hugs all around, I was introduced to Paul, John and Cynthia, and Ringo. They were just concluding an interview with Murray the K, but although the interview was over, he made no move to leave. In fact, during the next few days, he glued himself firmly to The Beatles, dubbing himself "The Fifth Beatle," the first of a whole battalion

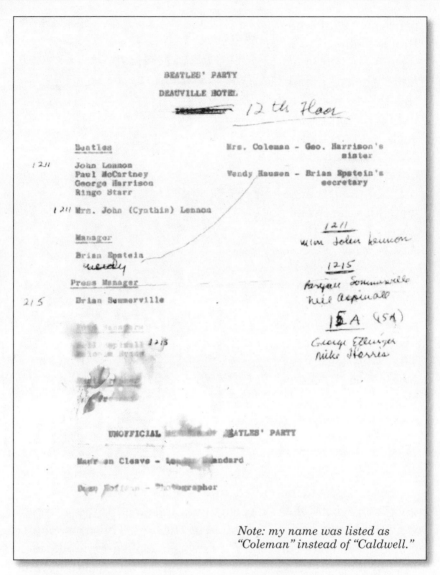

Note: my name was listed as
"Coleman" instead of "Caldwell."

of Fifth Beatles as we were soon to discover. Privately, we thought of him as the proverbial clinging vine! I don't think they had Klingons back then; otherwise, *that* would have been the name we would have given him!

For those who may never have been in the Presidential Suite at the Plaza, back then, it consisted of three bedrooms, a large living room, a kitchen area, and I do not recall if there was more than one bathroom. John and Cynthia had one bedroom, Paul and Ringo shared a second bedroom, and George had the third one. The living room and each bedroom had a TV set, all tuned to different channels. (At that time, there were just the three networks: NBC, ABC, and CBS, plus maybe PBS.) All the networks were covering some aspect of "The Arrival of The Beatles in New York." The Boys were so excited. They were rushing from room to

FROM

BILL TURNER ~ Capitol RECORDS

Promotion Manager, Balto. - Wash.

4-4-64

Dear Louise,

Please bear with me a little longer for the copies of your picture - Have been so busy haven't even had my own pictures processed -

Kindest Regards,

Bill T.

room saying, "Hey, come and see what they're saying about us here," only to be called into another room to view yet another report. The TV reporters all seemed to be infected with the same hysteria exhibited by the fans. The atmosphere transmitted on our hotel TV sets was one of sheer jubilation.

Paul had a relatively new invention, a tape recorder, and he was playing back for us all the things he had recorded when they were on the plane. He had spoken to the cockpit crew—it was okay to speak to the captain back then—and I'm sure the conversation was one the captain would recall with pleasure for the remainder of his life.

In the midst of all this activity, Brian and his entourage arrived. We finally met face-to-face after the many communications we had had during 1963. Amidst the introductions and general euphoria, something rather unsettling took place. A New York City police officer arrived and began to gather up the very many boxes of chocolates, cakes, pies, and other goodies sent by fans. The officer told us there had been a threat against The Beatles' lives, and for our safety he had to confiscate all the goodies. Being Liverpudlians and not easily scared, we just came to the more comforting conclusion that this was a good excuse for the "coppers" to get a feast for themselves.

Meanwhile, George had disappeared into his room. Next thing, the hotel doctor, Doctor Gordon, arrived at our suite about 5:00 p.m. and went into George's room to examine him. When he came out, he announced, "This is one very sick boy. He has severe strep throat and a temperature of 104. I will have to send him to hospital!" Immediately, Brian began to panic, "Oh no! This **cannot** happen. We can't allow the press to hear of this. Can he be cured by Sunday night?" The doctor said, "Well, he seems to be pretty healthy; if we bring in a nurse and start a course of treatment, he may be able to be on his feet in time." Again Brian said "No, we cannot have outsiders knowing about this." At that point, I don't remember who it was, but someone told the doctor that George's sister is here and she would be better able to look after him than any outsider.

Doctor Gordon agreed, mentioning with a grin, "She is probably the only girl in New York right now who would not faint at the idea of being in the same room as a Beatle." And so my fate was sealed. The doctors' remark was duly noted in the press a few days later.

Mal Evans or Neil Aspinall and I went off to my sixth-floor room to retrieve my suitcases, which I had not unpacked. I was moved into the second bed in George's room. Over the passing years, I have seen many news articles depicting me as a Florence Nightingale during this episode. But, I have to admit that I didn't even like being around *myself* whenever I was sick, so I wasn't really the "nursing type." However, I had been raised to welcome challenges and deal with them to the best of my abilities.

Dr. Gordon had given George a shot, and he gave me a whole bunch of medications for him and an ice collar, plus a long list of instructions as to how and when these were to be administered. He also, in view of the raging storm of excitement going on both inside and outside of the suite, suggested that I try to keep George quiet and let him sleep as much as possible. The next day, George was to sign a photo or album cover, I don't remember which, for the Doc, but I do recall that he wrote, "Thanks for the jab!"

During the evening, the Lads received a large array of harmonicas. One was a contraption with a keyboard you could play while blowing into the mouthpiece. George was trying to figure it out. The remainder of the retinue left with the Capitol Records officials and George and I were alone— except for the very loud DJs and press in the hallway outside our suite.

There was so much racket going on in the corridor it was impossible for my poor kid brother to get any rest. He asked me if I could try to get them to leave, so I went outside into the corridor to try to get rid of these noisy "DJ-voiced" men. Naturally, I could not say George was sick, but I asked them politely to please leave. They started to plead with me; they explained to me they had all been promoting The Beatles like crazy ever since their single "I Want to Hold Your Hand" was released. The guys from one radio station told me their promotion had generated 40,000 postcards sent in to their station for a contest to win seats at the *Sullivan Show*. They begged me to accompany them to their station so they could show me all the mail. At that point, I had an idea. I told them, "Okay, I will just get my coat and come with you."

Back inside the room, I told George happily, "I've found a way to get rid of this bunch; they want me to go to their radio station." George was rather concerned by this plan. Back then, at 33, I still looked okay.

"But, Lou, I don't want you to go off with a bunch of fellows you don't know. It could be dangerous," George, always protective, replied.

I had noticed earlier that they were all wearing T-shirts with the station's call letters: WMCA Good Guys, so I reassured George, "I'll be safe enough, Luv. They're Good Guys."

He was still concerned, "How can you know that?"

I responded innocently and seriously, "Well, it says so on their shirts!"

(I told of this incident for the first time years later when I had been invited to New York City to present the Lifetime Achievement Award to one of New York's top radio personalities, Scott Muni; he had been one of those Good Guys.)

Leaving my brother to hopefully be able to sleep, I went off with the Good Guys. We arrived at the radio station. Although radio work had been my ambition since my college days, this was the first time I had actually visited a radio station. Before I realized what was happening, I was in a studio, wearing a headset, and chatting amicably and quite naturally with the on air DJ. Oh, yes, they did take me to see all the 40,000 postcards—the original excuse for my trip. After a few minutes, the station manager rushed in and told the DJ, "Forget the commercials and the station IDs for now; we just did a quick survey and we have over a million listeners, so just keep on going." I had no idea how they took surveys or how important IDs were, but we just kept talking. Suddenly, I noticed the clock, and I realized it was time for George to take his next medication. I told the Good Guys I had to call the Plaza right away. They handed me the studio phone with an outside line. George was still awake—it was around 8:00 p.m. by then. Meanwhile, he had received from the Hall family a twelve-string Rickenbacker guitar and was trying it out.

Despite the illness, George and the rest of our group were experiencing a tremendous natural hight from all the activity and excitement. Realizing I was speaking with George, the DJs naturally enough asked if he would speak with *them*. So he told about his new guitar and played a few notes and chatted for a few minutes. Soon thereafter, the Good Guys took me back to the hotel. Unbeknownst to us Harrisons—a pair of innocents in the city—WMCA had recorded George's little chat, and for the remainder of the weekend they replayed it every hour on the half hour!

Pretty soon, I found out from a very irate Brian that before coming to New York, he had made an agreement with Murray the K that he alone would have exclusive access to The Beatles during this visit. Our "clinging vine"—now actually living **in** our suite—was somewhat accidentally foiled, and his exclusivity vanished. Looking back, although this totally impromptu and innocent incident scuttled my relationship with Brian, I still think it made much more sense for the band's future relationships with the media that other radio stations in New York had access to The Beatles at that crucial time. Murray the K was a self-promoting opportunist, and Brian was, not surprisingly, becoming quite self-important. He had little understanding of the aggressive and competitive marketing here in the States compared with the easy-going and gentlemanly way business was conducted in Britain. It was therefore very easy for him to be duped by such an eager opportunist! I remember being shocked in my early days in the states by seeing an ad in a newspaper asking for "an aggressive salesman." In Britain, *aggressive* was always considered a negative attribute, one to be avoided at all costs. Being very much "the proper English gentleman," Brian—like the rest of us—was ill-prepared for the onslaught of aggressive "marketers" to come.

For example, one well-circulated story tells how the enterprising Beatles wig creators met with Brian to propose he give them licensing rights to sell these, and subsequently, many other Beatles-related items. They were prepared to settle for, as far as I heard, a 50/50 split of profits, but before they came to this part of the proposal, Brian—always protective of his boys, but not greedy—came up with the bid that if this deal was to happen, "The Beatles should get at least five percent!" Naturally, the sharks quickly agreed!

But, back to February 1964 at the Plaza. Still being treated for strep throat on Saturday morning, George had a temperature of 104° and had to remain in his room; however, the other three Beatles went out into Central Park with oodles of press in order to have a photo session. In the afternoon, they took off to the theater to meet Ed Sullivan, do a sound balance, and check camera angles. There were many other technical things that go into the smooth running of a show. A short while after the others left, I got a frantic call from Brian saying I must get George to the theater to take part in these preparations. My first reaction was to call Dr. Gordon and ask his opinion. He came to our suite, checked George, whose temperature by then had dropped to 102°F, and shook his head doubtfully, saying, "Well, if he is *really* needed, take him, but make sure you stay no longer than an hour; otherwise, you risk the chance he could get much worse and not be able to do the show on Sunday."

Capitol Records had a fleet of limos at the ready, so George and I took one to the theater. As soon as we arrived, George was rushed to the other three, and the mob of reporters started taking pictures. There were so many cameras, I have never been sure by whom many of the photos I have since seen were taken, though I believe Dezo Hoffmann, our official photographer took several.

It was all so crazy and confusing that I do not recall whether they ever did all of the technical stuff required; however, being **very conscious** of Dr. Gordon's concern, I was watching the time.

When the hour was up, I went over to Ed Sullivan— to whom I had, of course, been introduced when we first arrived—and told him, "The doctor told me I must get George back to the hotel promptly if he is to recover in time for the show." Ed Sullivan had been privately made aware that George was very ill. I was also aware, by then, that an extra TV performance was scheduled for Sunday afternoon. This was to be taped a few hours prior to their live United States TV debut and shown on TV later in the month as the third Beatles' performance. Dr. Gordon and I were already very concerned regarding George's ability to even stand up for the evening show, let alone an additional one, hours earlier.

The second of the three Ed shows which aired at that time, was broadcast live from the Deauville Hotel in Miami the following Sunday.

Despite the overwhelming excitement and euphoria, the sight of my terribly sick kid brother valiantly trying to keep up with all the many things expected of him, gave me quite a few teary moments of apprehension. I was thinking, *"In my eagerness to have my kid brother become a star, I didn't realize what might happen. I see him now being treated as a mere "product" to be sold to the highest bidder with absolutely no regard for his well-being. What have we done? Will he be able to recover?"* I admit show biz lost a lot of its attraction for me in those few days. The *price* seemed way too high for the *prize* to be worthwhile. *(See photo on page 205.)*

Once back at the hotel, George was only able to rest for a short time before he had to go to yet another press conference. I think that was the one when asked if they ever had haircuts, George replied, "I had one yesterday." I know this created much laughter, but it was the truth. I had spoken to him in Paris a couple of days before and—having seen a current photo of him with his hair almost covering his eyes—I had jokingly suggested that he trim his bangs a bit so he could see where he was going! He had actually done this himself, and photos of him at that time do reveal a rather "handmade" job!

The press conferences were a blast! The Boys could not suppress their amusement at the idiotic questions constantly being asked. When asked the inevitable question, "What are you going to do when the bubble bursts?" their inventive minds would create answers such as "take up scuba diving," "take up weaving," "take up knitting," "join the Salvation Army," "climb Mt. Kilimanjaro," etc.

One senior press corps lady asked a very convoluted question ending with "...so what would be the greatest threat to your success, a nuclear bomb or dandruff?" Without the slightest hesitation, Ringo quipped, "The nuclear bomb; we've already got dandruff." Their hair was actually sparklingly healthy, but this reply was certainly a good put down to the often contemptuous and ignorant questions. At one point, John—in frustration—commented, "How do these people get jobs as journalists? Some of them don't seem to have ever gone to school." But this problem soon went away! The playful, good-natured humor and innate charm of the Boys quickly captivated the press. The press eventually entered into the joyful spirit of the occasion. They were enjoying themselves too, therefore, their questions and subsequent reports soon became less hostile and much more positive.

One reporter who later became a good friend was Al Aronowitz, of the *Saturday Evening Post*. His report of the Central Park Beatles outing caused me to write a letter to the editor for the first time in my life. He had written in his article that George was absent from the Central Park Saturday morning outing—*due to overindulgence*. Any one of the thousands of folks who have met me over the years will have some idea how furiously I would react to such a remark. Knowing first hand just how ill George was and how much he had been expected to do that weekend, I was in tears of fury when I read this. Even during the afternoon and evening Ed Sullivan tapings, he still had a temperature of 102°. Anyone with less dedication and integrity would have just languished in bed, but there was my kid brother bravely doing all that was asked of him, with as much humor and energy as he could muster. Well, I can tell you now, that if I had at that moment come into contact with Al, I would have felt like tearing him into little pieces. Of course, I have never actually had the strength to carry out such actions, but no one "messes" with my kid brother without bringing down my ire. In later years, Al did apologize for writing such misinformation. George and I came to know him well, and I have even visited his home in New Jersey. This event was also notable because it foreshadowed my public role as Protector-in-Chief of The Beatles' reputations by correcting the constant misinformation generally being dispersed about them. Ergo, the main reason for this book! I hope no one thinks I'm doing this for fun!

On Saturday, and again after *"the shew"* on Sunday, the whole entourage went out together, including a reluctant George. We found ourselves at places like the Playboy Club and the Peppermint Lounge. Right now, I do not recall which night we went to which club. *(See photo on page 205.)*

At the Peppermint Lounge, most of us were pretty exhausted from all the hectic activities, though Ringo was in rare form. He was twisting and doing all the other dances of the day until we were all gathered up and dropped off at the Plaza.

We had received an invitation to the Playboy Club, which I believe was a private club. This incident was incorporated in a different context into the *Hard Day's Night* movie. We all had a wonderful meal, and as we were getting ready to leave, Mal and Neil, our roadies who dealt with all the necessities, were getting ready to pay for the twelve or so dinners our group had consumed. The manager, however, came up and said, "Oh no, it's our pleasure to have you all here. You are our guests, and we would not think of having you pay."

I was standing beside John at this moment, and his reaction mirrored all that John has ever represented. He said quietly to me, "Isn't that just typical? When we didn't have enough money to buy a cheese sandwich, no one would even lend us a thripenny bit, but now that we can afford to pay, it's all this stuff about 'our pleasure to have you.' That's the difference between the way the poor and the rich get treated in this world!"

(How correct, I won't use the word *right*, he was. I have lived enough years and had enough experiences since that night to know how insightful his remark was, especially now in the 21st century! I recently met with some of the 99%ers at Occupy Wall Street, as I wanted to show my support. They were pleased to meet "George's sister" and impressed that I was sufficiently sincere not to show up accompanied by the press. I gave Harrison Hugs to many of the 99%ers and told them that from my experience of John's views, I believed, "If John were still on this planet, he likely would have pitched

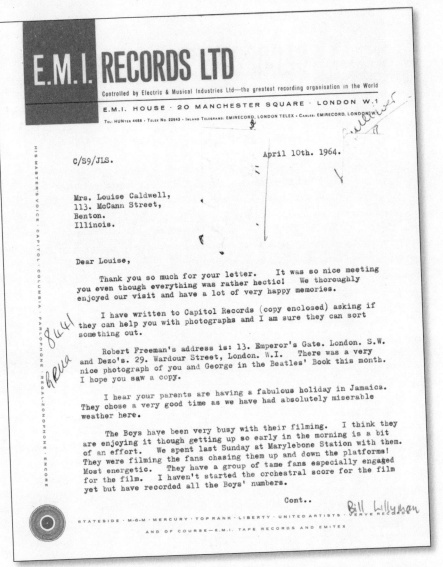

E.M.I. RECORDS LTD

Controlled by Electric & Musical Industries Ltd—the greatest recording organisation in the World

E.M.I. HOUSE · 20 MANCHESTER SQUARE · LONDON W.1

Tel: HUNter 4488 · Telex No. 22643 · Inland Telegrams: EMIRECORD, LONDON TELEX · Cables: EMIRECORD, LONDON W.1

C/S9/JLS.

April 10th. 1964.

Mrs. Louise Caldwell,
113. McCann Street,
Benton.
Illinois.

Dear Louise,

Thank you so much for your letter. It was so nice meeting you even though everything was rather hectic! We thoroughly enjoyed our visit and have a lot of very happy memories.

I have written to Capitol Records (copy enclosed) asking if they can help you with photographs and I am sure they can sort something out.

Robert Freeman's address is: 13. Emperor's Gate. London. S.W. and Dezo's. 29. Wardour Street, London. W.I. There was a very nice photograph of you and George in the Beatles' Book this month. I hope you saw a copy.

I hear your parents are having a fabulous holiday in Jamaica. They chose a very good time as we have had absolutely miserable weather here.

The Boys have been very busy with their filming. I think they are enjoying it though getting up so early in the morning is a bit of an effort. We spent last Sunday at Marylebone Station with them. They were filming the fans chasing them up and down the platforms! Most energetic. They have a group of tame fans especially engaged for the film. I haven't started the orchestral score for the film yet but have recorded all the Boys' numbers.

Cont..

Bill Lillyman

STATESIDE · M-G-M · MERCURY · TOP RANK · LIBERTY · UNITED ARTISTS · VERVE RECORDS
AND OF COURSE—E.M.I. TAPE RECORDS AND EMITEX

one of the first tents in Zuccotti Park." During that week in November 2012, I'd been involved in a media blitz in New York to promote The Beatles Hamburg recordings. In 2010 I had been approached by Iambic Media in Britain. They were putting together a documentary about The Beatles' next gig that week—all the activity at the Coliseum Concert in D.C. Watching Iambic's footage helped me remember more clearly all the happenings during that occasion.)

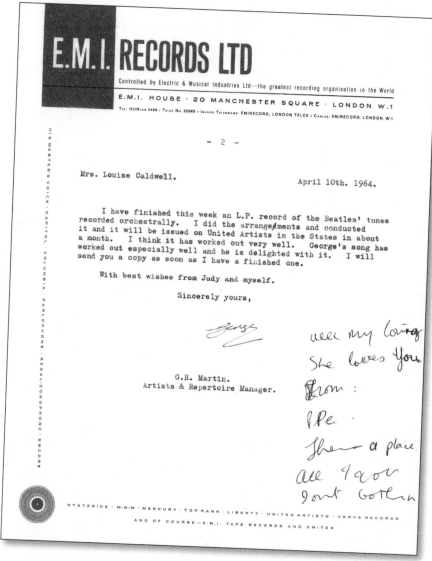

E.M.I. RECORDS LTD

Controlled by Electric & Musical Industries Ltd—the greatest recording organisation in the World

E.M.I. HOUSE · 20 MANCHESTER SQUARE · LONDON W.1

Tel: HUNter 4488 · Telex No. 22643 · Inland Telegrams: EMIRECORD, LONDON TELEX · Cables: EMIRECORD, LONDON, W.1

- 2 -

Mrs. Louise Caldwell.   April 10th. 1964.

I have finished this week an L.P. record of the Beatles' tunes recorded orchestrally. I did the arrangements and conducted it and it will be issued on United Artists in the States in about a month. I think it has worked out very well. George's song has worked out especially well and he is delighted with it. I will send you a copy as soon as I have a finished one.

With best wishes from Judy and myself.

Sincerely yours,

George

G.H. Martin.
Artists & Repertoire Manager.

all my loving
She loves You
From :
P Pe .
There a place
all I got
Don't bother

STATESIDE · M-G-M · MERCURY · TOP RANK · LIBERTY · UNITED ARTISTS · VERVE RECORDS
AND OF COURSE—E.M.I. TAPE RECORDS AND EMITEX

The original plan, that February in '64, had been to fly to Washington, but due to a sudden severe snowstorm, the plans were changed and we went by rail instead. Of course, this made it easier for the hordes of press to come along and capture every move we made.

Throughout their entire visit to the States, we were accompanied by a few official photographers, including Dezo Hoffmann and Harry Benson. They took many photos of all of us, including some that I don't think they would mind if they find their way into this book. The Maysles Brothers were also officially on board to make a video film of the trip. They were two wonderful young fellows, and I felt such sympathy for them as they struggled through the throngs carrying a huge video camera and sound recording equipment. It was Albert Maysles who operated and carried the camera on his shoulders all the time, and it

E.M.I. RECORDS LTD

Controlled by Electric & Musical Industries Ltd—the greatest recording organisation in the World

E.M.I. HOUSE · 20 MANCHESTER SQUARE · LONDON W.1

TEL. HUNTER 4488 · TELEX No. 22643 · INLAND TELEGRAMS, EMIRECORD, LONDON TELEX · CABLES: EMIRECORD, LONDON, W.1

HIS MASTER'S VOICE · CAPITOL · COLUMBIA · PARLOPHONE · REGAL ZONOPHONE · ENCORE

C/S9/JLS.

May 27th. 1965.

Mrs. Louise Harrison Caldwell,
113, McCann,
Benton,
Illinois,
U.S.A.

Dear Louise,

Sir Joseph has asked me to thank you very much for your letter to him, and as I have the details you want asked me to reply to you.

The Beatles have so far received 22 Gold Discs. These are made up as follows:- 4 United Kingdom - 16 U.S.A. - 1 Canada - 1 Japan. They have of course received many trophies and I am afraid I cannot give a complete list. There are several from various magazines etc. which we have no note of here. Perhaps Tony Barrow could help over this.

I hope you are well and enjoying life. I can imagine how busy you must be with all the fan mail etc. and running a home. The boys have been working extremely hard on the film and must be glad to have rest now.

With best wishes from George and myself.

Sincerely yours,

Judy

For: G.H. Martin.

STATESIDE · M-G-M · TOP RANK · LIBERTY · UNITED ARTISTS · VERVE RECORDS

AND OF COURSE—E.M.I. TAPE RECORDS AND EMITEX

was really heavy. Technology was not what it is today! His brother, David, took care of the sound recording. They did a wonderful job despite the difficulties, and I do hope anyone reading this book has availed themselves of a copy of the Maysles' Beatles First American Visit footage. From the point of view of family legacy, it is rather a pity that although I was in most of the original footage, I—unfortunately—ended up on the cutting room floor. Let's face it, I didn't have a Beatle hairdo!

We all had a lot of fun on that rail trip; the Boys were goofing off for the press. At one point, George—who by then had pretty well recovered from his strep throat—climbed into the luggage rack, and at another point dressed up as a steward and came into the coach carrying a tray. I'm sure many readers have seen the photos.

Meanwhile, Ringo collected cameras from most of the photographers in the entourage. He draped them around his shoulders and staggered through the train saying, "I am a camera!" I think there had been a recent movie of that name. I had been given a promo copy of their *Meet The Beatles* album, and I gathered the Boys' signatures. There is a photo of me with Paul as he signed to me "from your older brother." I had been teasing him about his strong resemblance to my brother Harry. *(See photo on page 203.)*

Eventually, we arrived in D.C. and went off to the Shoreham Hotel. All in our party were issued badges with 7777 on them, to give us secure access to the seventh floor, which I guess had been designated for "our gang."

I'm not sure now exactly where we were when the following little incident took place, but I think it was before we left to go to the British Embassy. On that occasion, as we were getting ready to leave, George, who had now recovered from his strep throat, came over to me with a very bashful expression on his face and in whispered tones drew back the cuff of his jacket sleeve to reveal his cuff-links. He said to me "just look what some rich fan gave to all four of us!" Holding his cuffs together were cuff-links made in the shape of beautifully crafted gold figures, posed in what is commonly known as "the 69 position." He grinned at me very sheepishly and said, "Isn't it amazing what rich people can do with their money?" He quickly added, "I hope I haven't offended you?" Being then in my "hey-day" I assured him with a laugh, "Not at all, but I am sure my husband will be envious when I tell him about these cuff-links, and not just about the gold!"

Once all were ready to leave, we were taken to the British Embassy. I remember ascending this really impressive staircase. The walls were covered with huge portraits of Very Important People. Of course, as usual, the Boys were joking. As we went past the various portraits, they were imitating the stern, important expressions on some of the faces, and we laughed all the way up the impressive staircase.

Next, we found ourselves in a ballroom at a charity ball. I was introduced to Lady Ormsby-Gore, the wife of the ambassador, and Cynthia and I were invited to sit with her at the back of the room. The Boys were sent to officiate at the "prize drawing" for this charity. It was—as usual at any Beatles appearance—very noisy, and total confusion reigned. Suddenly, Ringo came striding over to the table where the Ambassador's wife, Cynthia and I were seated. He was really upset and asked could she please get him a car so he could go back to the hotel. She was concerned and asked kindly, "What happened? What is the matter?" Ringo turned and showed us where a big clump of his hair had been cut with scissors. Apparently, an invited teenager—hearing beforehand The Beatles were to be present—had prepared himself, and armed with scissors, made his attack. (More about the outcome of this incident in the next chapter.) The Ambassador and his wife were both sincerely apologetic at this indignity, especially happening to a guest who had been invited to help with a charitable event.

A little while later, the rest of us returned to the hotel to prepare for the show at the Coliseum. We left the hotel in different limos and in the confusion, Cynthia and I were dropped off quite some distance from the door and we found ourselves being helped over snow banks and into the building by Tommy Roe. Cynthia and I sat together. We had also been together at the Ed Sullivan evening live TV show, but at the two Ed shows, I hadn't been conscious of much except how George was doing and whether he was able to stay on his feet long enough to get through the songs.

But now in Washington, I was more able to take an interest in the actual show. The building held 7,000 screaming fans, plus all the usual retinue of press. From the configuration, I guess the auditorium was usually used for boxing matches. The boxing ring being used as a stage was in the center. For the Boys to be seen by each quarter of the audience, they had to play a few songs facing in one direction, stop, and then move all the equipment to face the next section of the audience. I remember Mal and Neil, the roadies, had their work cut out for them that night. There were a couple of opening acts; Tommy Roe—our savior from the snow banks—was one of them. Eventually, organizers of Beatles shows realized it was pointless to have "opening acts"; it was just humiliating for these poor souls to be there—not a single person in any of their audiences was the slightest bit interested in seeing or hearing anyone but the Boys. Not that, as we all know, the Boys themselves could ever actually be *heard!*

I have no recollection of how we arrived back at the hotel after the show, but we were able to chat and have fun. For once we had the rare opportunity to relax, just the four Lads and Cynthia and myself. (No fans or press, what a relief!)

I had grown up understanding and practicing the typical Liverpudlian "put-down" humor. But, during my first few days with John, I found his sharp, cynical wit to be rather intimidating, and at times I felt that it was directed at me personally. The next day, when speaking to Mum by phone, I expressed my concern that maybe John didn't like me. She then told me, "Lou, that's just his protective wall. He is a very sensitive soul, so be kind to him." She also told me that since his mom had been killed in a car accident, she herself had tried to fill that void as much as she could. And because Paul had also lost his mom during his teens, George became super-concerned about our Mum, always telling her to be careful. She became the only Mum to John, Paul and George, and had a particularly comedic and goofy relationship with John who matched her own goofiness. I guess no matter how big a superstar one may become, a mom is always important. After Mum's reassurance regarding John, I was better able to interact with him on a friendly basis.

The day after the Washington Coliseum Concert, we were back in New York. Behold! Surprise, surprise, the Carnegie Hall concert. This extra addition to the schedule had sold out so fast that we, The Beatles entourage, had to sit on folding chairs at the back of the stage, behind the Boys. Again, Cynthia and I, the only really close relatives of the Boys, sat together. When we came out of the theater, we tried to find the limo and driver to whom we had been assigned. We found to our dismay that the limo had been commandeered by some Capitol Records executives. So here we were, virtually stranded. Naturally, the Boys had been rushed out very quickly, before the audience left. We had no cash with us— we had been warned not to carry any when in the city—and neither of us knew where the Plaza was located in relation to Carnegie Hall. (In the '70s, when I lived in New York, I knew it was within easy walking distance—especially for two English girls. But at that time we had no idea how to get back.) So I hailed a cab, not an easy task in those crowds. But one stopped, and I asked the driver if he would take us to the Plaza and explained our predicament. I don't know if he believed us, but we told him we would pay him once we arrived and went to our suite. I think he just told us it was okay about the fare and dropped us off at the Plaza. All of this had taken probably more than an hour, and when we arrived at the suite, the Boys had been ready to call "missing persons" and have them send out a search party to find us!

Although George suggested I stay with them and go on to Miami— after all I did have a babysitter for a week—I missed my children, and even for me, that much excitement in just a few days was enough. So, the next day I returned to Illinois and comparative sanity—ALMOST!

Chapter Ten

ACCIDENTAL RADIO CAREER

*F*ebruary 13, 1964, I arrived back home in Benton. Whilst in New York with my brother, I had received a phone call from a DJ with an Evansville, Indiana, radio station. I had met Jack Comer when I was visiting radio stations trying to get airplay for my kid brother's band in 1963. He and his family had visited me in my home in Benton and we had become friends. Apparently, after the Feb 9th *Ed* show, he had suggested to his now "very much on board Beatlemania radio associates" that since he knew me, he could maybe arrange a contest where they could have George agree to make a personal phone call to a contest winner. In view of the "hullabaloo" going on across the United States, and the fierce competition for a taste of anything "BEATLE," his suggestion was greeted as a stroke of genius. Anyway, after I took Jack's call at the Plaza and heard his request, I asked George and, always obliging, he readily agreed. So it was that the Evansville radio station set up a contest whereby the lucky winner would speak with Beatle George Harrison by phone. This was to be the same day The Beatles were to play their second *Ed Sullivan Show,* this time from the Deauville Hotel in Miami.

George, Jack and I made these arrangements: When the "lucky winner" was on the phone with the radio station, Jack would call the hotel, get George on the phone and all would be peachy! However, due to the chaos and high security at the hotel, Jack was unable to reach George. In desperation and in fear of losing his career, Jack called me in Benton and together we were able to solve the problem. The next unique part of this story is only possible in the audio version of my story, and for my listeners, here is the recording of the conversations leading up to that fateful contest. In the printed version of my memoir I can tell you that after much "sweat and almost tears," the contest winner *did* get to speak with my twenty-year-old kid brother.

Whilst I was dealing with this particular drama in Evansville—I was disturbed by a news report on KXOK in St. Louis, regarding our visit to the British Embassy earlier that week. The report stated that Lady Ormsby-Gore, the wife of the Ambassador, had wrestled Ringo to the floor and cut off a chunk of his hair. Once again, the Harrison sense of honesty came into effect. The insulting story about this gracious lady made me furious. I immediately called KXOK and asked to speak with the Program Director, Bud Connell. Fortunately, he remembered me from all my solicitations on behalf of The Beatles throughout 1963. Right away he asked me to go on the air to correct the erroneous report.

Though I had accidentally "made my radio debut" with the WMCA Good Guys in New York a week earlier, I was still shy about being in the public eye, so declined. One of the regular newsmen happily told the true version and, to my relief, the corrected story went nationwide to the wire services. All is well, I thought.

But overnight, Bud Connell had been doing some constructive marketing thinking! On Friday, he called me and made a suggestion that changed my life. He said to me, "You were right about your brother's band! There is so much excitement about them now, so many crazy stories going the rounds, and you are in the position to know what is really happening. Would you consider writing 60-second reports, two a day, five days a week, calling them in each Monday, until the mania subsides?"

Radio had always been in my blood, plus protecting my kid brother and his band's reputation—attempting to put the crazy stories to rest—was in tune with the values I learned from my parents. So I replied, "I'm just a housewife and have no experience at anything like this, but if you wish, I will try."

He said, "Great! The union rate for a 60-second feed is $17, which we will pay each week. Is that okay? "

Wow, $17 a week!" I thought. At that time, I was receiving a couple of hundred Beatles fan letters every day, and—as Mum had urged—was trying to answer them all. My husband, who never really approved of the whole "Beatle thing," complained about the money for postage—three cents a letter, plus stationary. So my reaction to his offer was this: "Yes, $17 a week will help me pay for a lot of postage stamps and stop my husband from yelling at me!"

Bud laughed and said, "No, it is $17 per feed, which for 10, would be $170 a week!"

I could not believe my ears. Maybe for three or four weeks I could earn that much money to buy stamps and have the opportunity to tell the fans the real story, but I still had to find out if I could do it! I remembered what my parents had always told me: "No one knows how to do anything when we arrive on this planet, but if we are determined and put our minds to the task, we are likely to succeed."

George was in Miami getting ready for their second live Ed "shew." I called him at the Deauville and told him about Bud's idea. George—also eager for the truth to be known—right away started feeding me information, saying, "Well, today we've been water skiing, and we are spending time at some millionaire's houseboat." He suggested I make an international call to Mum once a week for accurate updates because he and our parents were constantly in touch. I relayed this conversation to Bud, and—to reduce problems with my husband—he offered to have the radio station pay for a weekly transatlantic call, which in those days was pretty expensive.

Next week, KXOK began to broadcast my Daily Beatles Reports. To my total surprise, I found I had a gift for writing friendly, interesting anecdotes. Once they started to air, Bud was delighted with the reaction from the public/fans. I composed the reports Monday mornings, and called them into the control room for their engineer to record. Each week, the tape from the previous week was erased and recorded over. (Isn't it a pity we did not know then what we know now about The Beatles Story? We could have had a treasure chest of material had we known to save them!)

The reports aired for five weeks, and Bud told me the station was getting lots of positive feedback from listeners. Apparently, they particularly enjoyed the "English accent," but the reports did nothing to reduce the fan mail coming in—just the opposite. I now started getting mail directed at me! At the five-week point, Bud called and said, "Well, Lou, this has been really great. Our ratings have sky-rocketed, but I think this mania is about played out, so we will go ahead and stop the reports."

"OK. Now I will have more time to answer the mail," I thought.

But that was not to be. A few days later, a stressed out Bud called me and asked, "Hey, can we start up again? The day we stopped the reports we had over 500 calls in one hour! They wanted to know 'Where's Louise?'" This time, he made a different offer. I have never been motivated by money, so have not known how to take advantage of financial opportunities; however, Bud was really smart. I still speak with him occasionally. Beatlemania being rampant all over the country, he realized that my reports would also enhance the rating of the other Storz group stations, so he suggested, in addition to KXOK, I also call in my reports to WQAM in Miami, WTIX in New Orleans, and WDGY in Minneapolis. Each would pay me $30 per week instead of the $170 for just one station. Now, instead of taking half an hour a week to call in the reports, it took a couple of hours reaching four different engineers It didn't occur to me at the time that I was doing four times the work for $50 a week less. Dummy!

A funny thing happened about six months into this venture. I was phoning in my reports to one of the stations, and I stumbled on a word. Aghast, I did an OMG! The technician just laughed and said, "That's okay, Lou. We can just splice, or dub. It's no big deal!" Then he asked, "You act like this has never happened to you before?" Embarrassed, I said, "Yes, I'm really sorry."

Then he told me something I found dumbfounding. He asked, "You have been recording these reports now for six months, more than forty, 60-second spots a week, and this is the first time you've flubbed your lines? That has to be a world record for accuracy!" This comment made me feel pretty good because before that, I had no idea what the normal standards were or if it was okay to make a mistake.

Another interesting thing was happening: Many times fans would be on vacation in areas where my reports were aired, then when they arrived back to their home towns, they would eagerly tell their local radio stations about the reports.

This led to enquiries from all over the country asking if the Beatle reports could be made available elsewhere. So this totally non-business-like housewife was soon running a "syndicated radio show" all over the United States. Of course it never occurred to me to go back to the $17 per minute feed; I just went with the $30 per week for ten reports, two per weekday. Altogether the reports ran over a period of eighteen months on about twenty major AM stations, including WNOR in Norfolk, VA; WBZ in Boston; WINS in New York; KIMN in Denver; WSAI in Cincinnati; WHK in Cleveland; WKNR in Detroit; and stations in LA, San Francisco, and others. WLS in Chicago, however, just had Ron Riley call for "free" interviews every so often. It never occurred to me that WLS was getting for free that for which others were paying a small fee. For me truth—rather than money was always the motive.

Regarding the widespread appeal of these reports, I recently had a card from a longtime fan. She said, "For me, from the beginning, it was always John, Paul, George, Ringo and Louise." She said, "That's how most of us kids saw the Beatles phenomenon."

As this "career" was developing throughout 1964, I hired a full-time housekeeper and a live-in secretary. When I put an ad in the local paper for a housekeeper, one of the applicants was Mrs. Parris, the mother of the young boy who had spotted, and quickly returned, George's billfold during his visit to my home in Illinois the previous September. At that time, she was working as a dishwasher at a local restaurant from 5:00 p.m.

until 1:00 a.m. and making $25 a week. I offered her $30 to clean, cook, do laundry, and take care of my children. My son had started school, and she walked him to school and back each day, or on bad weather days—I ordered them a taxi. The house was easily cared for; thus, she had lots of free time to read or watch TV. She loved both her job, and the children.

Our German shepherd, Sheba, always accompanied Mrs. Parris to and from school. After a week or so, in the afternoons, the dog would pick up her leash and rattle it at Mrs. Parris when it was time to pick my son up from school. There are times when animals really show just how smart they can be.

Joyce Kirsch became my secretary. Originally, I met her through her fan letters to me. She lived in St. Louis. The "Uppercrust Convent" I had attended took the attitude that their students would, naturally, have an army of servants and office staff should they need them. So I had not been taught how to type. Fortunately when she knew how overwhelmed I was with all the fan mail, Joyce offered to become my secretary. The house was large enough for her to have her own spacious room. Her pay was $30 a week, plus room and board. She had excellent shorthand and typing skills, and we devised a workable system for the mail.

Most fan letters, after the usual comments about their favorite Beatle, then asked questions. There were about ten or twelve recurring, or "most asked questions." We set up a numbering system for each question and wrote out an answer to it. Most of the questions were childlike and simple in their innocent curiosity. For example, some frequently asked questions were, "What is George's favorite color?" and "What is The Beatles' favorite cereal?"

Each morning, I would spend about two hours reading the 200+ letters. According to the questions, I would mark the answers needed for each letter. For example, Letter one might require answers #2, #8, and #5; letter two, answers #1, #6 and #8. Then Joyce would go to the little Wizard typewriter and personalize each reply. Later, I would sign each of them. With this system, together, we were able to get through an enormous amount of mail. This was my simple/ crude version of an assembly line!

Of course, I was still writing and recording The Beatles reports, which had escalated to around twenty stations. I usually called Mum on the weekend for the latest Beatle info. I wrote the scripts on Sundays, and calling the distant radio stations to have the engineer record the feeds was always my Monday "task." I had a weekly subscription to the *New Musical Express* out of Britain and was receiving the monthly *Beatles Book* publication. By using these resources and calling Mum, I kept pretty accurately up-to-date on the latest Beatles doings. Although KXOK had at first paid my overseas phone calls, when other stations signed for my reports, this stopped, and so my phone bills, magazine subscriptions and mailing costs were quite high. But, I was earning the money to cover these costs, as well as pay for my housekeeper and secretary, which, instead of pleasing my husband, actually seemed to enrage him, especially after his evening drinks.

The next development started with WDGY in Minneapolis with a DJ named Bill Deihl. He was also a journalist with the local newspaper and hosted sock hops throughout the area. He suggested to the radio management that they have me co-host the morning show for a couple of weeks in January 1965. Due to the great reception this effort received, Bill later arranged for me to attend several of his teen sock hops throughout the state.

Before I accepted this offer, however, I had much to consider. In the past, except for the visit to New York for the ED shew, I had seldom been away overnight from my children. But, considering this offer, I knew I had a loving and competent "staff" at home to take care of things in my absence and I was able to pay them adequately for the extra work involved. The radio station offered me (for those days) generous terms for the two-week guest host visit. They included accommodations at the Leamington Hotel, a heated car to pick me up at 5:30 each morning, and—the "big benefit" for me—the opportunity to communicate with the fans in a more personal way than just through the "Reports."

Before starting my two weeks, I suggested a promo for the show. It consisted of a male announcer saying, "We're going to have a *new* morning man!" Another voice questioned, "Well, who is this new morning man?" The reply was The Beatles singing, "She's a Woman!"—from their latest hit. The promo went on to announce that Louise would be co-hosting the morning show for two weeks. Apart from my Beatle reports all over the country, a female voice was still quite rare on radio.

This two-week morning show was very well received by all *except the telephone company!* The volume of calls coming into the station each morning was jamming the lines and causing quite a headache for them. (Sorry!)

One morning, a really charming incident occurred. I received a call from a priest, who said, "I don't suppose you are getting a cup of hot tea these mornings?" I laughed and said, "Yes, you're right about that!" He then offered to come on his motorcycle with a tea kettle and the fixings for a cup of real English tea. He arrived on his bike a little while later, even though the temperature was thirty degrees below freezing on that early January morning. We had a great visit whilst he brewed my tea.

This gesture was just one of the many exceptional acts of kindness and love I have received over the last, almost, fifty years. Mum and Dad were absolutely correct when they advised me to reach out to the Global Family of Beatle People to return the love on behalf of the Boys and let them know that we—the same flesh and blood as The Beatles—appreciated the support and affection showered upon them. Due to Mum and Dad's own dedication and their encouragement to me, I also have dedicated my life to "giving back the LOVE!" I have found it to be true what they told me, "The more love you give, the more you get back."

Subsequently, I made lots of personal appearances in many of the areas airing my reports. Minneapolis was perhaps the most frequent. I was invited to a sock hop there in August, which coincided with my thirty-fourth birthday. During the event, I was signing autographs. There must have been about 600 or 700 teens present, and as they approached, I had a short chat with each one.

At one point, I was asked, "Isn't your hand getting tired after all this signing?"

I admitted, "Yes, a little bit."

Then the youngster suggested, "Why not sign a bunch of them at the hotel before you come?"

Knowing that the majority of "autographed" Beatles photos were actually signed by Mal and Neil, I replied, "Well, I wanted you to know that it was really **me** signing them." To my surprise, I then received one of my most treasured compliments: "But we know you wouldn't cheat us, Louise."

Moments like that are what made all the hard work really worthwhile. That same evening, my naïve approach caused quite a lot of laughter. I guess Bill Deihl had arranged to have a large cake delivered to celebrate my birthday. Whilst I was on stage chatting with the teens, an announcement was made: "A birthday cake with candles is over at the refreshment stand in the back corner of the room." At that news, I invited the audience. "Won't you come join me in the corner and have a piece?" Everyone burst out laughing, and one young male teen shouted out, "You're all right, Louise!"

I was invited to speak at Beatles-themed events in the auditorium at Dayton's, a major department store in downtown Minneapolis. The first time at Dayton's, they gave me a desk and a chair onstage. A live band was playing Beatles music and the fans were allowed to come up on stage with items for me to autograph. Besides being unable to hear anything being said to me, flash cameras also bombarded me. As each person approached, a flash would go off, leaving me temporarily blinded. The auditorium was on the seventh floor, and I recall hurtling in the limo after the event, round and around in an ever-descending circle in the parking garage trying to get us down and out of reach before the fans arrived at street level. Between the flash bulbs, the noise, and the circular escape, for the first time at one of these events, I felt pretty queasy!

But I was not the only "almost casualty." The fire marshall was pretty upset with the store because they had far more people in the auditorium than fire codes allow. At all my future appearances in the Minneapolis area, fire department officials attended with counters, stamping the hands of all who entered. When the legal fire capacity was reached, all others were turned away. That was part of the "downside" of reflected glory, but occasionally there was an upside, too. On one occasion, Bill and I were late getting to a sock hop, so he was driving a little "hastily." A police car stopped us, but when Bill explained the situation, we were allowed to proceed, with a friendly wave—after I had signed a Beatle photo for the officer. For over a year, the mail each day from the twin city area alone exceeded 100 letters.

The largest event I attended in that radio market was the Twin Cities' Winter Carnival, I think in 1966, with a "legitimate" audience of 15,000. Another challenge surfaced due to the popularity of the Daily Beatles Reports. (Of course, the subject matter was the chief reason for their popularity.) My English upbringing—plus the Harrison Family Curse— did not prepare me for the fiercely competitive nature of the US radio business. Apparently, prior to the Daily Beatles Reports on WDGY in Minneapolis, a rival local radio station had been Number One. I received a call from this other station offering me double my weekly fee, plus three more stations within their network, also at double the fee if I would switch from WDGY and feed my reports to them. I explained—very truthfully—that I wasn't doing it for the money, but to enable the fans to separate the facts from the copious fiction. I also pointed out that if I were to switch radio stations for "more money," my integrity would be in question. Considering how Mum and Dad raised us kids, I would never let *that* happen. So the rival station's next move was to report to The American Federation of Television and Radio Artists (AFTRA) that I was "performing" on radio without being a union member. They said I was "taking a job away from an AFTRA member," which made no sense to me; after all, how many AFTRA members qualified as a flesh and blood connection between The Beatles and their fans? Just who was out of a job because of me?! When I told WDGY about this threat, they told me it was all about the loss of ratings for this other station. However, the matter was quickly settled by having me become an AFTRA member.

Due to my relationship with WDGY in Minneapolis, I was invited to The Beatles concert there when they were on tour in the United States. The plan was to have an on air call-in show the day before the concert. I was to introduce the Boys at the concert, and finally have a follow up call-in show the day after. For some reason, which I never discovered, the promoters did not allow me to make the introduction, though.

I was booked for those few days into the same motel as the Boys in order to spend time with my brother. After the concert, we all retired to the motel. I think we had a few beers sent up, and the Boys and I gathered in one of the rooms. The exhausted Beatles flopped down on the beds to watch TV and, as usual, to hear what was being reported about them. I sat on the floor, leaning on the bedside cabinet between the two beds. The next day's newspapers reported on the "orgy taking place, with *girls* in the Beatles' rooms." Naturally, this was *really news* to all of us! The lads certainly missed it. Boo-hoo! So if our little innocent family get-together to watch TV could be termed "an orgy," it certainly opened my eyes to the amount of fabrications being circulated about The Beatles in the general media. It definitely convinced me of the necessity to keep on making my honest, non-sensational, and non-titillating tell-it-as-it-really-is Beatles reports.

Appearances at other cities brought a variety of adventures. WTIX in New Orleans invited me to Mardi Gras in 1965. Sixty thousand of my listeners had signed a petition asking that I be made an honorary citizen of New Orleans.

I was to receive a certificate from the mayor, and so, for the first time in my radio career, my engineer husband wanted to come along. The early events planned for me included

Nanny French, my maternal grandmother, with Eddy, my youngest uncle.

Photos Mum and Dad, Louise and Harold, exchanged during their courtship.

My uncles, Jimmy, Eddy, George and John.

Our Lady of Good Hope Roman Catholic Church in Wavertree, Liverpool.

Uncle Eddy performing at a display of the Liverpool Mounted Police Academy.

Having my "photograph taken."

George and I in Scotland waiting on a ferry to the Isle of Skye.

Me and my three brothers.

My brothers and I celebrate V-J Day with the children from Arnold Grove.
There is part of an air-raid shelter behind us.

The Cunard Building and Liver Building at the Pier Head in Liverpool.

Mum, Dad, Peter and George standing in front of Gwyrich Castle in North Wales.

Oh, so demure and holy at Our Lady of Good Hope Catholic School!

Me with my son and daughter just before leaving Canada to go to Peru.

Marcia Schafer Raubach was the first person in America to interview a Beatle when she did so with George on WFRX in West Frankfort, Illinois. The station was also the first in the US to play Beatle music on a regular basis.

The V.F.W. Post #3479 in Eldorado, Illinois where George accompanied the local band, The Four Vests, in an impromptu set.

George also set in with The Four Vests at The Boneyard Bocce Ball Club near our home in Benton, Illinois.

Here we are in downtown Benton, Illinois during George and Pete's visit in September of 1963. George is holding his niece, Leslie.

The Four Vests, a popular local band in Southern Illinois, whom George accompanied at a couple of performances during his visit there.

On the train from New York to their Washington, DC concert appearance, Paul autographs a copy of their new album for me. February, 1964.

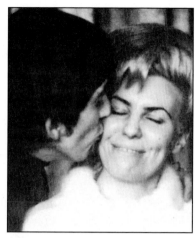

George and I hadn't seen one another since his visit to my home in Illinois the previous fall of 1963. Here we are backstage at the Ed Sullivan Show in New York waiting for them to go on and perform for the largest television audience there had ever been.

This is George on the Ready, Steady, Go! show playing his 1962 Rickenbacker 425 guitar that he bought at Fenton Music Store in Mt. Vernon, Illinois on his visit to see me in September, 1963. He paid about $400 for it, including refinishing it from red to black to match John's Rickenbacker. It sold recently for $657,000 at auction.

We are being greeted by Ed Sullivan, shaking hands with George, who had missed the rehearsals due being ill. George and I had to show up so that George could participate in the pre-show preparations. He was still running a fever. Beatle manager Brian Epstein is to my right.

Following the Ed Sullivan Show performance, we all went to the famous Peppermint Lounge. Roughly from left to right you will see me, George, John and Cynthia Lennon, Paul, and Ringo.

My children and some of their cousins hanging out with The Beatles.

Mum's own ticket to the World Premiere of "A Hard Day's Night."

Mum and Dad surrounded by and answering some fan mail.

Mum, Dad and I pretend to perform on stage at the famous Cavern in Liverpool where the boys had created such a stir over the previous few years.

Mum making sure the boys don't fall as they are watching The Rolling Stones perform from backstage awaiting their turn as the main act at WGH.

One of the photos taken during the WGH promotional trip.

During my WGH trip to Britain, I join Mom in answering Beatle mail.

Back cover of the All About The Beatles album.

George and Ringo dancing with their mothers at a party following the Royal Command performance.

Mum and John had a warm and goofy relationship. After he lost his mum, both he and Paul "adopted" George's mum.

Mum helping George pack for yet another tour.

Mum and Dad often attended fund raisers for orphanages.

For Louise Harrison
With Love
From:
Mark Richman

The Beatles at Busch Stadium, St. Louis Mo. 8/21/66,
About 9:15 P.M. ... It was raining ... No one noticed!

These three photos (above and at right) were taken by my friend Mark Richman at The Beatles concert at the then new Busch Stadium in St. Louis, MO, not too far from our home in Illinois. These photos were taken at about 9:15 p.m. on August 21, 1966. Eight days later they would complete what was to be their last tour ever in San Francisco's Candlestick Park. Note the makeshift stage cover due to the unforeseen rains.

George Harrison and Pattie Boyd posing with loved ones during their wedding reception, January 21, 1966. Left to right: Brian Epstein, Mum and Dad Harrison, Paul McCartney, Pattie's mother Diana Gaymer-Jones, and Pattie's Uncle John Drysdale (Diana's twin brother).

The Harrison family getting together, late 1960s.

Me exploring ancient South American ruins.

Sarasota in the 1980s, my "stress free" decade.

This photo was taken some 20 years after my brother was alarmed at me wanting to "try out" for the "girl on the beach" scene in HELP!

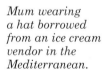

Mum wearing a hat borrowed from an ice cream vendor in the Mediterranean.

Here I am part of the team from the University of Illinois with our experimental hybrid electric vehicle in the summer of 1994.

Teams from universities all across America competed in the HEV Challenge. Today hybrids are common production models.

*Photos taken
at the Clinton
Library opening
in Little Rock.*

Photos from Drop-In days at Beatlefest. In all three photos, I am wearing T-shirts made from recycled soda bottles.

Neil Innes and I clown around for some fans. Neil was the brilliant musical force behind and co-star of The Rutles movie, a Beatles-spoofing documentary. George was a close ally and supporter of several other Monty Python projects over the years.

Cynthia Lennon and I first met at the Ed Sullivan Shows in 1964 and became good friends. She still is today.

Victor Spinetti and I. Victor is the only actor besides The Beatles themselves to star in all three of their feature films.

With artist Wyland in Sarasota.

Picton Clock Tower, which was very near Arnold Grove in Wavertree, Liverpool.

With the help of Chicago DJ Terri Hammert, Marty Scott and I have this photo to treasure.

Peter Noone singing in the rain in Florida.

Some shots of the Liverpool Legends. For more, see Liverpoollegends.com.

Just me doing what I like best... talking to our Beatle family.

appearances at Godchoux, a major downtown department store, and also to be present on the WTIX remote broadcasting location on Canal Street during the daytime.

The mayhem started when we landed at the airport. The city officials arrived in an open convertible to pick up my husband and I. There was quite a significant motorcycle escort, but even so, about a dozen fans leaped into the convertible pulling at our hair. I was getting to be fairly accustomed to this kind of thing, but my poor husband was in shock! We had dinner with our hosts, and then were dropped off at our luxurious hotel.

The next morning, we were driven to the department store, only to find the whole city block besieged. The people bringing us to the store paused the car near the entrance, and my husband and I had to make a "dash" for the door. On the way inside, I temporarily lost my shoe when the heel got caught in the street-car rails. New Orleans was fortunate to have a decent public transport system. Inside, arrangements had been made for me to sit at a lovely Louis the Fourteenth desk on the bridal floor. The regular elevators were so overcrowded they could not move, so we were ushered into a maintenance elevator. When we arrived at the bridal floor, again the crowds were packed like sardines. The idea of the fancy desk in the center of the room was abandoned, and my husband and I were taken into a rather flimsy partitioned storage area along one side of the entire floor. Guards were set up outside the door, and the fans were lined up and allowed in—a half dozen at a time—and sent out another door. Each time the door opened, an avalanche of fans would crash inside. I felt so sorry for these poor kids. Many had their clothes ripped and were sweaty, battered, and bruised. But, I was able to greet them all, chat and sign items for them, and they left quite happily.

When the two-hour scheduled appearance ended, we had to again be taken out in the maintenance elevator, which went underground to the basement, and through to the next door restaurant. From there, we went to the WTIX float, or remote broadcasting center, on Canal Street, which was

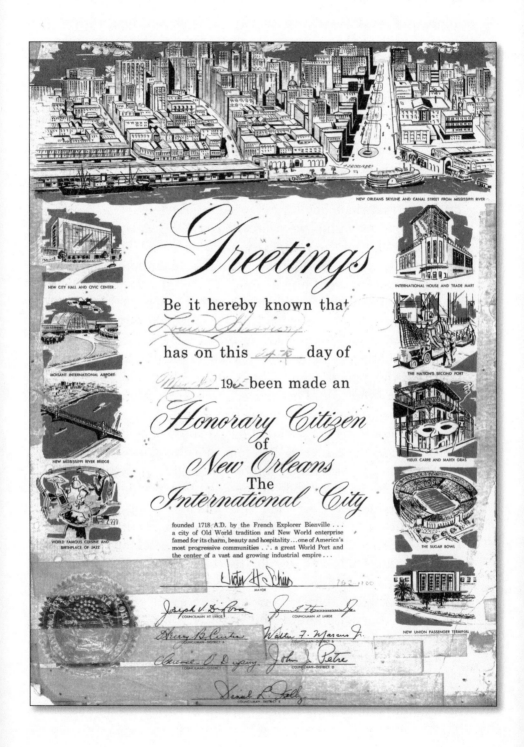

another challenge! But, this one was a lot easier to manage. Although we were safely high up on their remote facility/float, fans could come up and hand us hats, shoes, books, albums, etc., to sign. Suddenly, the crowd made a huge roar, and who should come striding through but the great Al Hirt! What a thrill! There was such a huge crowd that we were unable to talk very much, but he invited my husband and I to view the evening Mardi Gras parade from the balcony of the hotel suite, located on the parade route, where he and his family were to assemble to watch. He gave our driver instructions and continued on his rounds among his fellow citizens.

At some point during the afternoon, the mayor of New Orleans presented me with a proclamation making me an honorary citizen along with the key to the city. It was a small gold key I could put on my charm bracelet. I still have the proclamation *(previous page),* but—like so many other precious items—the key has long since vanished.

My husband and I spent a wonderful evening with the Hirt family, meeting his wife and eight children. Al confided in me that when The Beatles first arrived, he was not too thrilled. He had spent years and years playing trumpet, practicing for hours every day—then when he finally had his number one hit, "Java," along came The Beatles and knocked him to second place! However, he laughingly admitted, in order to fit in, he very quickly became a Beatles fan because all his children were stricken with Beatlemania! I kept in touch with the eldest daughter, Gretchen, for quite some time afterwards. Incidentally, although he was delighted to meet Al Hirt, my husband did not attend any other Beatles events with me. It was all too much for a dour Scotsman! During these radio report days, I also took on the duty of trying to track down and dispel some of the many crazy rumors always swirling around the Boys. That had been, of course the original purpose of the reports. One of their venues was in Indianapolis during the 1964 tour. Early in the summer my daily fan mail started to include dozens of letters pleading with me to make sure The Beatles did not fly into Indianapolis. The reason—it had been "reported" that the well-known psychic, Jeanne Dixon, had prophesied that The Beatles would die in a plane crash heading into Indianapolis that summer. Sympathetic to the heartfelt concerns of these young fans, I felt it my duty to get to the bottom of yet another rumor. I tracked down Jeanne Dixon—which was no easy task in those days prior to the internet—and spoke to her husband; he reassured me that no such prediction had been made and, not only that, Jeanne had, thus far, not meditated on The Beatles. He also sent me a transcript of an interview she had done regarding The Beatles. So armed with legitimate information, I was able to pass this on to the fans in my next report and let them know that this was just another unfounded story invented by those with nothing better to do than cause problems and perhaps sell more newspapers. Naturally armed with the information that the rumored air crash was false, I let the boys know in order that they not be worried. Their peace of mind was, of course, the most important reason for my search for the truth of that particular story.

From information I obtained recently, it appears my brother and his mates did not receive my report which would have reassured them as to the fabricated rumor. I hear from Larry Kane, an official reporter along with the boys on that flight, that they had no idea I had received information from the Dixon family about this story, and were very apprehensive during that flight. As you all know, some years after the Jeanne Dixon incident, we had another scary invented story, yes the infamous "Paul is Dead" saga. Although many people thought this was "an in house publicity stunt," the last thing any of The Beatles needed—or wanted—at that time was additional publicity! Paul himself, when asked about it, said something to this effect:

"Well, if Paul *is* dead, I guess I'll be the last to find out!"

Another experience related to my radio reports involved WQAM in Miami. The Beatles were to appear in Jacksonville, Florida, in early September, and WQAM set up a contest for listeners to win tickets to the Jacksonville show. The

JAMES L. DIXON & CO.
Realtors

1144 EIGHTEENTH STREET, N. W.
WASHINGTON, D. C. 20036
FEDERAL 8-7200

1430 N. UHLE ST.
ARLINGTON, VA.
JA. 5-7110

SALES   LEASES
MANAGEMENT   LOANS
INSURANCE   APPRAISALS
RENTALS   REPORTS

August 31, 1964

Mrs Louise Harrison Caldwell
113 McCann Street
Benton, Illinois

Dear Mrs. Caldwell:

  Thank you for calling my office this morning – and I am so glad that I was in at the time and able to talk with you, for I am very interested in this matter of 'false rumors' which are circulating concerning the 'Beatles'.

  I appreciate your bringing these new 'rumors' to my attention. Among the many fan letters that come in, I have established a regular file for 'The Beatles' – and I received so many letters from youngsters – and adults, too, who are so interested in the success of the Beatles – asking if the rumors were true. I am enclosing a copy of the Herald Examiner of Thursday, March 26, 1964 which carried my denial of these so-called 'predictions'. I have continued to make such denials whenever I was on a radio or television program.

  Your interest – and your help is certainly appreciated, and if at any time you can have any one of the Beatles – or all of them to 'give me a ring' – I would be most happy to talk with them and do my best to encourage them and assure them that I have not made any such forecasts about them. I wish them every success – and I feel that there is great success ahead for each of them – each in his own field and according to his own talents – not necessarily as a 'group', for I do feel that each will be successful fulfilling his own 'purpose' in life.

  Please let me hear from you again, and if there is anything I can do to help in this regard, feel free to call me at any time.

Most sincerely,

Jeane L. Dixon

JLD:m   *A Complete Real Estate Service*

winners also won a flight to Jacksonville from Miami. Part of the "prize" was for me to be on board the flight and chat with the winners during the trip. That, by the way, was the first time in my life I was ever considered to be a **prize!** As it turned out, our flight into Jacksonville coincided with the tail end of Hurricane Dora. The flight bounced all the way up the Florida coast. I was expected to be sociable with the passengers and wander up and down the aisles chatting. Always dutiful, I chatted, but occasionally hit the ceiling and the floor on the way up and down the aisle.

Once we arrived in Jacksonville, I was united with my brother and the rest of his entourage. We were housed in a medium-sized trailer, but with the winds still pretty strong, we didn't feel awfully safe. I think we joked a bit about "gone with the wind" and "over the rainbow." A meal was provided for the Boys, but when it arrived, it was cold and unpalatable. I recall the meat spread on the plate was sitting in a bed of congealed white fat. I witnessed many occasions when they either missed being fed altogether or received less than decent quality food.

Rick Shaw, a legendary DJ from Miami, was with us. I recall Ringo being very taken with the ring Rick was wearing—the initials "RS" in gold. Ringo pointed out these were also *his* initials! *Hint, hint!* However, Rick did not part with his ring! He still had the ring when he and I joked about this incident years later when we met again at a Beatles Day in Miami.

Another adventure involved WNOR in Norfolk, Virginia. This happened very early on in The Beatles' saga. A DJ named Gene Loving contacted me shortly after the 1964 February *Ed Sullivan Show*. His station offered me an all-expense-paid trip to Liverpool to visit my Mum and Dad. Once again, in my innocence, I did not recognize how "self-serving" for the radio stations were all these wonderful offers and ideas. By taking advantage of having me along, their DJ had access to The Beatles and their families without having to pass security. Pretty smart of them, Eh? However, I did not understand anything about "Big Business," and I did enjoy the interaction I had with the public. Besides, here was a chance to see Mum and Dad, and my brothers. So I set out from Norfolk to Britain along with Gene and his camers. I do still have some of the photos taken on that trip. I believe I have the right to include them in our photo section. *(See photo on page 208.)*

Besides visiting Mum and Dad in Liverpool, Gene and I also went to the New Musical Express Annual Awards ceremony at Wembley Stadium in London. The Beatles were, naturally, the headliners. Mum and I spent time with the Boys in the dressing room until it was time for them to perform. We watched from a window under the stage as The Rolling Stones performed. Obviously Gene was there too. I have a photo of George standing on a chair to watch, with Mum holding on to him so he wouldn't fall.

I was already getting some idea of the stress and confinement fame was inflicting on the Boys. Before the show, George had wanted to take Mum and I to a famous restaurant in London, but due to the crowds, we were unable to leave the hotel until time came for **"the almost spy-movie drill"** it took to move the Boys from one location to another. George commented on the situation, "Now that we can afford to go to a really nice place to eat, we mostly end up with trays of half cold food from room service."

During The Beatles' 1964 and 1965 tour of the States, I was able to see the Boys quite often. Many of the radio stations using my reports would bring me into town the day before The Beatles show. We would have a couple of hours of open phone lines during the evening when I could speak with fans and generally get into the mood for the show—not that anyone needed any encouragement to get excited!

One such promotion was with WBZ in Boston. Their program director was Squire Rushnell, and he arranged for us to do "a remote broadcast" from a mobile unit in a shopping mall. Once again, they featured me as part of a **prize!** This time the contestants sent in postcards; I was to draw the ten winning entries during the "remote." The winners would all be transported to a famous Boston lobster bar to have dinner with me and the DJs prior to the concert. A huge metal drum the size of a beer keg was full to capacity with cards piled high on top, with lots more cards on the floor around the outside. When the time arrived for the live, on air drawing, they led me to the container, where my hand was gently guided toward the cards bulging out of the top. I took a card, and then, with the impulse to be really fair, started to dive way down into the container and into the cards stacked on the floor around the outside. WBZ had a broadcast signal that went halfway across the United States, and many of the cards I drew were from states other than Massachusetts. Later, I learned from Squire that the cards had been sorted in such a way that the ones coming from "nearest to Boston" had been put on the top of the container, and those from far away were the ones I had dipped deep down to pick out. Since the prize included all expenses to travel to the lobster dinner, the cards I picked out cost the station quite a hefty amount of money. However, the whole promotion turned out to be wildly successful, so Squire was able to laugh and say it was just as well I did the drawing the way I did. It turned out to be more fair than if all the winners had come from "just around the corner"— not that the listening audience would have been any the wiser!

After having dinner with the winners, we all went to the show. As usual, I was able to spend time with the Boys backstage. Once the show was over and Mal and Neil were packing up the gear and the Boys were getting changed, I walked out by the stage. Fans were coming up, tears running down their faces. With motherly concern, I asked, "Why all the tears?" The answer: "We'll probably never ever see *them* again." Many fans merely wanted to touch the stage where The Beatles had stood. That was when I began to understand there was a much deeper significance to Beatlemania than people simply appreciating a genre of music.

For me, the best thing about my radio experience was having the opportunity to visit my brother at so many of The Beatles' shows. A few times I was able to catch a ride with them on their private plane—an Electra—taking them from gig to gig. A couple of "backstage" incidents I have told to audiences throughout the years include the following stories:

We were in either Cleveland or Cincinnati. When you are being rushed from plane to limo to hotel in a mad turmoil, eventually you have no idea what part of the planet you are currently on. Anyway, I was sitting with George before the show. We were chatting when he took up his guitar and started to tune it. I asked, "Why are you bothering to tune up when no one is going to hear anything anyway?" He looked at me with those gentle, loving big brown eyes and laughingly said, "Well, I always have this scary feeling that one day they might stop screaming, and I will be out of tune!" That dedication was so typical of all four of those boys; no matter if anyone will hear or not—they wanted to give it their best.

When they played at the Stockyard in Chicago (1964), I was also with them. We were chatting in a hotel room before the show. When it was time for them to be onstage, a man appeared on the fire escape at the window to lead them safely into the auditorium out of sight of the crowds. I will always remember the look in George's eyes as he climbed through the window onto the fire escape. It was one of those "deer caught in the headlights" expressions, and at that moment I felt such compassion for him—big sister just wanted to bring him back into the room and say, "You don't have to do this anymore; you can go back to just being my little brother George." But, unfortunately, that was impossible.

(Even now, as I am writing about some of these incidents, tears come to my eyes, and I can still feel the same heartache and compassion I felt back then for those four "so eager to please" young men. To me they were, and are, my very dear and kind kid brother and his pals. And although I am sharing some private memories with my readers, you may have noticed that intimate details are few and far between. The purpose of this book is *not* to "tell all" as some media outlets have claimed, but merely to tell the truth and give you a flavor of what I experienced as one who was there *from before the beginning,* before they became rich, before their privacy was lost and their lives became so "delved into" and complicated.)

A few minutes after he left by way of the fire escape, I was brought into the auditorium through the hotel in a normal fashion and allowed to stand behind the sawhorses and the line of police. The stage was about 6' tall and I'm merely 5'1", so I was not visible to the audience but positioned right below George. During the show, the fans showered the Boys with jelly beans. The avalanche of jelly beans rained down, and every few moments, George would push a bunch lying at his feet onto my head, chuckle, and give that impish grin. Years after that Chicago Stockyard concert, I heard from many fans how surprised they were to find such a jolly George at that particular event. He was known for his serious dedication to his playing at most shows rather than for being jolly. So I would explain, "That's because his sister wasn't usually below to kick jelly beans onto."

In their early days in Britain, the Boys had been asked what their favorite sweet/candy was." They had flippantly replied, "Jelly Babies," which, in fact, was no more strictly true than when on February 9, 1964 on their way into the *Ed Sullivan Show*, they were asked "What is your favorite song?" and John quickly replied "White Christmas by Bing Crosby." Always joking! However those British sweets were soft gelatin, a little softer than Gummy Bears. The British fans had started throwing these onstage during concerts, which was okay because the candies were soft and cushiony. However, in the United States, the jelly babies translated into jelly beans, a much harder, and when thrown from a distance, more dangerous projectile.

Another adventure took place in Spring of '65. I was invited to be the guest host on one of the very popular Dick Clark Tours, which back in the '60s travelled around the United States to the great enjoyment of the public. The line-up for our tour included "The Tradewinds," a male vocal group; "Reparata and the Delrons," a female vocal group; and Lou Christie, male vocalist of Lightnin' Strikes fame! Also included was another male vocalist, Round Robin, "Land of a thousand voices," and as announcer and poem reader, me!

We spent three weeks criss-crossing three Midwestern states and in the most awful weather. We drove through thunder storms, tornado warnings, and lots of rain almost every day. Members of the cast did the driving. The audiences we played to were most appreciative, and we, as a very mixed group got along very well. But this tour was to open my eyes to a facet of "living in America," the existence of which I had been completely unaware.

Apart from the problems the weather caused in our travels, we experienced yet another problem when it came time to stop to get a meal. It happened that our Round Robin was known in those days as a negro. It also happened that segregation was still very prevalent. When looking for a place to eat, one of our little troupe had to enter the potential "eatery" and find out if they were segregated. Then we would ask Round Robin what he wanted to eat, leave him in the car out in the storm and get our meal and bring his to him. As I recall, there was only once in those weeks we found a place where he could come inside with us. Can you imagine how thrilled we were to finally have him treated as a human and not an animal to be "left in the car?" It was the most joyful meal we had. When George had come to Illinois to visit me in 1963, it was a mere few weeks after the March on Washington. At that time he had noted the nasty attitude toward blacks, crowds holding signs protesting against "equality." Although I had lived since 1963 in Franklin County, Illinois, a proudly KKK area, I had not experienced personally the realities of what it meant to be black in America.

Except for this one lengthy tour, my travels were not too frequent. The Beatles daily reports were written and phoned in from my home. The time I was able to spend with my kid brother was limited to the few Beatles tour events that coincided with Beatles report cities, but all was not going well on the domestic front. Throughout the summer, our family went camping in the many lovely areas in southern Illinois, and some in southern Missouri. Often, we would arrive home to find a bunch of strangers on the front porch, visiting the house which by then was beginning to become known as a location George had visited in September 1963.

Fans would run screaming up to my husband and say, "Mr. Harrison, it's so great to meet you!" Unfortunately, the dour Scotsman was not amused! Being very chauvinistic, most men—including to some extent even The Beatles—tended to be that way in those days, he resented the fact that his lowly wife was perceived as important and somewhat of a celebrity. This situation made him very angry. He was also bitter that my kid brother, who was a mere eight or nine years old when first they met, was now a worldwide, highly paid celebrity.

To be fair, he did have a valid point when we consider the huge amounts of money made by sports stars, movie, and recording stars, etc., compared to the income made by scientists, engineers, teachers, first responders, and others whose *real* contribution to society is actually of greater value than someone who, for instance, runs up and down a field chasing a ball or who sings a song. Intellectually, I had sympathy for my engineer husband's viewpoint, but his use of alcohol in his leisure hours was becoming a real problem.

During the months I was involved in The Beatles reports, I met Grahame Richards, the CEO of the Stortz Group. He was very happy with the work I had been doing for his stations and came to me with a business proposal. The idea was for me to have "live-on-air interviews" in several major radio markets. Guest questioners would be selected by a promotional contest. The live shows would take place and be recorded at a major hotel in each city. Then the tapes would be edited into a lively album format. *(See photo on page 209.)* This seemed like a good idea to me, and my husband agreed. The proceeds from the album were to be split three ways, and I was to receive one of the thirds! Finally, it seemed I could justify all my hard work trying to promote the Boys during 1963, which led to getting into trouble with my husband. Although money was never my goal, at least maybe now my husband would see my efforts could now contribute to our financial well-being. But I reckoned without the blow it would be to a Scotman's pride to have a mere wife contribute substantially to the family coffers.

After much preparation and travelling, the live interviews were completed on WMEX in Boston, WNOR in Norfolk, WHK in Cleveland, WKNR in Detroit, and KIMN in Denver. Then the album was edited and finally pressed, the photos were selected for the cover, and the title was chosen: *All About The Beatles*. Only 5,000 were pressed, and fans across the United States were eagerly awaiting the release.

Then guess what happened? Apparently at that time, there were so many entities leaping onto the bandwagon and putting out all kinds of stuff blazoned with the word "Beatles"—that Eppy's legal people issued a "cease and desist" order for any items using the word "Beatles" that The Beatles themselves had not recorded. *WHOOPS! "Another bump appeared in the road!"* The company financing this venture was Recar in Minneapolis. I do not know if they ever recovered their investment in time and money, but I do have one, rather-battered copy of said album. I do occasionally meet a fan who has a copy and wishes me to sign it. But back then, this turn of events just afforded me a rather "snippy," "I told you so" from my securely superior husband.

Throughout most of those early Beatle years we remained in Benton, our first home in the United States. Later in the '60s, my husband and I moved to Galesburg, Illinois, and he tackled a problem for Bixby Zimmer Engineering. They made screens for use in mining that separated the valuable minerals from the waste. The problem he was brought in to solve was to produce a screen so fine that more of the "good stuff" would be saved. This, again, he solved successfully and rapidly. During our time in Galesburg, both children were at school, and I took a job with radio station WGIL, known as Wiggle, writing commercials, keeping the logs, and doing what was known as "continuity," setting up the FM automation machine. I also had a program called "Lunch with Louise." Our chief engineer, who taught me all the technical stuff I needed to know, wanted me to apply for third-class engineer certification, but although I could have

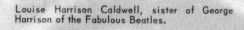

KIMN OFFICIAL Hit Parade

Louise Harrison Caldwell, sister of George Harrison of the Fabulous Beatles.

Lee Randall
Midnight – 6 a.m.

Don Martin
News Director

Paul Anderson
6 a.m. – 9 a.m.

Bob Scott
City Editor

Boogie Bell
9 a.m. – 12 noon

Chuck Duncan
Newsman

Robert E. Lee
12 Noon – 3 p.m.

Mike O'Meara
Newsman

Jay Mack
3 p.m. – 7 p.m.

Hear Louise IN PERSON on KIMN starting November 10th at 7 p.m. Call her--talk to her in person--ask about the Beatles. She'll answer your questions, give away autographed pictures of the Beatles, Beatles albums, Beatles Monthly Books, and other prizes. Listen to KIMN-950 for full details including personal appearances by this famous sister of George Harrison.

Tim Findley
Newsman

Pogo Poge
7 p.m. – 12 p.m.

Chuck Buell
Week End

Don Fortune

Lee Anderson
Weather Girl

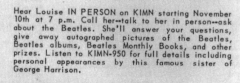

passed the test, I could not have been accepted because I was not an American citizen.

Having an enjoyable and successful radio career, unfortunately, was *not* what this Scotsman expected of a dutiful wife. His drinking and general behavior became worse and worse. My parents were worried about me, especially when they learned that there were times when I showed up at my work with my face smashed and bruised. The children were always being yelled at, especially at meal times, and my son developed a stomach ulcer. Mum and Dad invited the children to go to stay with them for an extended visit. Mum, bless her heart, thought that with the children elsewhere, my husband and I would have a "second honeymoon." She, like me, was innocent when it came to understanding anything about alcoholism. Mind you I was beginning to learn, and about that time started attending Al-Anon meetings.Though my home life was really bad, my job was a source of great satisfaction to me.

Some of the businesses for whom I wrote commercials were very appreciative. One childrenswear store would bring me garments for my kids each week. When I furnished my children's bedrooms with "built in" cabinets and beds with ample storage, the furniture store whose commercials I had been writing charged me only a fraction of the retail price. I researched, wrote and produced commercials for a farming supply company, explaining how farmers could increase the yield per acre by using certain products. These spots were run at 6:30 a.m. I soon found that the many farmers in the area enjoyed the infomercials, and dubbed me "the fertilizer lady."

It was during my time at WGIL writing commercials that I began to understand one of the major societal and cultural differences between the US and the UK. In Britain there is the British Broadcasting Corporation (BBC), which is government funded, thereby owned and influenced by taxpayers. Each radio owner paid a small annual fee and *that* paid for the programming—no commercials. When I was living in Britain, the BBC Radio consisted of three channels or programs. With no need for dozens of individual "sponsors" each bringing their own viewpoint and agenda— as so far as I know it is still true today—their world news coverage has the most objective content of any of the other world news organizations, though CNN and MSNBC come close. These three different radio outlets provided material for a wide variety of interests. The Third Program catered to the more intellectual topics and classical music listeners. The Light Program provided "popular" music, comedy shows, etc.; the Home Program consisted of dramatic productions, sometimes in serial form with a new daily episode; and readings of short stories, and so on.

I remember one spy series called *Dick Barton Special Agent*. Our George thought they were saying, "Dick Barton Speculations," and before long, the rest of the Harrisons also adopted his version of the title.

Working in radio and charged with writing commercials really opened my eyes to the major differences between the US and UK cultures. Most of my life my parents had shown me love with a hug, a pat on the head, a smile, and maybe a box of crayons at Christmas. We knew we were loved without a display of gifts; when we did get a gift, it was not wrapped in fancy paper! But in the United States, I found myself writing persuasive copy to encourage more and more buying!

The not so subtle threat in the commercial indicated:
- "You'll be in real trouble if you forget to buy gifts for this person or that event."
- In February, everyone has to buy gifts for their loved one on Valentine's Day.
- In March, the excuse to purchase is St. Patrick's Day.
- Easter means bunnies, baskets, and bonnets.
- Then God forbid you forget Mom on Mother's Day, or... Dad on Father's Day. Without a card or a gift on this specific day, you obviously have no respect or love for your parents. Wow!
- Independence Day means we have to acquire and dangerously explode tons of pollution into the air to

celebrate freedom? (A great boon/boom to revenues for the explosives business!)

- Next, we all must buy tons of Halloween candies, masks and costumes, which of course mostly benefits the candy manufacturers and costume makers.
- Thanksgiving, we all know, is not a good time of year to be a turkey!
- Next event, the super extravagance of the Christmas season and the added expense and waste of electricity with all those flamboyant lighted house decorations (Is the purpose for all those lights to enable Santa's reindeer to be able to see where we live?), not to mention all the gifts that must be exchanged.
- To close out the year, lots of wonderful liquor gifts, and of course more fireworks to pollute the air on New Year's Eve and add to the explosive makers coffers!
- Throughout all of this, the greetings card folks and florists were doing quite well, too!
- Some most important words to use in commercials were "introducing" and "only" or "just." For some reason, tried and true products were never as good as the "New and Improved whatchamacallit we now were Introducing!" Also, you never put a price into a commercial without the word only or just in front. For instance: *"Introducing Sweeneys new and improved two ounce, super-sized burger! Only fifty thousand dollars each, two for just fifty three thousand, for a limited time only. So, hurry to Sweeneys and get yours today before supplies run out at Sweeneys!"* Yes I am being silly, but perhaps you have noticed these ploys also? Yes it was also important to name the client three times during the "spot."

I was finding myself involved in this mass manipulation. Commercials then tended to infer that the only way to exhibit your love for a friend or family member was to spend money, especially for things they really did not need, such as jewelry, alcohol, perfume, or clothing they may not like, etc.

You get the picture. I was becoming a tool in the scam of "spend, baby, spend." I was not happy with that part of my job and felt that I was not being as "true to myself" as Dad had raised me to be. But my husband had grudgingly agreed to me working, and I was not sure how much longer I could endure my home life, so did not want to give up a decent job.

(I have to admit, though, as bad as the commercialization was back then, it is a zillion times worse now. Then, only eighteen minutes per hour could be devoted to commercials. Now, I notice by timing various TV channels that twenty-six minutes are devoted to commercials and thirty-four to the actual show. (You can check this out yourselves.) Also, in the 21st century, the majority of commercials are for the insurance, pharmaceutical, financial investment, and similar industries rather than the cute little Pillsbury Doughboy! And what could be more ridiculous than taking a certain blue pill only to have your home vanish and find yourself in a bathtub somewhere in a field? Is this scenario conducive to "lovemaking?" Speaking of lovemaking...is sex the only way to demonstrate love to a partner? Maybe a man could more effectively demonstrate his love by taking out the trash without being asked, or fixing a leaking faucet, or even emptying the dishwasher and putting away the dishes. A real treat for any woman would be to have her male partner actually listen to what she is saying to him occasionally! These are all acts that would be appreciated, and no need to go off and buy something.

As we humans reach a certain stage in life, all the huffing and puffing and sweating of making "love" gets to be tiresome. After all, sex is *not* actually *love!* Consider when a woman starts to think *"Oh not that again!"* or a man has to resort to the blue pill. Could it be that actually there is nothing *wrong* with them? Our western sex-obsessed society does not need a pharmacy to develop a very profitable *cure*. These individuals have simply reached the stage in life when their minds and brains have finally become smarter and perhaps more powerful than their hormones!!!

Is that possible? Think about it!

21st century commercials are not only an insult to the intelligent, but are also degrading to the stupid as well. But our current problem of blatant product commercialization is *nothing* compared to the present day unabashed purchasing of politicians.)

Although my husband and I both had satisfying work, due to his increased nightly drinking, there were many days when, as I had reluctantly admitted to my parents, I would arrive at work with my face swollen and bruised from the violence inflicted by my drunken husband. Each morning, he would apologize profusely. I am sure many people reading this may have experienced this kind of abuse and understand, especially when children are involved, it is not easy to "walk away." Again, once he solved the current engineering puzzle of the fine screens, he became bored and returned to Freeman Coal in southern Illinois. My children had spent most of their early childhood in that area, and on their return from Britain, were happy to reunite with old friends. We bought a nice, modest home just outside Johnston City, another small town just south of West Frankfort.

Our house in Galesburg was for sale, and George offered us the down payment for our newest home while we waited to sell the Galesburg house.

One day, shortly after returning to southern Illinois, I received a phone call from a person who turned out to play a pivotal role in my life. His name was George Dodds and was the owner of an influential radio station WGGH in Marion, just a few miles from our new home. He had been aware of my Beatles reports during 1964 and '65. It was by now 1969, I think. Anyhow, Mr. Dodds called me into his station to ask if I would be interested in starting up a new morning talk show, co-hosted by an announcer named Larry Watts. I had been doing quite well in radio in Galesburg, and this seemed a perfect "fit" for my inclinations and abilities. So it was we started "Sound-Off," a morning call in talk show. We covered every subject of interest to our listeners, including many social and political situations.

Influenced by my "having grown up wealthy" husband's ideas, I was very much inclined to agree with his conservative views. I had read several of Ayn Rand's books, including *Atlas Shrugged*, and had sent a donation to Barry Goldwater's campaign and, later, was supportive of Nixon and Reagan.

Our radio show was very satisfying. I had a secretary at the station to help send out letters to solicit and book guests. Mr. Dodds would allow me to use his Lincoln auto when invited to attend special events, for instance with the governor of Illinois or to a rodeo in Missouri to meet Michael Landon, Little Joe of the *Bonanza* TV show. When speaking with Michael, we found we both had a daughter with the same name, and sitting with me in the back of a trailer in Sikeston, MO, he gave me a really great interview for our show. Other notables we had on the show were Wayne Newton and his brother. Politicians included Congressman Grey and Senator Percy. We had many other lesser known guests, and through our outreach and listener support we were even able to help get legislation passed, for example to build sewage treatment plants on the Mississippi and to establish the sensible idea of junior colleges. There were many other worthy projects. But, as happy as I was in my job (especially since I didn't have to write commercials), my home life was getting unbearable.

Mr. Dodds and his wife were very kind to me. My brother George—with whom I was constantly in touch—was also very concerned and supportive. Knowing how badly I was being abused, Mr. Dodds offered to lend me the money to engage a lawyer so I could get a divorce. I actually kept in touch with Mr. and Mrs. Dodds until his death at the age of ninety-two. My children had also been suffering from their father's abuse. As a toddler, my son, a very sensitive little boy, had developed a nervous stammer due to the traumatic accident he had witnessed in Gagnon. His father constantly made fun of him, calling him a "sissy." Subsequently, almost every meal time turned into a tearful event. When my son was eight, due to so much stress he was diagnosed with a stomach ulcer. My husband's behavior was such, that he later shot and killed my daughter's beloved dog. So when I asked my children if they thought I should get a divorce, they both said, "Yes, Mommy, you are too gentle to be with Daddy." So on January 29, 1971, my divorce was final. Thus the mistake my teenage hormones led me to—a rather challenging marriage—came to an end.

George, always there for me, offered to have me and the children move into his Middle Lodge at Friar Park. In order to return to England, I booked passage on the *QE2*. But again, my life veered in a different direction from the one I planned.

Chapter Eleven

THE BANGLADESH ERA

*I*n January 1971, I was now single and thirty-nine. I remained thirty-nine for twenty-five years until I became sixty-four! I had no choice but to "move on" at that point because a couple of thousand Beatle people were singing to me "When I'm Sixty-Four." I did protest that this was actually the 25th Anniversary of my 39th birthday. But they just insisted on the sixty-four thing! As George once remarked, "It is difficult to pretend when millions of people know more about you than you know about yourself!"

The summer of 1970 I spent time in England during our Mum's final days. After the funeral, George and I left Dad's home in Appleton and drove down to London in his bright red Ferrari. I will always remember being forced back against my seat by the terrific "thrust" when he put his foot on the accelerator to take off!! George was in the process of purchasing Friar Park then, so I spent a few days with him when he was able to show me around. The entire property was in a terrible state of abandonment, the grounds as well as the house itself. He had a video made showing the condition of the place when he bought it, and when I first arrived it was in that shape.

George and Pattie had bought the house from a group of nuns who had run a school there. The house had been built by Sir Frankie Crisp, a rather eccentric millionaire of the 1800s. Everything about the house was in excellent taste, and extremely expensive materials had been used. Unfortunately the nuns had, at one time, received a donation of many gallons of pale cream paint. This they used to paint over the beautiful wall coverings in the hallways and many of the rooms. The dining room in particular had leather wall coverings with designs carved into the leather. This did not escape the cream paint either. At the time George had many friends in the Hari Krishna movement, and for many weeks they patiently toiled at gently scraping off the paint in order to restore the wall coverings to their original state wherever possible. I recall that George had a sampling of some of the original 18th century wallpaper and took it to many manufacturers to try to match it up. He was finally able to find a firm in New York (I believe) to restore much of the house to its original unique and very whimsical character. Which I must admit, *did* rather match my kid brothers own unique and whimsical character. I expect many of my readers will have seen a couple of music videos which were shot at Friar Park, including the one with Neil Innes dressed as a nursemaid pushing a "pram" up the driveway to the strains of "Crackerbox Palace." That particular nickname for Friar Park came from a chance meeting George had with a man named Mr. Grieff, if I recall correctly, somewhere in the south of France, whose own rather whimsical home he dubbed Crackerbox Palace. Naturally this name appealed to my brother's sense of whimsy, thus the song and the connection. Many of his songs in that era reflect Sir Frankie Crisp's influence, songs such as "Let it Roll" and "The Flying Hour."

Throughout Friar Park, the Friar theme was very prominent. All the light switches were miniature friars heads and the actual switch was the nose!

In the acres of gardens were three connecting man-made lakes, complete with little waterfalls and stepping stones. Caves were accessible from the stepping stones, and the video of George's version of the "True Love" title song from the Grace Kelly/Bing Crosby movie was shot there.

Our other brothers, Peter and Harry, both had good jobs and were buying their own homes near Liverpool. George understood that, due to his high profile circumstances, he could not find anyone better than his siblings to protect him and manage this thirty-eight acre property. With a bit of friendly persuasion, he managed to convince them to move to Friar Park. Harry moved into the gate, or entrance, lodge and Peter bought a nice family home nearby. Although they both helped look after George, they were careful not to let it be known they were in anyway related to him. Harrison was a common enough name, so only a few close friends in Henley knew of the connection. In fact, Harry and Pete were so "turned off" by the behavior of Beatle fans constantly going through their trash cans that they could not understand why Mum, Dad and I would interact with the fans at all!

Realizing what a great opportunity this property afforded for him to have all of his family together, when Dad was not voyaging around the world he had an apartment in the "big house." Harry and his family were to live in the Gate Lodge, so George offered his Middle Lodge at Friar Park for the newly single me and my children, I booked passage on the *QE2*. However, we discovered that if we changed from the US educational system to the British system that my children, raised so far in the United States, would be two years behind the British school children in academic knowledge and,

To dearest Mum, on your special day.

'When you are joyous, look deep into your heart and you shall find it is only That which has given you sorrow That is giving you joy. When you are sorrowful too again in your heart and you shall see That in Truth you are weeping for That which has been your delight.' K. G.
With lots of love from George. Pattie

therefore, would be two years behind their own age group in class. Well, when you are a child, being put on the same level as children two years younger is a big blow. So, after

DARK HORSE RECORDS

'Lou'

2356 RIVIERA DR.
SARASOTA, FL 33582

LOUISE HARRISON
(813) 924-0463

much soul searching, we decided not to make that move.

Once again, it was Uncle Eddy to the rescue. He and his family had moved from Toronto and had bought a small motel, Greg Apartments, in Deerfield Beach, Florida. One of the units had two bedrooms, a bathroom, plus a small living room/kitchen. He offered this accommodation to me and the children and arranged for them to enroll in the local school. So with our trunks packed for the sea voyage, we went instead by rail to Florida. Pretty soon I found a job at a research laboratory, and Uncle Eddy helped me put a down payment on a Toyota.

Soon after we arrived in Florida, Dad came to visit us.

My son had difficulties at the school in Florida. As previously mentioned, he had already been traumatized in Gagnon and later was diagnosed with stomach ulcers at age eight. At the school in Florida, there was a swimming pool and he could swim, but "new kids" were put through a hazing. A group would hold the new kid's head under water until the child almost drowned. He was miserable. His sister, though younger, was tougher, and would fight his bullies at school in Florida. When the summer vacation time arrived, their father invited them to spend the summer back amongst their Illinois friends and enjoy camping once again. A couple of years prior to the divorce, we had bought a very nice camper trailer.

When I divorced him, I just wanted to "escape," so had not asked for any settlement. He kept the house in Johnston City for which George had sent the down payment. He also kept all the furniture, which had been more or less "gifted to me" from my radio clients, and he kept the camper, which had largely been paid for by my radio earnings. Although I had legal custody of the children, I was never able to obtain child support; he had other priorities for his money! All I had wanted was to get away from the constant drunken abuse, even though it meant leaving the career I really enjoyed, a really vital and socially significant radio talk show and the children leaving all that was familiar in their lives, too. I had for some time been a member of Al Anon, a support group for relatives of alcoholics, and understood it was useless to hope for a change unless, and until, the alcoholic wanted to quit.

So, although I was apprehensive when their father invited the children to spend the summer with him, they were unhappy with their treatment at the Florida school and really wanted to see their friends and their dogs, two German shepherds from one litter named Bonnie and Clyde. Although Uncle Eddy provided us with a free motel room, and I had obtained a position as a lab assistant at a research laboratory nearby, it was difficult to provide adequately for the children on my $90 a week pay. So worrying about doing the right thing, I considered that their father had the home, etc. and a very good income, although he refused to pay child support to me. So, I knew that in Illinois, they would not suffer from lack of food and shelter. Then I bought rail tickets for them to spend the summer with their father. I knew he was stern, but had never physically harmed them (as far as I understood at that time).

At the end of the summer, I received a really nasty letter from the children. They told me they were going to stay with their father. He was not drinking and had promised to buy our son a motorcycle and our daughter a horse, two things they had always desired. They also said he told them I was a whore and not fit to take care of them. I knew he was merely using them to hurt me. Though I had legal custody of the children, I resolved not to put them through a court battle as long as it seemed he was treating them right. I replied, saying they had my blessing to stay. I did make it clear that I was ready at any time to have them come back to me, should the need arise. They always had my phone number. George also constantly reassured me by affirming, "Whatever happens, I am never farther away than the other end of the phone."

Around this time, George created the Bangladesh Concert. His good friend Ravi Shankar, the world's greatest sitar player with whom George had studied, approached George in distress. He told about the terrible events taking place in his homeland of Bangladesh. When he asked George if there was anything he could do to help. George immediately suggested, "Why don't we gather up some of our friends and have a concert to raise money?"

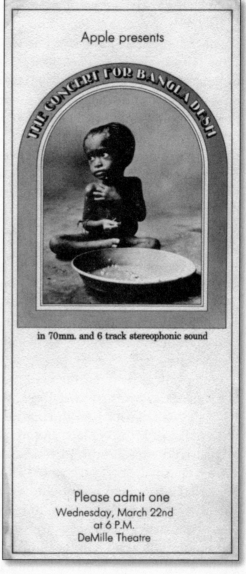

Apple presents

THE CONCERT FOR BANGLA DESH

in 70mm. and 6 track stereophonic sound

Please admit one
Wednesday, March 22nd
at 6 P.M.
DeMille Theatre

George brought Dad in to assist him in this venture, and I too flew from Uncle Eddy's motel in Florida to New York to spend the week or so prior to the show with them. This undertaking was quite daunting for my kid brother, and he relied on Dad's calm strength to help him pull it off. We had lost Mum the previous July on Ringo's birthday, July 7, 1970. Not only was this concert a first for George, but also such a rock and roll benefit was the first for the *whole planet!!*

All the participants stayed at the Essex Hotel on Central Park South. We were back and forth to Apple and Madison Square Garden during the week. Dad and I were able to take on some of the mundane tasks involved in such a venture and take a little of the load from George, but still it was a huge burden on his slim shoulders. The first thing we had to do was to find a large enough venue and a suitable date for the concert: Madison Square Garden on August 1, 1971. Once that was confirmed, there were a zillion more details to deal with.

The more notable amongst the "Friends" were Ringo Starr, Leon Russell, Billy Preston, Eric Clapton, Bob Dylan, Klaus Voormann, Jim Horn, the band Badfinger, and, of course, Ravi Shankar and his band, which consisted of Ali Akbar Khan (on the Sarod), Alla Rakah (on the Tabla), and Kamala Chakravarty (on the Tamboura). During this tense and significant week, we all became close and supportive "teammates."

One comical incident for Dad and I occurred the night of the concert. We were with a family from Long Island who had been penpals with Mum during her life. Dad kept in touch with many of Mum's longstanding pals even after her death. We arrived early and had ten seats, located about twenty rows from the front, stage right. The aisle seat was empty, so being a short person, I thought, "Okay, I can see better down the aisles from here," so Dad and I sat down. As the concert was about to begin, one of those "self-important suits" tapped me roughly on the shoulder and said, "Young lady, you are in my seat! George Harrison himself invited me!" In typical Harrison fashion, Dad and I just said, "We're so sorry," and without another word moved the whole gang along to give Mr. V.I.P. his seat. Dad and I had quite a chuckle to ourselves, and naturally we did not bother to reveal to him *just who* had invited *us*.

After the Bangladesh show, we—the participants and many others—all went to Jimmy Weston's Supper Club for an after show party. Phil Spector was in rare form that night and took to the piano on the small stage and made up songs about some of the people there. I recall one about Paul McCartney, who had intended being at the concert, but did not actually arrive. The ironic off the cuff lyrics mentioned something about Paul being known for "Yesterday," but now he's just "Another Day." A member of the Who also performed and at one point stumbled against a cabinet at the side of the stage, crashing it to the floor; unfortunately, it contained all the china belonging to the club. Poor George had to pay for the damages! Jim Horn and his group played also. George jokingly referred to them as "Jim Horn and his Horny Horns!" A day or two after the concert, I returned to Florida.

Although George was mostly in Britain and other parts of the planet, he kept in touch and knew all that was happening in my life. He had one of the CPAs from Apple in New York "put in charge of my well-being." This CPA, Eugene, explained to George that it would be to his advantage so far as his income tax was concerned, to help support me and my children financially and claim me as a dependant. This George did a few years later.

Whilst my children were still with me at Uncle Eddy's motel, and before they chose to stay in Illinois, George wanted to buy me a home in Boca Raton, close to Uncle Eddy. But at the time when his CPA arrived to purchase the home, the children had made it clear they wished to remain in Illinois. After much discussion, it was deemed a good idea for me to move, instead, to New York. George was there often on business—plus, I would be close to the folks at Apple. The CPA found me an apartment on East 70th Street. Being city bred and after spending so many years living in small and often remote mining towns, it was—for me—a relief to be once again in a city, especially The Big Apple.

During the next couple of years, I was able to spend a lot of time with my brother. He was working on the album and movie version of the Bangladesh Concert in order to create more revenue to send to the country in need. We spent many evenings together at the mixing studio near the Columbus

Circle. Here is one perhaps little-known factor about the album: During the concert, when playing "My Sweet Lord," Eric was frustrated by the complex riff repeated throughout the song, and for the album, George had to "dub over" Eric's rather fumbled version on the soundtrack recorded by the fourty-four microphones at the event.

Of course, it is now a well-known and admitted factor that Eric was having some heroin problems at that time. I know George was concerned about several of his peers with similar problems, and having himself relinquished drug use for more spiritual reasons, had been very helpful in aiding their recovery. Not too many people are aware of that aspect of George's life, but at this point, I am certainly not revealing anything he would have wished to be kept a "secret." Eric has since built and funded a rehabilitation center and been a great advocate for persons similarly afflicted. Ringo, also, has confronted and defeated addiction problems and advocates the benefits of living an alcohol and drug-free life.

Once the Bangladesh album and movie were ready, those of us involved had a private preview at a tiny movie screening place, I think on 5th Avenue. The invited audience included Bob Dylan and his wife. We chatted quite a lot, and although I have never been "into" jewelry, I was intrigued when the couple showed me their matching emerald-studded wedding rings. While we were watching Bob's portion of the movie, he expressed concern that all the rest of the concert showed a group of friends singing together for the purpose of helping those less fortunate. Bob said, "I look so big headed, standing there all by myself, when all the rest of the show is like one big happy family!"

George's rather comical, but to the point reassurance was this: "Well, Bob, you don't exactly write sing along with Dylan type songs, now do you?" All present had a chuckle and had to admit George "nailed it."

But many problems lay ahead for my brother. Due to the integrity with which we had been raised (THFC), he had expected that this good effort would go smoothly. Unfortunately, he found the truth in the saying that *"No good deed goes unpunished."* The money from the concert itself was sent by check to the United Nations Children's Fund in the amount of $243,418.50. He also wanted to personally deliver the proceeds from the album and movie as soon as they were available directly to those in need in Bangladesh. He was concerned that on many occasions the money raised for folks *in need* instead found its way to folks *in greed.* I don't know all the details, but I do know he was having problems with Capitol Records and the IRS. In his concern to be able to help others, he had not known that in order to disperse funds charitably, one had to have a 501(c)(3), in other words file for a tax-exempt status. So, the IRS insisted the money be taxed before it could leave the United States. Also, Capitol—involved in record distribution—did not want to give up their profits, so after all his hard work and the efforts of many of his friends, he was hitting his head against a bureaucratic brick wall. However, now that he knew about charities and 501(c)(3)'s, he set about learning what had to be done in order to comply, so that any future efforts to aid others could go more smoothly.

He discovered that one had to incorporate, then have the corporation apply for the tax exempt status. Also, said corporation had to have a board of directors, trustworthy people who would oversee the corporation's operations. There were many "helpers" around though not an awful lot George regarded as "trustworthy," so at that time he asked me if I would become a board member. I remember replying that I didn't know anything about business, and he laughingly added, "Obviously with this mess on my hands, neither do I!" We had a chuckle, rare in those weeks, and that was that.

I later came across the following paragraph from a book by R. Buckminster Fuller, a 20th century intellectual I regard with great respect, and I think it may well be appropriate to insert it here.

"In your musical-education world and in your professional meetings, I think it important that you realize that within the next ten years the world of

*science and the world of seemingly very pragmatic
affairs may be turning to the world of music for
leadership in fostering the spontaneous development of
the most powerfully coordinate capabilities of evoluting
life. Rather than being a pleasant sideshow for the
more serious central affairs of economic life, you who
deal with the music of the universe and the innate
coordinate capability of man to tune in the music of
the new life, may be recognized as dealing with the
sensitive mainspring of life itself, because of which you
may find yourselves called by society to perform its most
responsible task allowing life to succeed."* (from *Utopia
or Oblivion: The Prospects for Humanity*, New York:
The Overlook Press, 1969. 78-79)

Seems Bucky had a point, and one I have taken to heart
presently. More later.

To promote the album and movie, George was invited to
appear on the *Dick Cavett Show*. Before the show, we had
dinner with Leon, then we all proceeded to the studio. There
was a live audience, of which I was a member, and poor George
was as nervous as can be. All his life, although he was relaxed
when performing with his band, he was nervous being alone
in the public eye. The tape of this show is "out there," so I
expect many readers have probably seen it. It was a ninety
minute show. After just a few minutes, George said to Dick,
"Well, I really have nothing to say." With about 80 minutes
to go, Dick almost fell off his chair in shock. If you have not
seen this tape, I recommend you take a look; it really was
comical. George at one point—due to the frustration he was
undergoing trying to get help to the victims in Bangladesh—
actually shook his fist at the cameras and mentioned Baskar
Mennen, at the time head of Warner Brothers, with whom
George was in conflict. Although involved closely with George
on a personal level, only a fragment of these details are
known to me. Other comical happenings during that the *Dick
Cavett Show* occurred each time the studio monitor appeared
with the inevitable commercial. When George spotted the

message, he immediately began to read it out loud to Dick's surprise and amused dismay.... "You don't have to do that," I think he told George. However, by then finding a way to amuse himself, George was starting to enjoy this experience.

As we were leaving the studio, George said to Dick, "You ought to talk to our Lou." At that point, he introduced me, saying, "She's really good at this talk show format. Had a successful show on radio and she lives in New York now." A month or two later, I had an interview, which George told Apple to arrange, with John Gilroy, the Producer of the *Dick Cavett Show*. Dick's ratings at that time were slipping, and Apple's proposal to Dick's producer argued that the addition of the only "Beatles sister" could improve the demographics of the show. John and I hit it off, and after a lengthy conversation he seemed quite satisfied at my potential as co-host. As I left, he said, "I'll get you in here next week to sign a contract and let you choose the colors for your dressing room."

George and I were thrilled. He was pleased with himself for being the one to introduce me to Dick and eventually his producer. Finally, I was to get an opportunity to show that more than one Harrison had talent. He also knew that, although he was always there to help me, I did have abilities and as a Harrison would much prefer to be able to help myself. But as you now know, I was never cast as co-host of the *Dick Cavett Show*. No, ABC cancelled the show that same weekend. Naturally, we were bitterly disappointed.

However, before long, the CPA at Apple—along with two business partners and myself—formed Jet Cloud Travel and rented office space on the 33rd floor in the Sperry Rand Building next door to Radio City Music Hall, on 6th Avenue. Most of our travelling clients were other recording artists. In those days it was possible for an airline passenger to book a flight and change it numerous times before actually flying. All these changes were at no charge to the passenger. We came to dread the times when Waylon Jennings was touring. Every time he booked a trip, we had to change the flights frequently before the actual date when his group departed. It was also true that in those days each ticket had to be written out with a very firm hand because there were several carbon copies. It seems strange that airlines no longer give refunds and charge extra for EVERYTHING!, yet the tickets are generated automatically by electronic means, thus no need for the expense of an employee. This was an early step in the ongoing process of eliminating tasks that require human participation, thus less employment opportunities.

One incident I recall from my days in New York happened on the 25th of February. My brother called me from London. Due to The Beatles "fame," they had to have their phone numbers changed quite often to preserve their privacy. George's number had been changed the day before, so, knowing I did not yet have his new number, he called *me* so that I could wish *him* a Happy Birthday. I remember that call so well, and was so touched at the thoughtful way he made sure I was not thwarted by being unable to reach him.

We had an interesting little adventure one Saturday afternoon during my New York days. Pattie was in town, and also Ringo and Klaus. Pattie wanted to see some museum or library. George, Ringo, Klaus, Pattie, and I set off walking up Park Avenue. We felt we were pretty inconspicuous as we strolled along, but Ringo has such a distinctive walk—perhaps a slight strut? Pretty soon we were being accompanied on the other side of the avenue by a small crowd of Beatle People. They were very polite and on that occasion did not bother us at all. At one point, we stopped at a shoe store. Ringo noticed some high-platform running shoes and wanted to try them on.

We all went inside, and I guess this was a pretty high class joint because the staff brought us wine in boot-shaped glasses. One male staff member was so overcome at seeing our George that he came over and knelt at George's feet to pay "homage." Naturally, George was embarrassed and pulled the fellow up to sit beside him and join us in a glass of booted wine! Meanwhile, Ringo, the natural comedian, was trying on these ridiculously high platform running shoes. He tried one on and kept his regular shoe on the other foot and was walking very lop-sidedly up and down saying, "These fit perfectly," to the screams of laughter of everyone present. When we left the shoe store, we passed by a jewelry store. Pattie saw an item in the window and asked George to buy it for her. Before heading into the store, George said to me, "Is there anything *you* would like, and I'll get it for you." I looked at the displays and found a relatively inexpensive item—an ornament in the shape of a tree with Jade leaves—so he went into the store and bought the items for Pattie and me. This little jade tree is still one of my more treasured items and one that—so far—has not been "requisitioned" by visitors to my home.

After we accomplished our intended visit to the library/museum (I don't recall which), we went back to my apartment and had a meal.

An Austrian family lived in the next door apartment. They had a young daughter named Chrysanthi, who was about nine and had made friends with my children when they spent Christmas with me. Anyway, on the many occasions George visited me, he would wave to her because the window of her bedroom was at right angles to mine across the fire escape. When his most current album, *All Things Must Pass,* was released, he knocked on Chrysanthis' door one evening and gave her a copy.

Many years later, she told me this story: The next day at her school was "show and tell," and though she did not have the album with her, she excitedly told how George Harrison had come to her door the previous night and given her his latest album. The poor child was severely reprimanded for making up outrageous lies and made to stand in the corner for ten minutes. If I had known this at the time, I would have gone to her school and set them straight right then! Several years after this event, her mother died. She tracked me down at that time to ask me if I would be her new Mom; naturally, I said yes. She is now married to a physician and has a child of her own.

I spent quite a lot of time at the Apple offices, especially when George was in town. Obviously most players in the

Beatle saga would be in and out too. I became good friends with Judy Gilbertson, Alan Klein's executive secretary. Occasionally I would spend lunch hour with her in her office. One day we were chatting quietly when the large door to Klein's office burst open and hit against the wall with a crash. Startled, we looked up to see a diminutive figure wearing high heeled, exotic creature animal skin boots stride through the doorway. She paused, then pointing her finger imperiously at Judy yelled, "**Two chicken noodle soups!**" She then turned on her heels and this time the door crashed closed behind her. Dumbfounded, I looked at Judy and asked "Just what was that supposed to be?" Judy, casting her eyes to the ceiling, said with a slight sigh, "Oh, that's the way she orders lunch for her and John." I won't repeat my comments–I do want to get this book printed!

The absolutely perfect sequel to this incident occurred about a week later in this same office. My brother was leaning against the filing cabinets reading fan mail and chatting to Judy and I. He finished one of the letters, and putting it down, he turned to Judy with a smile and said (his exact words), "Judy luv, is there any chance you could get me a cup of tea?" His words and demeanor did not surprise me, but I was gratified at his courteous manner and the respect he was showing to an "employee." My thoughts at that moment were, "Mum and Dad, I appreciate the values you taught us." Mum always stressed to us that the royal family, as a mark or indication of their royalty, would treat even the lowliest of their subjects with courtesy and consideration and never yell orders like a bully. To Mum and Dad, being impolite to others indicated a lack of self-esteem. End of segment!

I really enjoyed living in New York and would walk to 6th and 51st Street from 1st and 70th Street each day. I would take a different route most days until I grew to know that part of the city pretty well. Sometimes, before walking home, if it was raining, I would stop at one of the many business folks' bars nearby. One evening, I was at The Office Pub when the man standing next to me at he bar whispered in my ear with a note of desperation, "Please, would you pretend you know me? There's this awful woman I'm trying to get away from!"

Reared to be kind, I immediately turned and said, "Wow, it's so great to see you again, how have you been?" That moment became the prelude to my relationship with Walt, husband number two. Within a week, he moved into my apartment with me. He was the northeast regional sales manager for the Corning Glass incentive marketing division and was one of their most promising sales executives, highly regarded by Corning.

Naturally, I was in constant communication with my children, but a month or so later, when I wrote telling them I had met a person I really liked and may possibly marry, their father once again became Mr. Hyde. He shot and killed my daughter's dog and inflicted much more abuse, which there is no point in mentioning. I guess he thought if the children fled back to me, it would mess up my new relationship, especially since my new soon to be husband was much younger than I. But, Walt had a very kind heart, and soon I made reservations for the children to fly to New York and move into my 70th Street apartment with us.

Shortly after this, Walt was relocated from the Corning office in the city to their office in White Plains, NY. We married in the town of Harrison in New York State in July 1974. He soon found a larger apartment in Harrison, which could better accommodate a family of four. It had hardwood floors throughout, and we bought a 9'x12' area carpet for the living room. He also insisted on paying the extra fee in order that the children, who were heartbroken over the murder of their pet in Illinois, could have a German shepherd puppy. We named him Bandit because he looked as though he was wearing the kind of mask worn by movie bandits. My daughter has always been fantastic with animals, and within a week or so, Bandit knew not to step onto the carpet. The children would take him for walks, and altogether we finally had a loving and happy family atmosphere. Walt's mother, quite naturally, was rather alarmed at her twenty-nine-year-old son taking on the challenge of an older woman with two teenagers. However, she soon became a real grandmother to the children, and whenever we visited her in New Jersey, she would load us up with tons of food from her fridge. She often gave me wonderful outfits from her abundant collection of "high-end" clothing.

That same year, 1974, George was on tour. Amongst the crew, it became known as the "Harry's on Tour." Again, Dad was along for moral support. For the final show of the tour— at Madison Square Garden— we were all invited and spent time before the show with the participants. My son and daughter had a great time with their uncle and grandfather. One memory really sticks out: Dad was walking along backstage with his grandchildren, and my daughter had her arm around his shoulder. She was 5'8", and for the first time in my life, I realized that my dad, at 5'7", was actually quite a short man! Wow, to me he had always seemed the biggest man in the world!

After the show on December 20, 1974, we went to the aftershow party held at a club called the Hippopotamus. My son was quite pleased when one of the guests asked him if he was a guitarist, saying, "You have the same long fingers as George." I suppose family DNA could account for that. At some point during the '70s, we moved from our apartment in Harrison to our own home in Danbury, Connecticut. Whilst there, my son joined the United States military and began to train as an air traffic controller.

Another couple of interesting events connected with my brother occurred during that same era. Around Christmas, George and his retinue were staying, once again, at the Plaza. For a joke, whilst he was sleeping—he was known to sleep soundly—his crew entered his room with seventeen fully-decorated Christmas trees and set them around his bed. They also set about a dozen alarm clocks, each to go off at minute intervals.

When I heard about it later, I did not think it was funny. I don't recall George's reaction, but it seems he took it in stride.

Also, when staying at the Plaza, George was alerted one night that one of Frank Sinatra's employees was attempting to reach him to try to persuade him to write and produce an album for Frank. To avoid having to say no to Frank Sinatra because he was so busy himself, he spent the night hiding in a broom closet on his floor at the hotel. You may remember that Frank did record his own version of "Something." To the amusement of most Beatles fans, he was famously quoted to have said that, "'Something' is the best love song Lennon and McCartney ever wrote." But, obviously he learned of his error, hence his attempt to have George write and produce an album for him.

Anyhow, I guess it was in the late '70s when Walt left Corning Glass Company and started his own marketing business. We moved to Daytona Beach and, with the proceeds from the sale of our Danbury house, were able to pay cash for a very nice doublewide mobile home in an all-adult community. By then, my son had married and was an air traffic controller in the armed service. My daughter was able to have her own apartment and work at one of the many hotels along the beach.

Within a very few years, our marketing business was doing so well that we were able to move to Sarasota, on the much lovelier Gulf Coast, and put a 50% down payment on a golf course home, 2,400 square feet with A/C and a huge garage and a caged pool. This is where I was living when—with very little animosity—my second and final marriage failed. However, due to a friendly settlement, which George helped negotiate, and a pension George provided, I was able to remain in this lovely home.

Those years, in the '80s and happily single, provided with a modest pension and living in a lovely home in Sarasota, were definitely my happiest years. In retrospect, they were the closest to a relaxed retirement I have ever been able to enjoy. During our marriage we had travelled constantly with our business, thus I knew very few people in Sarasota. However, in order to make some new friends, I invited one or two of my radio friends to a "First Friday of the month Happy Hour" at my home. I provided a very low cost, homemade extensive buffet with homemade rum punch and sangria. The home had a large caged pool, a huge family room complete with table tennis and a darts area, so it lent itself well to parties. Before long the parties were being attended by as many as 150 persons. Sometimes we played volleyball in the pool. Most attendees were show biz folks and we never had any spilt drinks, cigarette burns, or for that matter anyone misbehave in any way. These parties continued for about fourteen months. Notably, my guests observed that not once did it rain on my party! Thanks, rain god.

Throughout the years, George had been in the habit of sending me wonderful gift baskets at Christmas with Dom Perignon and other goodies—quite a treat! After he built a home in Maui and whilst I was living in Sarasota, one year I received a different Christmas gift. A van pulled up to my home and the deliveryman came to the door with what looked like a coffin for a small person. It turned out to be a box containing a dozen or more exotic blooms direct from Maui. Each flower was huge! The only containers I owned large enough for them were a couple of buckets. However, my next door neighbors, who had their own hothouse, came to my rescue and provided me with vases capable of holding the lovely flowers.

Time proceeded into the '90s. By then I had two wonderful grandsons, my son's son, born November 29, 1988, and my daughter's son, born November 26, 1990. Life for me was very pleasant. I had many friends and most days walked the six-mile round trip on Crescent Beach with my pal and roommate, Jan. *(See photo on page 216.)*

I loved my home and really enjoyed my social life. My brother had set up a modest pension for me and my parties cost very little, but just like many thousands of equally unsuspecting souls, I allowed myself to get caught in the trap laid by the seductive and urgent cry from the banks; "Why not re-finance and make use of some of the equity in your home?"

What they did *not* tell the public was this: *Do this and you are virtually giving the banks an opportunity to ruin your life. An adjustable rate mortgage means that your thirty-year* *fixed rate of maybe $212 a month, can now keep going up and up until you are paying far more each month than you can afford, thus making it less likely you can keep up the new payments and retain ownership of your home. Are we not still reaping THAT harvest today?* So, this self-confessed dummy refinanced a home that was almost fully paid for. Then, my manageable monthly payment of just $212 skyrocketed to $1,300 a month. I had foolishly used some of the "equity" to upgrade my auto and had payments on that, too. Although I've never fancied myself as having a "business head," I was so embarrassed by being so badly bamboozled, that in order to "save face" and not admit this error of judgment to my family, I regretfully sold the house for the equity I still had and moved into a much more modest condo.

Soon, however, the responsibility of grandsons caused me to look much farther into the future. Then it became clear to me due to a couple of centuries of unthinking human activities and ignorance of the delicate balance of our eco-system, the health of our planet was in peril. So, also was the future of our species and my two precious grandsons. Recognizing problems and trying to find solutions had always motivated me, so shortly after moving from my lovely home to the small condo, I incorporated as an environmental non-profit organization called We Care. Remembering the solution to the problems George endured over his "efforts to help," I knew enough to incorporate, and this time I offered George a spot on my board, but he, just as I had, said no thanks!

Now, onto my next challenge: the environment.

Chapter Twelve

DROP-IN ENVIRON-MENTAL
ORGANIZATION

*S*ince I had been a child conversing with my dad, I've always been very much engaged in knowledge of world affairs. With the arrival of two grandsons, my concerns focused a lot more on the future of Earth's finely tuned and delicate ecosystem and the potential for long-term survival.

From my earliest days in the United States, I was impressed with the sensible and eco-sustainable way our original Native Americans conducted their culture and lives. I became familiar with the famous letter in the 1800s from Chief Seattle to Washington, and so totally agreed with his observations that I have recorded the letter as a voice demo tape.

Since my second, and final, divorce, I'd continued to work in radio, but in 1989 fate intervened and as a relatively new grandmother, I took a position as Nanny for a lovely lady stockbroker, mother of an eleven-week-old baby boy, Marsh. He was a delight. Just after his first birthday, he accompanied me to meet my newborn second grandson. As they grew, the three toddlers, Marsh and my two grandsons, became buddies, I often took them to the Jungle Gardens in Sarasota. They also spent a lot of time at Marsh's home. His house had a swimming pool with spa attached. All three toddlers soon learned to swim, and we had a wonderful time together. George's music videos were popular with them, too. On TV they loved *Shining Time Station* with Ringo playing the tiny Mr. Conductor. I noticed how they were riveted to the TV when Ringo was in the episode, but when George Carlin played the part, they would get restless and wander away. I concluded Ringo held a lot more appeal for little children.

When Marsh took his afternoon naps, there was a monitor in his room so I could keep "an ear" on him. When he was about eighteen months old, I had shown him the new video George had sent me of "Blow Away." Imagine my surprise and delight when I heard this little guy singing himself to sleep, *"Bo way, bo way, wuv you, wuv you, Duckie!"* If you have seen this video, you will understand; if not, try to find it on the Internet.

Marsh lived in an affluent area on Siesta Key. The house had been remodeled and a huge addition built on. In Florida, the most practical flooring is ceramic tile, which was installed throughout the house. I had it in my home, too; it was easier to maintain when you are walking in from the beach with sand on your feet all the time. It was best to avoid carpet, with its risk of mites, bacteria, mold and mildew as well as the flea population. As in most Floridian homes, a pest company would spray the home each month with pesticide to keep the fleas and larger Palmetto bugs away. When Marsh was close to two years old, he developed a serious asthmatic condition, which necessitated him having to spend fifteen minutes, three times a day, breathing from an inhaler strapped to his face. Witnessing this tot trying to remain sitting still whilst on his breathing machine just about broke my heart.

Once again, when confronted with a challenge, I started to research, this time childhood asthma. In the previous twenty years, this problem had increased 200 fold. In other words, for every one child with this problem in 1960, in 1980 there were 200. Besides the danger to small children from pesticides, the other major danger was indoor pollution. One of the causes was the build up of mold, mildew and the decaying bodies of vermin and bugs which collected in the heating and cooling ducts in most of our "conveniently climate controlled homes." It did not occur to most homeowners that the ducts, in some cases more than thirty years old, might, once in awhile, be in need of cleaning.

The incidence of brain cancer and leukemia in children had also increased rapidly during those years. I will spare you all the details, but briefly—during WWII, Germany had built up a vast stockpile of weapons grade nerve gas, which they eventually decided **not** to use as a weapon during the war. After the war, this stockpile was available to the commercial world market. And so it was that an enterprising business person had—as business persons often do—a "wonderfully profitable" idea! *"Let us take this nerve gas, dilute it somewhat, and use it to kill undesirable species such as insects."* The brilliant idea continued in the context that *"although these insects may have an important role to play in the ecosystem, which we neither care about, nor understand—we don't want them in our homes, and we can make a killing!"* Yes, they did. In every way possible! Profits poured in—and more and more small humans fell ill.

Of course, in the 21st century, to certain interests, health is not nearly as important as wealth. Billionaires, who can purchase candidates to legislate in their favor, have their priorities, after all. Fortunately not all rich folks are greedy and selfish, let's face it: I had a brother who was rich, and he paid taxes in the 96% bracket, hence his "Taxman" song. But, he and the other Beatles cared about the health of our planet and the future of our species. I'm pretty confident 90% of my readers are literally "on the same page" when it comes to the forces we need to view with caution. We are not the ones who say, "What can I do? I'm only one person." No, we understand the power of good people "Coming Together" to get something done.

As my research continued, I was learning a lot more about the disasters happening to our precious planet's life support systems due to the greed of the uncaring few. These self-serving idiots were reaping profits by destroying the life support systems of our mutual home. Yes, idiots is not too strong a word, because they don't believe in science, nor do they take nature's warning signs seriously. They do not have the sense to understand that they, too, need clean air to breathe, pure water to drink, and unpolluted soil in which to grow our food. We also need insects to pollinate all plants, including those we find edible. With ever ready pesticides and our obsession about being insect free, we are even endangering our so called beneficial insects—those very same insects who diligently help pollinate the plants we use as food. So this Harrison became sufficiently steamed up to decide to reach out to her global family of Beatle People to see if together they could stem the tide of destruction.

A few years earlier, I had been at a Paul McCartney concert in Orlando and hung out with his children Stella, Mary and James on the sound equipment console. Paul had large screens at both sides of the stage showing documentary film provided by Friends of the Earth and PETA. Many fans spoke to me, applauding Paul's dedication to this cause and said, "Wouldn't it be great if there was an environmental organization for Beatles fans; we could 'Come Together' and try to 'Save the World!'"

I remembered this conversation while still doing research into environmental problems when another event took place to really "kick my butt into gear." Hurricane Andrew! When that disaster happened it occurred to me, although I was powerless to prevent the suffering, the displaced surviving families might appreciate a little "cheering up." I had many friends in the entertainment business, so I went to the local newspaper with a plan.

The *Sarasota Herald Tribune* initially put out an article which helped me "round up" volunteers. I called upon my moderately famous show biz friends, to help me organize free concerts for the displaced tent community in Homestead, in southern Florida. Because of the enormity of the devastation, I did not wish to cause security problems by suggesting to "big-name" friends—for instance, Paul or other major stars—that they show up. I contacted the mayor of the city of Homestead, and he connected me with the Army's 10th Mountain Division, who constructed the tent town. There were many others who helped and to whom I owe thanks. The Army built a stage for our use at one end of a field where most of the tents were located. Many of my show business friends took part. Of these the most well-known to the general public was Butch Gerace, a member of Sam the Sham and the Pharoahs. For several weeks we made the trip from Sarasota and other parts of the state to perform for the displaced.

Apart from the air raids, which I survived as a child, I had not previously personally witnessed the aftermath of such a disaster, but merely scenes as reported on TV. So I can tell you truly—the *on the ground sights,* and *particularly smells,* are overwhelming. Most visible human remains had been gathered when my little entourage arrived. But, there were still many rotting animal corpses as well as spoiled refrigerator contents strewn over acres of ground. Just to see and smell it makes one wonder, *"How can it be possible to ever make things right again?"* Fortunately, the majority of our species is capable of compassion, courage, and an attitude of "Let us do our best to get the job done." We were not involved

GOOD WORKS

SAVING THE PLANET: When the board of directors of "We Care" Global Family Inc. has its monthly meeting at the Hard Rock Cafe in Orlando Nov. 17, it will be the occasion to celebrate the environmental organization's first birthday since its incorporation Nov. 30, 1992. Formed by Louise Harrison, the sister of George Harrison, the group's musical theme is Harrison's "Save The World," which is used in a series of PSAs on its behalf. Louise Harrison plans ior the 2   er- sary of the moon landing—to be followed each year during a Countdown To 2000 on the same date. Harrison, who prefers a lighter touch to reach more people and help the environment, says a cartoon series, "Drop," is being developed using the acronym for the slogan "Determined to Restore Our Planet." The Drop characters, who have come from outer space, are parents Ebb and Flow and their children Splish and Splash. "The already-con-

verted will watch environmental documentaries, most others won't because they perceive them as gloom and doom presentations," Harrison says. "People are in denial, because they are scared. We want to get the message out in a fun kind of way." For more info, Louise Harrison can be reached at "We Care" Global Family Inc., P.O. Box 1338, Tallevast, Fla. 34270.

GRANT ESTABLISHED: The New York Host Committee for the 1994 Gra Awards and Sony Music ment have estab- lishe e grant, in mem- or died last sum- mer. will be given each mys are in New Yo igh school musician. hairman of the com Mot- tola, preside. usic Entertainme the grant's first recip s- man, a pianist wh New Stuyvesant High party York—at a Grammy held at the Hard Rock Cafe Oct. 13. Tee played with such artists as Mariah Carey, Michael Bolton, and Paul Simon.

in the actual clean up, we were just there to cheer up...our little band of entertainers called ourselves "We Care." And we did.

This entire episode led me to be in a position, due mostly to publicity generated by our shows, to create an environmental non-profit organization. In December 1992, I incorporated

---

Sister of Former Beatle Organizes Fab Relief Show

This marks the first Public thing I did since John's death. It seemed a good enough reason to become visible.

D.R.O.P. IN!

~~WE CARE GLOBAL FAMILY, INC.~~
~~P.O. BOX 1222 TALLEVAST, FL 34270~~

FOLLOW UP *On The News*

Lou Harrison launches environmental group

After aiding Hurricane Andrew's victims in South Florida, the sister of ex-Beatle George Harrison has set her sights on a new goal that she hopes will take on national and, ultimately, global proportion.

Lou Harrison, who lives in Sarasota, has founded an organization called We Care Global Family to enlist others in protecting the environment.

"Who knows how far it'll go. My brother and I both come from the same genes and you know how far his group went," she said, half-kiddingly.

Her desire to lend Mother Nature a helping hand was reinforced recently in Homestead when she saw huge piles of debris being burned, polluting the air.

Harrison had gone to South Florida to stage free outdoor concerts with Miami-area bands, cheering up residents who had lost their homes and were living in tent cities. When she saw children dancing alongside the soldiers who had been brought in to provide security, Harrison knew the two concerts she helped arrange had made a difference.

The tent cities were dismantled in late October before Harrison could schedule more concerts.

Her desire to help others has taken a new twist as she launches her environmental movement, starting with "good Earth-keeping tips" she

plans to record for radio bro and a quarterly newsletter to porters. She hopes the radio will begin being broadcast in 1993 on 20 radio station tionwide.

"As we head toward the 21s tury, I'm confident that We Global Family will grow into a erfully positive force, demon ing our determination to resto planet for future generations said.

Harrison — who delivered "Beatle reports" daily on the when her brother was a risin nearly 30 years ago — figures not only have the ear of Beatle in her new endeavor, but tha 61-year-old grandmother, she' appeal to older listeners.

"As a member of the Beatle ily, which was perhaps the firs global family of people united common bond, I believe I h unique opportunity to reach t ceptive ear of many millions w still favorably drawn to the Be ideas and music," she said. "A a grandmother and a senior, I c example and encouragement, vate many of my generation selfishly say, 'There's enou last my lifetime.'

"You don't have to worry a the environment unless you br air, drink water or eat food gro soil," she added.

We Care Global Family will have tax-exempt status, she Anyone who would like to lend port may contact her at ~~P.O.~~ ~~34998, Sarasota 34234.~~

— *Mark Zal*

"We Care Global Family," though we later changed the name to the less cumbersome "Drop-In." This name was based on the O'Leary theory of "turn on, tune in, and drop out." In my estimation, "dropping out" did not work, but we did need to Drop In and take responsibility for our planet's health. DROP was an acronym for "Determined to Restore Our Planet!" I used the word "determined" because Dad frequently urged us to pursue our goals with determination.

Remembering the difficulties George had encountered in the

D.R.O.P-IN! ™
Determined to Restore Our Planet – one drop at a time

D.R.O.P-IN! is a loose creative consortium of artists, writers, cartoonists and musicians who use the entertainment medium to bring heightened awareness to our planetary problems, both social and environmental.

D.R.O.P-IN! is headed by founder Louise (Lou) Harrison (fondly nicknamed The Flying Mum, by her family of Drops.) Lou is a tireless campaigner for good who is unwavering in her dedication to leave Planet Earth a better place than now, more like it was when she arrived some 65 years ago in Liverpool England. Her tenacity in this goal is evident in the name she chose for her organization, which is an acronym for

Determined to Restore Our Planet

D.R.O.P-IN! has several creative projects in development, including the following:

1. The Dear Beatles Book, subsequently called "This is Love"…a compilation of individual Beatle-related stories from people all over the planet. Completed Volume One, 1998.

2. THE WHEE FAMILY OF MolleCools.

3. Annual Magical DROP-IN! Tours.

4. Establishing July 20th 2000 as Interdependance Day.

early '70s trying to accomplish a good deed without a 501(c)(3), I immediately set out to obtain this status from the IRS as soon as I incorporated.

We gained our 501(c)(3) status the next year. Recalling the success of The Beatles reports I had written and broadcast during the '60s, I decided to create PSAs called "Good Earthkeeping Tips." Radio was still the best means to reach the public. George offered his song "Save the World" to use as background music. Because we had learned as children never to waste anything, George and I were both concerned about the environment. Two major environmental organizations, World Watch Institute in DC and Union of Concerned Scientists in Cambridge, Mass., cooperated with me in the creation of the PSAs sending their current publications to me for my research. When I composed the text of the announcement, I would then fax it to them to make sure that in my efforts to make the often technical information easy for the average person to understand, I had not altered the meaning. Once approved, I then would record

each "spot" at a local recording studio, Paradox, whose owner donated his time and studio facilities for the cause. In all, we produced 170 PSAs in eighteen months. They aired on a total of 9,200 radio stations. Yes, a lot of work, but very satisfying and hopefully helpful. This initial environmental outreach all took place, more or less, at home, on radio, and involved no travel or use of polluting fuels.

We even created our own Good Earthkeeping Seal of Approval. It was a seal balancing the Earth on its nose and clapping its flippers together in approval.

At the time of John's murder in the '80s, George had been concerned about my safety, saying that there were so many disturbed people in the world who would feel justified in gaining publicity by murdering somebody closely connected to a celebrity. He was concerned that his fame could be putting me in jeopardy should I become known to the public. Due to his concern, for many years I had remained very much in the background. However, in 1992, due to my strong feelings regarding our planet's health, and the potential future of my grandsons, I came to the conclusion that since I was already older than Mum when she died and almost as old as Dad was when he died, was not inclined to be fearful anyway, and my connection with George might possibly "lend me an ear" to benefit the environment, it was worth a try. There was more at stake than any possible risk to my well-being.

Around Marsh's third birthday, Drop-In was becoming a full-time challenge. It now involved a lot of travel for me in order to gather members, whom we called DROPs. Reluctantly I resigned from caring for the child who had inspired all of this. I had for several years been receiving a modest pension from George, so felt I was able to manage okay financially without a salaried job-in order to devote my energies to the task at hand.

To gain support for my fledgling organization, I began attending Beatles Conventions run by Mark Lapidos. There I could invite the Beatle people who had initially inspired me, to "Come Together" and join my effort to "save the world." *(See photos on page 219.)* Mark was very supportive of my efforts and became one of my board members. Our "all volunteer" board members included, Charlie Walsh, who was head of Human Resources at Universal in Orlando, Florida, and John Audette, who when we first met, was in administration at the PBS station in Miami and later worked with Edgar Mitchell, famous as one of our moon walking astronauts. Our Secretary was Linda Garcia, whose husband had a very successful band, Omni, at the Columbia Restaurant's Patio on St. Armands Circle in Sarasota. Steve Glumm was with the Hard Rock Café in Orlando. Steve and Hard Rock Café, being in the same ecological wave as I, helped by hosting many of our board meetings. Michael Allen, a CPA I met at a Beatle convention in San Francisco, became our pro-bono treasurer. Ricky Landers Friedlander, from Toronto was another staunch supporter and board member.

As an ardent admirer of the Native American lifestyle, I was fortunate to be able to confer and cooperate at times with several Native American tribes throughout the country. At one time, I was invited to be a grand marshal at a parade in Arizona. To my delight, I was allowed to ride beside the driver atop a stagecoach. On another occasion, I was invited by Tom Gallaher to the grand opening of the museum for the Seminole tribe in south Florida. I hope you will understand that as "Mom" or "Mum" of this global Beatle family, I ask you to think about our present-day self-indulgent lifestyles.

George had offered his song *"Save the World"* to back my PSAs, so I invited him to join our board, but at that time he was dealing with partner-problems and stressed so he said, "I don't want to have to sign any more forms or deal with any more legal stuff," which I totally understood. He also added, "You seem to have tapped into a power far greater than any help I could give; this is your task or dharma."

The Beatles conventions, hosted by the Lapidos family, were in essence a huge family reunion. I was able to gain support for my environmental concerns and, greeted at all these gatherings as "the global mum," I really enjoyed meeting and becoming friends with the many thousands I'd long considered my extended family. Although the Beatle family individually agreed with my purpose, they were on the whole a little reluctant to give much financial support. I'm sure this same scenario must happen often to "relatives of stars"? People think we also are wealthy. Thus, my suggested membership donation of $25 per year for a family was greeted by some with, "Why should this millionaire take $25 a year from us? She can surely save the world without our help?"

I did have the $2,000 a month pension George had started for me when I became a single senior, but without much additional income it was not quite enough to succeed with the task of "saving the world." I sometimes joked that "I've never had a number one hit," and am just an ordinary person...but that fell on deaf ears, and the perception that I was extremely wealthy, unfortunately, continues to this day! *What about all those theatres and resorts I supposedly bought in Branson!?* I struggled on until the end of the century, travelling, giving talks and putting out newsletters until, with credit card bills in excess of $80,000, I had to admit to being "a fool on a hill." Reluctantly, I had to close my organization. I joked that the **non-**profitability exceeded my wildest dreams.

But during the life of Drop-In, with the aid of numerous talented "drops," there were many very worthy projects in the works. We started a movement to create an international Interdependence Day on July 20th, Moon landing day, each year. We also created a family of cartoon characters, or Mollecools. They were modeled on my own family, and the parents of this family of water drops were Ebb and Flo, the children were Splish, Splash and Splosh. Splosh formed a band called "The Puddles," whose other members were Squish, Spiffy and Bongo. A movie treatment was registered in LA with the Screen Writers Guild entitled "The Time is Now!" Regarding that creative project, I spoke at many conventions outlining the general idea behind this wonderfully creative environmental story. I was hoping to gain the interest of a possible producer.

An advisory committee comprised of many very prominent and influential people was also created. But, with the lack

---

PRESIDENT'S ADVISORY COMMITTEE

7/14/95

Linda Bavaro, Founder President of Retrieva. Atlanta Georgia.

Bohrman Caren, Movie,TV Literary Agent, Beverly Hills CA.

Patrick Carson, Environmental advisor to Canadian Govt. Toronto Canada.

Alan Clayson, British Songwriter/Author, Books on Orbison, Starr, Harrison, "Backbeat"

Alex Cruz, Owner, American Sublimation, Phoenix Arizona.

Romulo Dulapan, Physicist, Scientist, Inventor, Davenport, Iowa.

Ricki Landers Friedlander. Movie Production Co & Promoter Beatlerama, Toronto Canada.

Alison M. Gardner. Stockbroker, Sarasota Fl.

Tony Gerace, Formerly with Sam the Sham & the Pharaohs, Venice Fl.

Dwina Murphy Gibb, writer/illustrator children's books, Miami Fl

Jody Glisman, Associate Director Capitol Records. Hollywood Ca.

Dan Gottlieb, Associate Producer Captain Planet. Atlanta Ga.

Luke Halpern, formerly teenager on TV series, Flipper. Deltona Fl.

DR Jean Houston Ph.D. Scholar , writer, teacher. Pomona NY.

Neil Innes, Song writer, actor -comedian (Rutles/Monty Python) England

Alain Jehlen, former Producer Nova. Now producer WGBH. Boston Ma

Dan Johnson, Staff writer, National Audubon Society,Washington DC.

Joe Johnson, Radio Announcer, Hosts Beatle Brunch on 18 stations nationwide.

Hal Kane, Staff writer, WorldWatch Inc. Washington DC.

Mark Lapidos, Promoter Beatlefest. Newark NJ.

Mary Lawler, Attorney Warner Brothers, Cartoon Division, Los Angeles.

Lisa Max, President/Founder Betterworld, Inc, Pompano Bch FL

Angie & Ruth McCartney, singer songwriter. Nashville TN

Ingrid Melody, Director Institutional Affairs, Fl Solar Energy Center. Cape Canaveral.

Rev William Metzger. Editor Quest Magazine. Theosophical Soc. Chicago.

Michael Misch, Childrens environmental songwriter, Medford ,Oregon.

Bob Moll, Artist/Animator. Creator of our Mollecool tm. Characters.The Whee Family.c.

Martin Nethercutt, singer/songwriter. Nashville TN.

John Obie, Founder President of Enviro-mint and Enviro-wood, Chicago, Ill

Butch Patrick, Formerly Eddy Munster on TV. St Petersburg, FL

Phil & Lynn Reed, Partners in Theme Park project due to be completed 1996. FL

Theodore Roszak, Author, "The Voice of the Earth" Guggenheim Fellowship.Berkley,CA

Sherry Rothfield, CPA, Mediator, Miami, FL

William Ryerson. Exec VP. Population Communications International. VT

David Suzuki, Host of TV series "The Nature of Things" Toronto Canada.

Charlie Walsh, Director Human Resources, Universal Studios, FL.

Lisa White, Journalist teacher, writer, (Hillstreet Blues) Berlin Germany.

Bradley C. Wilson, 2 & 3D video graphics animator. San Diego, CA

Meredythe Dee Winter, Bob Marley Peace Award, Children's Director for WCGF. CA.

Wyland, World renowned for his 66 Whaling Walls, Environmental Artist.*

Also have verbal agreement presently with

Robert Watts, Movie producer, worked on Star Wars, Indiana Jones. Roger Rabbit etc.

Dan Wilcox. Screenplay writer, Mash, Newhart, Sesame St.

And with Victor Spinetti, of 'Hard Days Night ', 'Help'

---

of major funding, coupled with the global disinterest in environmental issues at that time, I really was "rowing against the current without a paddle."

However, a few years later I had a phone call from a lady who introduced herself as a close friend of my board member Ricky in Toronto. Knowing how closely he had been involved in helping with the movie, I spoke with this lady. She told me she had connections to Steven Spielberg, who was of course my number one choice to produce this movie.

After speaking with her daily for a few weeks, I sent her two or three complete packages about "The Time Is Now" including the treatment that had been registered with the Screen Writers Guild in LA during the '90s. Soon thereafter I was no longer able to reach her by phone or email. Her name is Mary Gleason. Since sending her those packages at least three years ago I have had no response or contact with her whatsoever. So, if anyone reading this is looking for help with a movie deal, take note of my experience. Be careful of potential "helpers."

Something that does remain—toward the end of our first year, we were able to publish our first newsletter, *Newsplash*. In the first editorial, we explain the whole concept of a DROP.

Obviously, in retrospect, I was a cock-eyed optimist! Not only did the wave never gain momentum, but I almost drowned in debt, finding the "non-profit-ability" exceeded my wildest dreams. Sadly, the people of our planet were not ready then, and still don't seem to be ready, to take on the task of saving ourselves.

During the life of Drop-In, I had an ongoing relationship with many other environmental pioneers and organizations. Together we came to the following conclusions:

a) **Fortunately,** our Creator had the foresight to endow at least a small percentage of our species with sufficient intelligence to partially understand the complex and intricate life support system that sustains all life forms.

b) **Unfortunately,** another small percentage are motivated only by greed.

c) **Unfortunately**, the remainder seem to be just decent simple folks who basically "mind their own business," enjoy their sports and other activities, and until very recently, trusted "those in power" to do the correct things. But, we are now recognizing that those in power do NOT always have the interests of the general population at heart and therefore....

d) **Fortunately,** we are now seeing the awakening of the 99%—or the 47%.

Happy First Birthday!

Newsplash

**Quarterly Newsplash, First Wave
November, 1993**
(First Birthday Issue)

"We Care Global Family • P.O. Box 1338 • Tallevast, FL 34270

From Me To You

Hello! This is Lou, in each issue you will find an editorial which will be called **From Me To You.**

As with ANY family on this planet, WCGF will be as dynamic, or as easily forgotten, as its family members! I'm just the Mum, or catalyst. It's my responsibility to help point us in the right direction. However, our daily accomplishments, plus the major goals we reach, will be the sum total of All Our Efforts. No single DROP can become a wave on its own. Each DROP has to connect with others before the full potential of the wave can be realized.

It is important that we each relinquish thoughts of calamity, doom or failure, and bring to this family all the creative ideas and enthusiasm of which we are capable. You see our planet itself is not in danger, the real danger we face is OUR ability to survive here. Our species, and most others, need fresh air to breathe, clean water to drink, and uncontaminated soil in which to grow food. So, if each DROP becomes part of the strength of the wave, then we can be a powerful force in the fight for our own survival and the task of restoring our life support systems for all future generations.

Think for a moment of the significance of Drops, one drop, the proverbial drop in the bucket, is rather puny, ineffective and doesn't even take the shape of the bucket! A larger number of drops, when contained, take on the shape of the container, conforming to its size, shape and capacity. In our present society, many drops are content to splash back and forth within the confines of their container!

But, when you have a great many drops, billions and billions of them, all with a common purpose, heading in the same direction, then you achieve momentum...an unstoppable force, which will move everything in its path in order to achieve its goal. We drops can become such a force, our goal, to live in harmony with nature and each other. The wave we create will be a positive one! It can turn the tide of destruction of our life support systems into one of healing, both for humanity, and all species with whom we are interdependent on our tiny spaceship. It won't be easy.

EACH ONE OF US MUST TAKE RESPONSIBILITY!
We must work together to find the right and sensible solutions.
Are "We" ready? OK!
Let's make a **Big Splash!**

Since 2012, I am a little hopeful that there will come a day when enough members of our species will be as dedicated, passionate and enthusiastic about events that ARE *really* significant to our well-being as they are now about the Olympics or a football or basketball match. I totally understand that it is much easier and much less stressful to devote one's aspirations to the outcome of a ball game, rather than "how to solve the problem of global warming." But, my fellow Earthlings, before too long, we *will* have to get serious about the health of our planet, and consequently our own survival. We must not continue to slide, all self-indulgent, arrogant and unaware into oblivion.

One who did understand was a dedicated artist named Wyland. His main focus was the fate of the whales. Because of their near extinction, he wanted to raise awareness that "If they go, so do we." During the '90s, he set out to paint, I think, fifty whaling walls in various parts of the world. He started out in his home state of California. If you do not already know about him, I'm pretty sure you can find him on the internet now. When I met him he had come to Sarasota to paint one of his smaller paintings on the wall at Mote Marine. Subsequently, I attended a number of his functions in various states. Later, he opened Wyland art galleries in several cities and I was present at the opening of some, including Key West, Sarasota and I think maybe Nashville. *(See photo on page 220.)*

Another aware individual was Dan Gottleib, the Producer of Ted Turner's *Captain Planet* environmental cartoon. I was also good friends with Ted Turner's secretary, Dee Woods (now deceased) and Susan Rook, who hosted a TV show called *Talkback Live* on TBS before it became CNN. To help promote Drop-In, I was a guest on several TBS shows, especially whenever George—during his solo career—put out a new album. TBS gave me an opportunity to promote them also. I never met Ted Turner, although I would have had a lot in common with him with regard to our concern about our planet. I did actually write a letter to him—but never mailed it—suggesting we create an environmental talk show, which would include many celebrities who were getting involved in Eco problems. As I have said many times in the past, *"There are problems to suit every taste. If each person was to choose the problem they are most concerned about and become part of the solution, we might start making some headway."*

Yet another aware person is Meredythe Dee Winter, I met her through "Drop-In" and worked with her on her Planet

One TV show. We also took part in Earth Day in Washington D.C., one year, along with her "Recycle Kids."

It is my belief that all problems we face are interconnected, interrelated, and interdependent. The most crucial underlying problem—which led to all the others—is overpopulation.

Unfortunately, although many experts understand this issue, and a number of years ago had an organization called Zero Population Growth, we are stifled by certain factions who, due to their religious superstitions, refuse to recognize this problem or to encourage education in family planning. In fact, the worst ones are even trying to eliminate Family Planning as an entity. It seems to me that during our lives, the single MOST important event we should put some thoughtful planning into is the responsibility of creating of a family.

You know, we use the phrase "bird-brain" to denote a lack of intelligence, but consider how carefully birds approach the task of becoming parents. They choose an area with plentiful food, select a tree, and then go about building a comfy nest, and find a mate who will co-operate in the lengthy process of sitting on the eggs. Then, once the nestlings hatch, the parents forage daily for food to nourish their chicks, pre-digesting it before feeding the babies, then, finally teach the little ones how to fly before leaving them to continue their lives. I ask the human species, *"What exactly is so 'bird-brained' about that behavior?"* Seems they care a lot more efficiently for their offspring than do many of our self-styled, super superior humans.

We constantly see charitable organizations pleading for aid to help the millions of starving, neglected and abused children worldwide. Again, I ask my intelligent readers, would not our money and our compassion be better spent by providing assistance to those living in poverty, to help educate them, so that they can safely and effectively limit the size of their families to the number they are capable of caring for and supporting? I know I am a voice crying in the wilderness with regard to this problem, and so long as we bow to the insane hold that the so-called Religious Right has on our society, we will never find a solution to this unnecessary suffering.

Another point that makes no sense to me is this: many religions believe in eternal life. The Soul or Spark of God within the body is believed to live for all eternity. Incidentally, thus far, no scientist has been able to locate this soul or spark, and there is no physical evidence, not in the brain or nerves, or anywhere else, of *"the actual entity which drives"* our flesh and blood container, or body. The conclusion drawn is that there *is* a non-physical vibrant component of a human, which is not subject to physical life and death and this life force is what we call the soul. Therefore, if we truly believe what most world religions teach us, that the soul is immortal, therefore not subject to physical-earthly laws and lives forever, it would seem a contradiction, or even blasphemy, to say we have the power to kill it? Surely, it is only the embryo of the physical vessel or body that can be disposed of by means of legal abortion. The immortal soul, if it was in any way actually connected to the physical vessel prior to birth, just lives on to perhaps, sometime later, inhabit yet another more suitable vessel, whose parents can provide for it.

I spoke of this contradiction in popular belief to the lady who was leading Republicans for Choice back in the '90s, and she totally agreed with me but sadly concluded that so long as extremists have control, they will continue to insist that *"those who commit the 'original' sin of copulation deserve to be punished by being forced to bear a child even if that child faces a life of pain and anguish and eventually becomes one of the millions who die of starvation every year."*

When will these extremists understand and admit that abortion, which is quite legal, is simply the termination of an unwanted or unplanned pregnancy and has *nothing at all* to do with killing babies. What it *does* is save many more souls the anguish of being briefly connected to a human vessel that will surely suffer a life of poverty, abuse and eventual starvation.

It does not sound to me as though these people have a compassionate, Christ-like attitude. It seems to smack more of vengeance and hate. It seems we are born with the capacity for love, but how and when do some lose it?

Many of the world's most knowledgeable scientists affirm that over-population is itself the most serious underlying cause creating all other problems. Now at over seven billion humans, and our natural resources being devastated by greed, waste, pollution and worst of all *apathy* on the part of the general public, I wonder, "is there any real hope for the future of our pathetically dumb though arrogant species?"

Unfortunately, the problem of overpopulation will not be solved until there is a world-wide change of attitude. For that to happen, we need more education and more people to not only learn to think with their minds, but to put that learning into action when they vote.

If we, as a society, would make a significant change of attitude regarding reproduction, we could solve many problems. To begin with, back in the days of our primarily farming economy, it made sense for farmers to have large families in order to take care of the very labor intensive work required, in order to plant and harvest crops, raise cattle and other livestock to provide food for our countrymen. Now, however, with automated harvesters, milking machines and so on, much less labor, therefore people, are needed to accomplish these same tasks.

In the general work force, the same thing is true. Elevator operators are just one example of this. Though not a very skilled job, an operator was needed for *each* elevator in *each* building in *each* city. I have no idea how many jobs "automated elevators" have eliminated, but if we then consider the amount of job loss due to the onset of mechanization and automation in factories, we can readily see that long before thousands of jobs went overseas, there was less and less need for "manpower." Therefore, by sheer proliferation of automation we are reducing the need for laborers. It is all very well to rant about "creating more jobs," but if most tasks are being performed by robots, or electronic intelligence, then it seems the *real* solution to unemployment is *to create less people*. If we continue to produce people at the present rate, we are surely condemning our future children to a life of unemployment and therefore poverty and starvation. We

Newsplash

**Quarterly Newsplash
1994 — The Second Wave**

February (Ripple One)

"We Care" Global Family • P.O. Box 1338 • Tallevast, FL 34270

From Me To You

With all the talk about Super Bowl this past month, I became keenly aware of the tremendous impact of this event! Millions of people shared in the excitement and suspense. At this event winners became heroes. *It is very clear we humans need our heroes.* Millions sitting safely on our couches watched as those heroes, using all the strategy, speed, strength and endurance of which they were capable, battled to the finish. Then, according to our preference, we either applauded the victors or denounced the losers.

It is very true we humans admire the talent, courage, skill, perseverance, determination and dedication required to *become* a hero or heroine. Music, science, sports, commerce, engineering, whatever the endeavor, there will always be those whose achievements we admire. But, there is another side to our human nature to consider!

"Let's get off the couch and participate in life!"

Often the adulation we heap upon our heroes or heroines can create "larger than life" expectations about those we admire. And yes, we constantly see when we create an image too big for us to handle, someone will throw mud, not caring if it is real or imaginary, in order to bring the hero down to size. I'm sure you can think of recent examples!

It will be easier for us to sincerely admire those who meet the challenges in the game of life with fortitude, energy and enthusiasm, when *we* get up from the couch and become players too! We don't need to throw mud at the world's achievers in order to gain equality. We need to give permission to the heroic part of our own nature to participate in the game of life. To accept the risks, and face the challenges with courage and determination. We can continue to love and respect our heroes and heroines when we are able to *stand beside them with pride in our own accomplishments!*

**TILL NEXT TIME,
CHEERIO!**

Why do you suppose this scenario occurs time after time?
Is it because, the **bigger** the hero, the **smaller** we appear?
Or, do we think if we cause their downfall, we will raise ourselves higher?
Or, is it that we just don't realize WE TOO can be HEROES and HEROINES?

need to wake up and understand more about the factors that dictate how life on this planet can more efficiently survive and prosper.

The solution is very obvious: folks need to just THINK in a sensible, rather than an irrational and superstitious, way.

We need to move into the future with a plan to moderate future population growth to better meet with the labor needs of our modern automated society. Now, I am aware we cannot change the numerical count of the present population, but we do need to change the mindset and educate our future parents—help them understand that our electronic automated society cannot accommodate many thousands of people when there are so few tasks that humans need to perform nowadays. If we are not to condemn thousands to a life of poverty, then we need to assist them by providing resources that will result in smaller families. It is a well documented fact that parental

Determined to
Restore
Our
Planet™

Newsplash©

**Quarterly Newsplash
1994 — The Second Wave**

June *(Ripple Two)*

"We Care" Global Family • P.O. Box 1338 • Tallevast, FL 34270

From Me to You

"Nobody made a greater mistake than he who did NOTHING because he could only do a little!"

Last year I used the above quotation in one of our Good Earthkeeping Tips. The source attributed it to Mahatma Ghandi. Recently I saw the same remark attributed to Edmund Burke. "Oh no!" I thought, "I wonder, who REALLY made that remark?" It then occurred to me, since Mr. Ghandi is no longer alive, it is unlikely that HE is concerned,

and maybe Mr. Burke is unworried too. (I'm not sure of the latter's earthly status.) Continuing to ponder on this, it also occurred to me:

Humanity *has* been around a very long time, many humans are capable of the same good ideas, and many sensible remarks are frequently repeated until they gain the status of a quotation. Ultimately, the **impor-tant** thing about a good idea is NOT so much who thought of it **first**, but the people who **hear** it, **think** about it, and also **act** upon it. *(We are not talking here about people stealing ideas in order to make a profit for themselves, that is inexcusable.)*

So let us resolve: When we come across good ideas which can help humanity find ways to live in har-mony with nature and with each

other, let us not worry too much about the origin, but rather let us **act upon and spread that good idea** as one worthy of repeating.

Now, what about the Ghandi/Burke quotation at the top of the page? It is great whoever said it! Let us think about what is meant!

In keeping with OUR ideas about the power of many DROPs joining together, let us always remain confi-dent, whatever little thing each of us does today, to help conserve our resources, when that small action **IS** added to the actions of many others, it **really does help.**

To quote a combination of some of the Fab Four's song titles: *"Come together, we can work it out, with a little help from our friends!"*

LET *US* NOT MAKE THE MISTAKE OF DOING NOTHING!
KEEP ON MAKING THOSE SEEMINGLY TINY DROPs OF EFFORT,
EVERY DROP *REALLY* DOES COUNT.

higher education is a factor leading to smaller families. So, education is a major factor in finding the solution. What a pity so many state governors are slashing funding to education these days! There is a great need for well-funded Family Planning Centers. This whole idea of sentencing people to have children they cannot support, then punishing them for being poor and unemployed. Well, I for one cannot see a much quoted Jesus sanctioning that cynical twisted mindset. It seems quite a contradiction to me. The very people who want to stamp out any form of public financial assistance to the poor are the very same people who refuse to fund Family Planning and other reproductive services.

Instead of applauding people for producing large families, we should be encouraging sensible, responsible reproduction. Unemployment is not the only problem caused by over population. With now seven billion people, we are more rapidly depleting natural resources. Consider just one mind boggling problem, the disposal of human sewage in a sanitary and healthy manner. We have already caused many of our rivers and oceans to become toxic. Then again, there's the rapid loss of many insect species needed to pollinate our edible plants, a task only *they* can accomplish efficiently. Those who do care about our common future can find many sources, now with the Internet, to help them understand and maybe find ways to become part of a solution;

There is a movie that I heartily recommend. If enough people pay attention to the message it could be very helpful. It has the very appropriate name: *Idiocracy!*

If any of you have seen the movie *Idiocracy,* I'm afraid if we do not change our present mindset, *that* scenario is the more likely one for our collective future. Perhaps if this movie was a part of the educational curriculum for teenagers entering puberty, our youngsters could avoid a lot of tragic mistakes, which in turn lead to lifelong suffering. And no, I do *not* have any financial interest in that movie, I just happen to recognize the validity of its "warning." The content is, to my mind, rather gross and tasteless, but the message of the movie makes a very valid point.

I *do* have a glimmer of hope, and that lies with you, dear reader. It is my belief that most of the people who are curious to read about my life and my connection with The Beatles, are likely to be capable of thinking in a reasonable and sensible way, and perhaps will also have the guts to speak out in defense of our fragile and badly abused Life Support System. That is why I spent those years in the '90s trying to gather my Global Family of Beatle People together. In that decade, not too many people understood how badly we humans have abused our planet. Now, though, more is known, a lot more oil has spilled, and perhaps if we can overcome the two major problems—Greed on the part of the rich, and Apathy on the part of the general public—we may stand a chance to stop before we go over the cliff! I am slightly encouraged by the movement to Get Money Out of politics, which is fostering protests in cities all over the world. It will be a thankless uphill battle, especially with all the clout/power in the hands of the most corrupt. Those who have been purchased by the wealthy few will continue to resist the will of the people. *Another factor that escapes notice is the absolute hypocrisy of certain elected people who vow to abolish "Obamacare." Yet those same people happily accept the health care provided to them as members of the so called "interfering government."*

If we, in the United States as seems to be happening, can overcome apathy and take back our democracy, which has been lost to the Corporate-ocracy, maybe we can gain justice and force the "Captains and Kings" of industry to bring back the still viable jobs from overseas and allow those fine citizens—eager to work, but unable to find a job—a chance to bring our economy back from the brink. It would also be a great relief to be able to purchase goods that do not fall apart in a matter of weeks!

Perhaps passage of the proposed jobs' bill would be a good start to the creation of new jobs, all the while rebuilding our crumbling infrastucture.

Healthcare is a respected provision of most "civilized" countries, yet in the United States the whole idea has been so distorted that the fellow who gave the thankful citizens of Massachusetts their healthcare plan, didn't even dare to admit to his followers during the 2012 elections that he "did good."

As the Russian comedian Yakov Smirnoff says, *"What a country!"*

I tried in the '90s to rally Beatles People to "do something," but the timing was not right. Now, however, it seems that just maybe the sleeping giant, namely the public, has finally been stirred into action. We seem to be ridding ourselves of apathy and are ready to engage the "Suits." Yes, it means taking a stand and not allowing greed to destroy all that is good, decent, and courageous in humanity. Let us face it— there are still millions of Beatles People across our planet, I'm sure many are already part of the current protests and if we, the people, do "come together," we can be an unstoppable force. I pointed out when I visited the Occupy Wall Street folks in November 2011, that if John had still been alive he would likely have pitched one of the first tents in Zuccotti Park. Most of what I am saying is really well-known Beatle philosophy, which is why I feel confidant these words are going out to the correct listeners. Hope you can hear this clearer than you could hear any of the Beatle concerts in the '60s!

I have to believe that readers of this book are very likely persons who regard *love* and *peace*, not just as words, but as a way of life. The awakening of the public has begun, let us join and make sure it continues to spread until we don't just have to "imagine," but "all the people will truly share all the world."

Chapter Thirteen

2001 – George Makes His Exit

*M*ost of my readers and friends, remember the significance of November 2001. Yes, the 29th was when I and the rest of the planet lost my dear, sweet youngest brother, George.

Due to the kind intervention of Dr. Lederman, who was caring for George, I had an opportunity to visit him on Staten Island two weeks before he died. Whenever we talked seriously, we held each other's hands to better connect—probably a practice started when he was a babe and I would sit and tell him stories. I recall years earlier in California when we were talking this way for several hours, his bewildered Hollywood friends, who had not met me previously, wondered, "Who is the new girlfriend?"

That was also the evening when he had with him the original acetate of "Miss O'Dell." On this acetate, which he gave to me that night, were two versions of the song. On one he sang the song okay, but the other version was when he kept making mistakes and bursting out laughing. I persuaded him to release the laughing version. As I pointed out to him—most people have a totally erroneous view of George as the quiet, gloomy, serious one, not the off the wall comic I have known so well all my life. He did put out the laughing version, but just on the B side of a 45 single [Give Me Love (Give Me Peace on Earth)]. Incidentally, the acetate had only those two cuts on one side. On the other were a number of songs that he had scored through. He had been going to throw it in the trash, but experience of being "bootlegged" prompted him to make sure the tracks could not be copied. How stressful it must have been for him (and his bandmates) to have to be so cautious about every move you made and every word spoken for fear of some member of our species pouncing on it in order to make a quick and dishonest buck!

At our final meeting on Staten Island, we were sitting together chatting about some of our comical early family experiences. Suddenly, George said softly "Let's see what's around this corner!" We looked into each other's eyes for a moment, then we both burst into laughter until tears rolled down our faces. Fortunately Dhani and his mother were in another room at the time, so we did not have to explain our hilarity. However, I will share it now as I think you will get a chuckle too!

Dad, working for the Liverpool Corporation Passenger Transport, had a two-week paid holiday each summer. He would book a cottage somewhere in the British Isles and we would set off on our annual adventure. Mum, who was very lively and vibrant was more of a "ringleader" than a Mum. She could infuse excitement into the most normal day. One time we were in North Wales at a location known as The Great Orme, a sort of large hill that jutted into the sea. Leaving the bus, we started walking to see the sights. We gazed in wonder at this huge "hill," then Mum said, "Oh let's see what is around this corner." With that we all set off "around the corner." On returning to Liverpool a couple of weeks later, our version of this story went like this: "We started off with mum around this corner, and the next corner, and the next...after about fifty corners we lost count!" Four days later (actually four hours in real time, but what is the point of an adventure if you cannot embellish a little?) we arrived at the other side of The Great Orme, having walked some four or more miles with no food or drink. We kept going around corners viewing magnificent scenes all the way.

Now that adventure alone would *not* have caused the hysterical laughter George and I enjoyed on our last visit.... but on many more occasions when on holiday, Mum was known to remark, *"Let us see what is around this corner, or along that path"* and we would react with apprehension. One time we ended up exploring the entire Cheddar Gorge, and another time we climbed to the summit of Mt. Snowdon, the highest peak in Wales, over 3,000 ft. Another time we went halfway up Ben Nevis, Scotland's highest peak at over 4,000 ft. So it was that whenever we would see that *"let's see what is around the corner"* look come into Mum's eyes, we would feign terror and say, *"Oh No, please Mum, not that! Not a corner, you never know how it might end. We will emerge three weeks later battered and bruised, half starved, having been treated to beautiful scenery all the way! Please Mum, not another corner!"* Of course one had to experience the adventure first hand to really appreciate how really funny, and enjoyable we found our wonderful childhood.

I just hope that many of my readers were fortunate enough to enjoy a similar wild and crazy, happy childhood. It was easy to cope with WWII with so much humor at our command.

We also spoke again about my decision, despite his concern for my safety, in the early '90s to "come out in public" to try to help the environment. I said to him, "I have been driven all these years by exactly the same power that was driving you." Before I had even finished saying it, he interrupted, "Yes, I understand that now, Lou."

From the many conversations we shared during his lifetime, I was aware that he was not at all reluctant to leave this life and proceed to the next "level"—hopefully to re-connect with his sweet Lord. Therefore, I did not view his departure as a loss, but rather as a stepping stone to enable him to begin his next great adventure, as I mentioned earlier.

When we were children, Mum had a habit. Many times when getting us up for school, she would say, "It's time to get up for today's great adventure," and so it is that I too have mostly regarded the dawn of each new day as the opportunity to embark on some new adventure. And believe me, writing this memoir is the ultimate one. (I should have stayed in bed!)

A day or so after George died, I was invited to appear on the *Today Show* in New York. I have always been very close with the global family of Beatles People, so it seemed to make sense that I should take this opportunity to express to all of them just what I felt George would want them to know. I recall sitting with Katie Couric, and I—being no stranger to TV—proceeded to address the viewing Beatle People, as usual, from the heart. When Mum died, George encouraged the family members not to be too sad, as he believed a family's strong exhibition of sadness and grieving, made it more difficult for the soul to embark on the journey to the "next level." Looking at the camera, I spoke directly to our viewers and conveyed George's view of death as a new beginning rather than an end.

I guess Katie's producers were telling her to "take charge," as she seemed very distracted whilst I had my say. Realizing she was under some stress, I quickly finished what I wanted to express and directed my attention to her. (Sorry, Katie, I did not mean to take over, but I did have a responsibility to our viewing Beatles fans.)

After the interview was over, before I left the studio, I received a phone call from someone for whom I have a great deal of love and respect—none other than President Bill Clinton. He wanted to offer his condolences and invited me to his office in Harlem.

When I arrived at his offices, I was rather teary-eyed, because I had been followed and was being hounded by an awful female British reporter, who was going on about some "rift" I supposedly had with my brother. This was news to me. Anyhow, when the President noticed my reddened eyes, he assumed I was upset about George. I soon told him "No, I think George was ready to leave, and I understand he is, hopefully, on to better things. The reason for my tears is the awful story this reporter was talking about." Then the President, who himself was no stranger to predatory reporters and bad press, told me not to be too concerned. He went to great lengths to explain how the press is so large and fragmented that most stories do not ever get into mainstream consciousness. Also, that the people who know you do not take the misinformation seriously. This was a great help and I knew he understood this subject very well, certainly better than most!

We spent time in his office talking about my brother and world affairs. It being a short two months after 9-11, I also expressed my regret that he, our former President, was not still at the "helm." I also met Maggie Williams and Jim Kennedy, who were at that time his closest aides. Just think of the global disaster we could have avoided had he still been "in office" at that time...Wow! "Past is gone, Thou canst not that recall," as it so wisely says, carved in stone at Friar Park.

Subsequently, I had other encounters with President Clinton.

Knowing how much he had yearned to be with "his sweet Lord," I went about my daily life without suffering pangs of grief for George. Early in 2002, I was invited to a "Flashback Weekend" in Chicago, designed to bring Beatles fans together for a remembrance and reunion. One of the "special guests" was a writer who had written a book about my brother. I had received a copy of the book some weeks earlier. During dinner that Friday evening, the publisher's publicist—who had mailed me the copy of the book—was seated opposite me and after introducing herself, asked if I had read it. Well, once again, the HFC kicked in when I heard myself admitting, "I did start to read it, but after a few pages, I had to put it down to calm my anger." The author happened to be sitting within earshot. This was not the first time my painful Harrison honesty had caused a social gaffe, and it certainly was not the last!

I met a person the next day whose presence in my life has brought great joy and an opportunity to work more closely with my family of Beatle People. (I truly believe this meeting was brought about by my brother in order that I should still have a brotherly presence in my life.) I will get to that event in a moment, but first I want to say this: from whatever vantage point George's Being now enjoys, I can imagine he is now able—without all that Beatles baggage that so weighed him down at times—to be free to see things more clearly. Looking into my heart, he is able to see the sincerity of my lifelong love for him and understand the fervor of my support for his chosen career. He also knows I miss his love and support of me. So this is what happened.

I spent most of Saturday "doing my thing," hugging Beatle People and sharing the love. In the evening, a Beatles tribute band took the stage. I found a seat at the back of the hall next to someone videotaping the show. I was happily enjoying the show, hearing all the familiar Beatles music, which for so many years had been part of my life.

Toward the end of the show, the young man playing George (Marty Scott) came onstage wearing the denim outfit and hairstyle from the *Abbey Road* cover. He started to sing "While My Guitar Gently Weeps." For the first time since George's death some six weeks earlier, tears flowed unbidden down my cheeks. The young man looked and sounded so much like my dear brother that my first thought was, *"It seems George has connected me with a substitute brother."* Later that evening, when we met in person, it was as though we had always known each other. We happily "adopted" each other and became brother and sister. Although he now says he is sometimes my dad, and other times my son; it is a well-rounded relationship.

Subsequently, I discovered that Marty shared personal characteristics of my brother, and I've since "adopted" his mom and dad. Yes, I still feel awful about being an orphan. Although they are both some ten years younger than me, they happily accept my calling them Mom and Dad.

The week following Flashback Weekend, it turned out that Paul was performing in Chicago. Marty invited me to stay at his home so that I could remain in Chicago to see Paul. Terry Hemmert—a dear friend and DROP supporter, who is a well-known DJ in Chicago—was able to obtain tickets and VIP passes for Marty and me, along with herself and her young cousin.

The four of us were escorted backstage before the show and were able to spend about forty-five minutes visiting with Paul. He and I shared some fond memories of George, and the conversation turned to Marty and his role as George in a Beatles band. As musicians will do, they spoke about experiences playing to audiences. At one point, Paul said, "You know, even though I wrote most of the songs I perform, every once in a while my mind will go blank and I forget the words." We all laughed, and then Marty said, "Well, that occasionally happens to us, but we just lip-read the people in the front row." *(See photo on page 221.)*

"That's a tip worth remembering," Paul replied.

Chapter Fourteen

A BACKWARD GLIMPSE
TO THE '80s

*T*hroughout 2002, I accompanied Marty and his band to many shows. Spending time with Beatles People as their Global Mum has been my role for most of the past few decades. Our parents were the original parents of the Global Family and had always encouraged me to "give back the love." They understood clearly that without the "fans," there would be no "famous Beatles." This concept was satirized in a scene from *"HELP."* The high priest complains, when unable to remove the sacrificial ring from Ringo, that without the ring there can be no sacrifice, without the sacrifice there will be no congregation and without a congregation, there would be *no me!* Most of my readers will recall the scene.

A topic George and I frequently spoke about was how horrible his life had become since he became *rich*. He once said, "Usually, when people make a lot of money, they become Tycoons—we just became Targets!" He was constantly "courted" by folks who undoubtedly were subconsciously singing, "Gotta get you into my life!"*

Learning of the stress this brought to his life, I became totally convinced I wanted no part of this "millionaire stuff." To this day, I will not buy a lottery ticket, nor will I put a dime into a slot machine in the fear that I might inadvertently win a million. Fearful in the event that ever happened, I might have to endure that same uneasy feeling he always had, as to the real motive behind the "love and adoration" expressed by those who thrust themselves into his life. At least I know my friends are there because they actually *like* me and not because of any financial benefits, or the occasional Porsche or Rolls I may buy them! Although, I do now understand that there have been quite a few instances when my relationship with my brother has been the direct reason why I also have been "courted" by predators. (A lot of good that did them!)

During the '80s, I was living in a rather affluent area of Sarasota, FL. The marketing business my former husband and I created had been generating a *very substantial* income. Our monthly net income averaged around $30,000, and to cover incidentals on our business trips, I always carried at least $1,000 in Traveler's checks in my wallet. My husband would joke about me buying clothes from the clearance racks and would often urge me to *"take $200 and buy a dress."* To me, the idea of spending even as much as $25 for *one* dress was pretty extravagant. Our parents had built our confidence to the point we knew the impression we made on others had little to do with our external appearance, including designer clothes or expensive jewelry, but rather on the way we conducted ourselves with regard to the care and respect we showed to those others. So even in my "wealthiest days," the riches themselves meant very little. Thus, when husband number two also became a victim of an alcoholic addiction, and before it followed the course of my previous marriage, we kindly and gently called it quits.

When my second marriage ended, the divorce settlement—with George's intervention—gave me possession of our house, but, since I was no longer part of our business, had no income to maintain it. Because George knew that both my marriages involved physical and mental abuse from husbands suffering from problems with alcohol, he had advised, "Do not get married again. I will provide you with an adequate income so that for the rest of your life, you can be secure and not have to be dependent on yet another person who might possibly mistreat you." He added, "In view of my own circumstances, there is no reason on this Earth why my sister should ever be in need." I gratefully accepted his offer, as marriage for me had not proven to be the "happily ever after" I had expected, when growing up in the security of my parent's loving relationship.

At George's suggestion, I had consulted with my two nearest neighbors as to the regular monthly costs of running their homes. At the time, I was unaware that both of these couples had no debts at all. Their homes, autos, furnishings, etc., were all fully paid.

They came up with a figure of $2,000 a month, which covered utilities, lawn and pool service, taxes, insurance, food, and an occasional meal in a restaurant. They did not include the costs of golf and country club fees because they knew I was not "into" that kind of life. And so, I told George $2,000 would be very nice, thank you so much. Initially, he set the pension up as a consulting fee, but when taxes rolled around that next year, I was billed $16,000.

When George heard this, he gave instructions to his accounting people to set up a tax-paid-up-front, lifetime pension to me of $2,000 per month. This proved to be a wonderful security blanket for me, and I have been truly grateful. Although most of my adult life I had been accustomed to being much more "plush," the frugality of my childhood years kicked in, and I lived very comfortably. I was making payments on the home, my auto, and the furniture, but I was okay.

When a $30,000 "balloon payment" became due on the house, George happily sent the check. There were still the regular monthly payments, of course. Unfortunately, like many other trusting souls, I fell into the "refinancing trap" set by the greedy bankers for a naïve public. Within a couple of years, my mortgage payments increased from around $200 per month to $1,300 per month, making it more and more difficult to hold onto my lovely home, which I eventually sold and moved to a small condo. There was no way I would go to George for help again for what I considered my own stupidity in managing money. The repercussions and extensive dire results of *that* cynical banking scheme are now being felt on a worldwide basis.

We have just re-visited some of the events of the '80s, but this part is about 2002, and in order to set the scene for what happened next, it was important to recall or revisit those details.

As you know, I arrived on this planet some eleven to twelve years prior to my youngest brother, and naturally assumed I would "leave" before him. So I was a little whimsically envious that he had apparently had his sentence shortened and was "let out for good behavior." It seemed to me a little unfair since I had, from the time of my earlier religious training, struggled to be "good." Oh well, I guess I have not finished my task yet! I recall George telling me that I have my own *dharma* to fulfill.

As the year 2002 progressed, there was much worldwide speculation about George's will. Since both he and I had expected him to long outlive me, his will was of no concern to me. However, I did have experience of how Harrisons took care of their kin. I knew when our dad died in 1977, he had left his small savings to be shared equally between *all four* children. And Dad's younger brother Jimmy, who had no children, also left an inheritance which was to be divided between all of his nieces and nephews. Although it was a small sum, about twenty of his heirs, including me and my brothers, each received a few hundred dollars. Equal shares for all, no favorites, and no one left out. This was the way the Harrison family designated the disposal of any money after their deaths. I was okay, secure in the knowledge that my precious "pension" from my brother was in place. But the day before Christmas in 2002, I received a short note from the lady who had been writing my monthly checks from George to the effect that these payments would no longer be made.

Naturally, this turn of events came as a serious shock to me. I was by now, however, receiving Social Security, and the amount at that time was around $600 per month. Although, in addition to my pension, by taking speaking engagements, I was able to pay off a lot, I still owed most of the $80,000 on credit cards from my "Drop-In" non-profitable venture into "saving the world." I was making payments on a property, which—although in the center of the United States—was in a remote spot in the country. I intended leaving this property jointly to my two grandsons and also to my nephew, Dhani. I had shown George photos of the property when I first bought it. He thought it was a beautiful, serene spot and was looking forward to occasionally being able to "hide-out" off the beaten path at this peaceful retreat.

It is a beautiful eighteen-acre area with three A-frame homes, about four acres of woods behind a four-and-a-half acre lake, and the remainder was meadowland. I was still very concerned about the health of our planet and hoped to be able to find sponsors to create a "renewable energy showcase." I envisioned photo-voltaic cells on the south sides of the A-frame homes, wind turbines, and wanted to create a geo-thermal system by drilling into the lake. I had installed two filtration systems, which processed household sewage into an end product of drinkable water. I think this method of waste treatment needs to be used in many more places.

I enjoyed the serenity living there, but because the area was so remote from other populated areas, my daughter was concerned for my safety, especially since—to her—I was getting to be *so old!* In order that we could be nearby in the case of "accident," she persuaded me to buy an inexpensive little house in the same town she lived with her husband and son. I did so, but because of my intention to keep my lovely country retreat for my family, did not attempt to sell the eighteen-acre property.

So it was that when my pension was terminated, I spent a really relaxed Christmas wondering how I was going to manage to maintain payments on all of this, with just $600 per month. At seventy-one, I was hardly a "must have" in the job market.

The first week in 2003, I received a registered package from a bunch of legal folks in England. They called themselves the Harrison Family Estate, although I do not know that any biological Harrisons were included. They said that it would be to "my benefit" to sign a whole bunch of documents called "non-disclosure." These documents mentioned the business ventures related to my brother and The Beatles. Since I had never known or been interested in any of these business ventures, it would not have been possible for me to "disclose anything." It is pretty common knowledge, that when someone wants to impose a "non-disclosure" thingy, it is usually because "whatever they are doing would not survive public scrutiny." What exactly was "The Harrison Family Estate" afraid of? I knew that apart from the well known use of "weed" in his early days, George had nothing to hide. Actually he couldn't hide, anyway, with the amount of media coverage on his every move. As he has said, *"they know more about you than you know about yourself!"*

As to my disclosure regarding my brother, any of about a million Beatles fans can attest to the fact that although I told stories of the many experiences I have shared with The Beatles after the onset of their public fame, I have always been adamant when asked, "What was George like as a child?"

My firm reply has always been this: "Since becoming a Beatle, George and the others have been so scrutinized and probed into every tiny aspect of their lives put under a microscope. Therefore, out of love and duty to my brother, I feel it my responsibility to keep private the time in his life when he was free to live as a normal child. There was never anything about him as a child I would be ashamed to tell about, but I simply will not talk about that phase of his life."

Although the audiences at Beatles gatherings and environmental expos were disappointed at my reply, they nevertheless always applauded wholeheartedly my commitment to protect my young brother's childhood privacy. Therefore, having no business knowledge to disclose, and confident of my integrity regarding George's childhood privacy, I was at a loss to understand just what, exactly, I was supposed to "not disclose."

I sought advice about this legal package with the businessmen who had been part of my board of directors with Drop-In. They included attorneys and a CPA, besides a couple of CEOs.

Although I had never heard of THFC at this point in time, the Curse did, however, kick in with a vengeance. The values taught to me by my parents caused me to look upon the contents of the package this way. I knew from history that during slavery days, entire populations of villages in Africa, including the Chief, were rounded up and herded into awful prisons, then into the filthy holds of ships for weeks until they arrived at the Land of the "Free(?)". And yes, the British had also been guilty of profiting from slave trading.

Families were then split up and sold to the highest bidder. Many times the chief, broken-hearted by the anguish of his villagers, would speak-up in protest. Again, I knew from history, that whenever a slave became "uppity" or troublesome, there was a sure-fire solution. The plantation or slave owner had a very easy remedy for anyone who spoke "out of place." Yes, in those days "knowing one's place" was very important. (Maybe those days have returned?) You may ask: what was that simple remedy?

Just cut the troublemaker's tongue out, and he will say no more!

So this whole "non-disclosure of things I knew nothing about anyway," smacked of a pretext to legally "cut out my tongue." The Harrison Curse of course would not sanction me becoming a victim to this skullduggery! Let's face it—if the German Bombs could not scare me when I was a child, I was hardly going to cringe in terror when a bunch of people—none of whom were biological Harrisons, but called themselves "The Harrison Estate"—attempted to "cut my tongue out." No, *this* Harrison has the same DNA as the one who composed "The Sue Me, Sue You Blues." Therefore, I had my legal friend write to say I declined to sign.

Meanwhile, the legal and accounting former Drop-In board members were telling me, "You know, Lou, it is probably just a formality to get your signature before they send a small bequest. Reportedly, George left 300 million dollars, or 500 million pounds, so in fairness, the *least* you and your two brothers would receive would likely be, maybe 10 million each. That wouldn't even put a dent into the total amount."

"But I don't want to be a millionaire!" I still protested.

"It won't be so bad," they assured me. "Besides, you could do so much good. You could create your renewable energy showcase that you wanted to do at the eighteen acres in

Macedonia, or give to the charities you admire, help your friends who are hurting financially, and 'Look on the bright side,'" they joked. "You would give it away so fast you would *un-millionaire yourself* in no time!"

I was still cautious. After all, I did not want the people who cared about me to be sneakily ousted by new ones who cared only about the money. But January was almost over, and the monthly bills were coming due, and I had only my Social Security check of $600 with which to pay them. So, I reluctantly called my lawyer friend and told him, "I guess they have me cornered. I will have to sign, but send the papers back as "signed under duress" or "under protest." This he did.

This is where the saga gets to be really hilarious! Even now, I am chuckling when I recall how I agonized about the potential terrors of millionaire-dom. I need not have worried. **The joke was on me!**

In due course, a check arrived from England. It was considerably less than the **annual** income my former husband and I generated with our marketing business. As near as I can figure, the Harrison Estate took one million pounds and divided it between the remaining Harrison siblings and their children. So the unwanted millionaire-dumb was not to be my fate after all. Whew!

However, after living in the "credit-driven society" for so long, it was a great relief to be in a position to pay off everything I owed. As my parents had always advocated, *"Buy only what you can pay for."* I was now able to reach that rare goal. There was just enough to pay off my two modest properties and the remainder of the credit card debt I had incurred with my, in every sense of the word, *non-profitable* organization. And thus my sudden wealth *vanished* just as suddenly.

"Hurray, hurray, I don't have to become a target!" I was pleased at both becoming solvent and escaping the fiendish millionaire thingy. It didn't occur to me that I might stay alive and have to pay bills for some time into the future. This self-proclaimed "old fogey" was not a viable "catch" on the job market and was still receiving a mere $600 a month. The social security did go up gradually each year, but with the aid of good humor and good friends, things turned out okay. Soon, my adopted brother, Marty, created a new career for the two of us—and joy for very many others. Watch out for Liverpool Legends!

*Footnote to this chapter. Out of respect for George's close friends—including musicians, the Monty Pythons, Formula One drivers, and others, famous in their own rights, many of whom I have met—I know he had no problems with the sincerity of those relationships. Mind you, being known as a friend of George Harrison was no drawback to any career.

Except, perhaps my own.... Many people keep assuming I own a theatre in Branson, or a mansion on the Riviera! No, but I enjoy peace of mind and count as *my* wealth, the smiles and love of my many dear friends. Apart from income I earn with my band, Liverpool Legends, I still have my social security to live on.

Thanks so much Harrison Family Estate! I guess with (as far as I know) no real Harrisons involved, years of Harrison family integrity was easy to dismiss?

Just like the Gerries in WWII, you lot don't scare me either! But anyway, I'm okay with having escaped the millionaire dumb. You're welcome!

Chapter Fifteen

LIVERPOOL LEGENDS

*I*n 2002, the Liverpool Beatles Convention invited me to attend. This was the first time they had sought me out in their more than twenty-year history. My new brother—Marty, a George impersonator—was also on the trip. I grew to admire his dedication to representing George with as much accuracy, humor and respect as possible. Marty's longtime friend, Kevin, was John Lennon in the band. When I say "was" John, that's exactly what I mean. Kevin could almost be John's clone! Even when not performing as John, just hanging out with friends, I get a feeling of déjà-vu, as though I was back in a room with the original John. His resemblance is uncanny, but without the spousal domination.

After our trip to Liverpool, Marty and I became very solid in our "sibling" relationship. But a few days before Christmas 2002, I received notice of the termination of my life pension. I was shocked by this, after all it was a lifetime pension, and I for one, felt sure I *was* still alive! Naturally I confided this development to my new brother. I felt sure he was the strong shoulder George had sent to be supportive, in his place.

Marty was earning his living by impersonating George, so his natural solution was to consider forming our own band and make me "manager." Then I could also earn an income. I'm thankful no one thought to put me in a clothesbasket and leave me on the doorstep of an "old folks' home"! (I probably would have escaped anyway.)

As I told in the previous chapter, several months later, I received the bequest, which I used to pay off my debts. The scary bequest turned out to be a mere hiccup—it was sucked up so fast. Quickly I was back to square one. My sole income was my social security check of $600 a month. I realized my future survival might depend on how well we could create and launch an excellent Beatles tribute band.

It never occurred to me to appeal the decision made by the "Harrison Family? Estate" to terminate my lifetime pension, though they probably knew I was, inconveniently, still not dead. It seemed obvious that the *real original* Harrison family way of doing things, such as looking after other family members as a priority, was no longer valid. So be it....

I know my Dad would have advised: "If someone kicks you in the gut, don't give them the satisfaction of seeing you 'down.' Get up and show you still have the guts to carry on." So, yes Dad that's what I did.

We originally dismissed the idea of adding to the hundreds of Beatle Tribute Bands. Our idea was to create a John and George duo, featuring Marty and Kevin as the "Passed Masters," I would be named their "manager" or as I put it, their mum. I felt comfortable lending my name to this venture because these two musician/actors were not only talented, but they were also the kind of fellows George would have enjoyed counting amongst his sincere friends. Whatever income we generated would provide for our needs. However, after a few dates playing as Passed Masters, Marty and Kevin came to me and said, "Lou, in order to do justice to the music, we really need to put together a full band." I was reluctant, saying, "I can honestly endorse you two with a clear conscience, but unless we can find other band members who will not bring discredit to my family name, I cannot do this."

So we went to work putting together what is now the much acclaimed Liverpool Legends. *(See photos on pages 222-223.)*

Now when asked, "How did you manage to find such an excellent group of musicians?" I have many times jokingly replied, "I have this 'twilight zone' feeling that wherever my brother's *Being* is now, he somehow helped me put this Band and career together." Although we Harrisons have never been afraid of hard work, during my later years he did provide me with a pension to make sure I would never have to live in poverty. So within or without his human body, I believe he has not let me down.

During the first year, we mostly played gigs at festivals and performing arts theatres. In fact, because a dear friend, Gary Sebescak who lives in Sullivan, MO, arranged for our first theater engagement to be at the Sullivan Performing Arts Centre—thus our very own Sullivan Shew!

Also—just as the original Beatles had played the *first* rock concert at St. Louis Busch Stadium—the Liverpool Legends played the *final* rock concert there before it was demolished to make way for a new stadium.

The past years "the season" in Branson, MO, has served as our home base. In the off-season, we played to sold-out audiences in many Texas and Oklahoma cities, and too many other venues for me to easily recall. One memorable show we played to a 3,000 strong audience in Santiago, Chile. What was remarkable about that show was this: although English was *not* the primary language, the audience was singing along, very loudly, in English, with just about every song we performed. In fact, there were times the volume from the enthusiastic audience almost drowned out the Lads on stage! Shortly after that, we toured eastern Canada, again to very enthusiastic audiences. In May 2013, we were honored to be invited to Israel to play for yet another super enthusiastic audience. In fact, our show sold out before we arrived, so we had to play two shows that same evening to accommodate all the Beatle People who wanted to see our show. We started at eight that evening and did not leave the stage until around 2 a.m., worn out but thrilled with our reception.

I am constantly told by Liverpool Legends audiences how much they enjoy our show, which they rate as the best reproduction of the original Beatles they have ever seen. Many even tell me emphatically, "This is the best show that I have *ever* seen!" To my amazement and—naturally—great gratification, these are people who routinely visit both Vegas and Broadway.

There was, however, one occasion when an audience member was not so pleased. An angry lady accosted me during intermission. Here is what happened: Marty, who has done an excellent job of producing a first class show, found the perfect role for me. He arranged to have me narrate a video telling "The Beatles history." This makes a perfect accompaniment to the way our show follows the musical chronology of The Beatles' career. In the video before the show opens I explain to the audience that everything in our show is *live*, with no pre-recorded tracks, overdubs, or lip-syncing. On the night in question this very irate lady came yelling at me saying, "You lied! I listen to Beatle music every single day and I *know* how they sound! You are definitely playing Beatle records!" Before I could reply, she rushed out of the theatre. I was pretty stunned—like George and our parents, I am known (as obvious in this book) for my often "too painful honesty." So her attitude was quite a blow. However, I later told my Lads, "Perhaps you could just throw in a mistake now and again so the audience will know it is really *you* who are singing." Mind you, these musicians are such perfectionists that they seldom forgive themselves if they *do* hit a wrong note once in a while! Let's face it, my brother and his mates only had to "get it right" **once** in the recording studio, not every night in a theatre!

Recently I was in New York City and was honored to be a guest with the legendary Cousin Brucie on his show. After we finished, he asked to listen to a CD I had with me of Liverpool Legends. I won't reveal his reaction, but I encourage you to try to catch his show on Sirius XM sometime; I would be happy for you to hear his opinion of my band.

I could write an entire 'nother book about my adventures with this "Make-Believe" Beatle Band; maybe one day I shall. The main purpose of writing at all, is not because I have any desire to tell about *my* life, but because so many people have asked for my personal experience of life as George's sister. They also asked for a more accurate account than the stories already "out there" of what really happened before, during, and after his involvement with the real Beatles. This is all I have tried to do without embellishment or sensationalism. I've just given the facts as I know, or witnessed them.

Will a book with no lies, hardly any sex, and no violence ever sell? Or even find a publisher? I guess I will find out.

People are already asking, "when can we order your book?" One young lady just insisted on prepaying for hers, I have her address, and she had a receipt from me for book number one.

Chapter Sixteen

BEATLE ADVENTURES

*H*ere are some of the adventures I shared with my brother during his Beatle years, including insights into the stories behind some of their songs.

I attended the *New Musical Express* annual awards at Wembley Stadium in London in, I think, 1964. This was one of the earlier events I shared with George. Mum and I had arrived from Liverpool the day before and we were staying at a hotel. When George tried to come pick us up, he was unable to get through the crowds because there were so many fans outside his hotel. He had to call us and tell us to go to Plan B, whereby we took a cab to meet him at the stadium. In those days we often had to go through plans A, B, C, and D to find one that could outsmart the devoted fans.

Incidentally, very few know George was responsible for The Rolling Stones gaining their recording contract. Years ago he told me how it happened. Apparently at a formal banquet at the height of the "mania," he was seated next to the Decca records person who some time earlier had rejected Brian Epstein's demo of The Beatles. (Just as most of the American DJs at the time told me, "This is not commercial and will go nowhere.") This gentleman told George how his career had plummeted due to that error of judgment. George's natural compassion led him to comfort the man. He asked George, "Maybe if I could find a new act, I could get my reputation back. Do you know anyone with potential that I might listen to?" It happened that George had been at a south London pub a few days earlier, and been quite impressed by a raw new band, so he said, "Yes, I saw a group the other day that you might like to take a look at, they were playing at...and they were called 'The Rolling Stones.'"

How does the saying go? And the rest is history...funnily enough, later on, once The Stones were established, the press tried to create a Beatles versus The Rolling Stones scenario; George merely shook his head at the manipulations the press work on the public and said, "There's space, and fans enough for everyone, without trying to invent rivalry."

The most exciting adventure was when I was invited to spend George's twenty-second birthday with him in the Bahamas. They were to film scenes for the second Beatles movie *HELP*. The James Bond movie *Thunderball* had just been completed, and a lot of the locations used in that movie were pointed out to me.

By this time in The Beatles saga, George had learned to let the security people know whenever I was joining him, thus preventing any more awkward situations like the one at the Plaza on February 7, 1964. Therefore, when I arrived at the Nassau airport, I was met by police officers and brought to the auditorium where the Boys were giving a press conference. As I entered the hall, John, seated on the stage with the rest of the band, leaned over to George and said, "Hey, your Lou just arrived with the security guards." This observation was noteworthy because John had very poor eyesight and could hardly see beyond his handsome nose! However, he had just been fitted with contact lenses and was thrilled with himself to be the first to spot me!

Walter Shenson and Dick Lester were the movie's producer and director, respectively. Leo McKern played the high priest. Victor Spinetti played the mad scientist. Eleanor Bron played the non-romantic female lead, as the priestess, and Patrick Cargill, the Scotland Yard inspector. I spent lots of time and had quite a few adventures with these actors during the filming. One day, the Boys spent an hour or two at a go-cart facility. There were some pretty steep climbs and dangerous curves, and they had a blast. However, the "suits" in charge put a stop to such activities due to insurance coverage. Let's face it, if one of the Boys had been incapacitated (or decapitated) it would have been quite a financial disaster. So, one drawback to fame was this: you couldn't have spontaneous fun anymore.

During that week, I met a lady and her daughter who have been good friends ever since. As you know, Paul lost his Mum to cancer early in his teens. His father had recently met and married Angie, a widow who had a four-year-old daughter, Ruth. Paul invited them along to the Bahamas for part of the movie filming, as a honeymoon trip. Naturally, we family members we introduced and spent a lot of time together watching the various scenes in progress. We have since kept in touch and have met occasionally at Beatle gatherings. Angie and Ruth run their own internet newsletter, at www. mccartneymultimedia.com.

The Boys were staying at a private house on the Island, and I was booked into a downtown Nassau hotel along with Neil and Mal. One evening, I guess the news that The Beatles were in town leaked out. My goodness, how could *that* happen? Mal, Neil, and I were having a drink at the hotel bar when we overheard a group of tourists/sailors talking about knowing The Beatles. One remarked, "I knew them in Liverpool when they all had dirty necks, and never took a bath." Well, they found out at that moment, you do not make derogatory remarks about The Beatles in the presence of Mal or Neil or Lou. Mal was a huge, intimidating fellow, and he approached these sailors in his "Super Beatle-Protective Mode." Towering over them, he told them quite vehemently to apologize or they could choose to "Drop Dead." They quickly left their drinks and scurried out of the bar, muttering to themselves. They had thought they were merely impressing the crowd at the bar with their stories. I expect this kind of thing is quite common and accounts for some of the wild stories and rumors about "my" lads.

The rooms in the downtown hotel did not have locks on the doors, and Mal went to a lot of trouble making sure no one could get through the barricade he constructed at my door! Although he and Neil are no longer on the planet, I can say with absolute conviction that The Beatles could never have found anyone—except their own families—with more dedication to their safety and well-being than their longtime "roadies" Mal and Neil. The pair had been with the Boys since high school days. They cared for me as a "younger sister," too!

The night of the 25th was George's 22nd birthday. A party was held at the house where the Boys were billeted...I recall the big cake. George found a sword or dagger somewhere in the house and proceeded to jokingly stab the cake into submission, before cutting it into squares or wedges. The room we were in had large ceiling-to-floor windows overlooking a large patio. Outside these windows the Boys repeated the trick scene in *A Hard Day's Night* in which they had held Ringo and carried him sideways past the moving train's windows. Victor Spinetti and I danced quite a lot and I even tried to smoke a cigar, but—unaccustomed to smoking, had to give it up pretty quickly!

One of the scenes in *HELP* had the Boys on bikes chasing the Bad Guys. As in most movies, the filming of any scene takes longer than the bit you actually see. The Boys were just having so much fun. At one point, the bikes were parked at the side of the road, kickstands down. John—walking ahead—suddenly realized he was supposed to be riding a bike. He stopped, turned, and whistled at the bike, in typical John fashion. To our amusement, the bike, standing alone on the road, promptly toppled over onto its side as if trying to obey his summons. In order to more easily record dialogue for the scene, the Boys were actually filmed riding the bikes round and round in a circle on the road. Naturally, no traffic was allowed in the area where they were working.

At noon, the crew took a lunch break. The Boys were sitting in an A/C limo learning their lines, not something these spontaneous individuals found easy—I also tend to be more comfortable being spontaneous rather than scripted! Everyone on the crew settled down to enjoy the sandwiches and drinks provided. I noticed that no food or beverages had been taken to the Boys in the limo, and asked the caterers to "see to it." They naturally did a "Whoops, we're sorry" and scurried to get what was left to take to the limo. I witnessed *so many* occasions when the welfare of the "stars" was overlooked; they almost needed to have Mum or I along to make sure they were properly cared for!

In another scene, I was in the "crowd" seated around the pool. The Boys had jumped into a vessel or fountain in a cave and resurfaced in this pool some distance away. Although I was seated amongst the tourists in that particular scene, I've never been able to locate myself whenever I've watched the movie. But I was there!

Another scene was called "The Girl on the Beach," where Paul strums the girl in the swimsuit as though she was a guitar. Back then I asked to be considered for this small part. I did look good in a swimsuit back then, as you will see from photos accompanying this book, but George was horrified that his sister would be seen in a swimsuit by the movie audience, so the idea was dropped. I still think they should have chosen me. The Shirley Temple in me is still alive and eager. *(See photo on page 216.)*

During the filming of *HELP*, I spent quite a lot of time talking with Sylvia, the continuity lady. She had the unenviable task of making sure the Boys were wearing the same clothes, etc., in the follow-up scenes. Sometimes part of a scene would be shot one day, and the next few seconds in the actual movie might not be shot until days later. So this poor girl had quite a task. The Boys had three sets of identical outfits, and one day George accidentally washed a pair of his blue jeans using bleach in the washer. The jeans came out with irregular greyish patches all over, so poor George had to try to make his other two pairs look the same. I was with him when he was painstakingly dipping his jeans over and over into a pail of water with some bleach. The results were rather crazy-looking, but, giving up on the task, he just said, "Oh well, the way things are going with this Beatles thing, everyone will be wearing jeans like this in another six months!" Lo and behold, the birth of the tie-dyed look!

Another interesting shared experience is the BBC TV skit based on some of Shakespeare's characters, Pyramus and Thisbe. Once again I was visiting my brother, and he took me along with him. The taping was far funnier than the end result, which audiences saw on TV. If only I had the "outtakes"—they were so comical I could re-watch them whenever I needed cheering up. You can imagine the opportunities John took to goof off, when dressed as Pyramus' female lover, Thisbe. His costume consisted of a gown and very comical blonde wig, complete with upturned braided pigtails. Ringo played the part of "Wall" separating the two lovers. Dressed in a flowing outfit with a brick design, he stood arms outstretched to keep them apart. There was, however, a hole in the wall through which they were able to pass notes. Paul played Pyramus and George was the moon. This skit is probably out there somewhere in cyberspace; you might try to find it. Unless the outtakes had been preserved, you wouldn't see all the spontaneous comedy I saw that night, but at least you'd get the general idea.

Here's an amusing little anecdote connected with the *Gone Troppo* album. When George became financially secure, he made a practice of showing up at Mum and Dad's home every few months with a paid vacation package for them. On one occasion it was to a seaside resort somewhere on the Mediterranean. During this vacation, Mum and Dad were relaxing on the beach one afternoon, when Mum spotted an ice cream vendor wheeling his cart across the sand. Well, she didn't want an ice cream, but this fellow was wearing an awesome hat. When Mum saw it she said to Dad, "Oh, I've gotta have a photo wearing that hat!" Dad, in seeing the hat recognized why this appealed to Mum's goofiness. So, he asked the vendor if he could borrow it and take a photo of Mum. *(See photo on page 216.)*

Moments later Mum was standing "in all her glory" wearing the hat. The photo also shows some of the other holiday makers staring in amazement at this apparition. I had a copy of this photo for years. Then one day round about the time of *Gone Troppo,* I was chatting with George and showed him this photo, which he hadn't previously seen. He roared with laughter, and said, "Oh how I wish I'd seen this before; it would have made the perfect album cover for *Gone*

Troppo. I have included the photo so you can see if you agree with him.

While I was living in New York in the '80s, George appeared on *Saturday Night Live* with Paul Simon. Again—as was his custom whenever I was in a nearby location—he invited me along. This time, his new brother-in-law, Walt, came, too. My daughter was a big fan of cast member Chevy Chase, and for once I had my husband get an autograph for her. Chevy asked him, "What shall I write?" and my husband said, "Whatever you like." So, those were the exact words Chevy wrote on his picture for her!

Again, having the opportunity to be present at the filming of a TV show turned out to be hilarious. Due to my brother's schedule—he was due to go to India the next day—this particular *Saturday Night* was not "live" but recorded the previous Wednesday night before an invited studio audience. The plan was for George and Paul Simon to sing two songs together. Paul's song was "Homeward Bound" and George's song was "Here Comes the Sun." Once they got going, George would get the words "the movies and the factories" mixed up and would joke with Paul about the complex lyrics. Then, when working on George's song, Paul would get the guitar part all wrong and joke back at George for writing such complex chords. Each time they made mistakes—which was often—the taping would stop. Once the huge cameras were rolled back into starting position they could restart. At one point, George laughingly suggested, "Maybe it would be a lot easier if you keep the cameras still, and Paul and I can just run around instead?" A week or two earlier, an offer had jokingly been made—on the air—to pay a fairly large sum if The Beatles would come on the show. So, in the corridor before the show, a short "joke" segment was filmed wherein George is pretending to ask for the payment promised. They tell him he can only have one quarter of the sum, since he is only one quarter of The Beatles. Again, the outtakes were much funnier than the show the viewing audience saw. I wonder if any of those outtakes still exist? Maybe they are also on the internet?

There was a very highly publicized Beatle adventure that took place during a visit to the Philippines. I heard a very full and detailed account from George when we were next together. That entire incident made a deep impression and reminded him of the dangers created by their fame. What he learned after the event was this: Some minor member of The Beatles entourage had apparently received a request or invitation from the Marcos family for The Beatles to visit the palace and meet with the President and first lady, Imelda. This message was never passed on to The Beatles or higher management. This is as close as I remember to George's exact words, "We were in the suite ready to have a meal before leaving. The TV was on and we heard the announcer saying—'Everyone here at the Palace is waiting patiently for The Beatles to arrive.'" He said they watched in fascinated horror the spectacle of "themselves—The Beatles *not* arriving at the Palace." You may recall stories of how The Beatles were mistreated, pushed and punched, and left to handle their own luggage at the airport by the angry mobs, who believed The Beatles had knowingly snubbed their President. But as George also said later when they learned more about abuses attributed to the Marcos family, "We didn't know anything about the invitation, but in retrospect, I am glad we didn't go."

I often speak with fans who can't understand the significance of many Beatles lyrics, especially the songs about parts of Liverpool. So I thought it may be of interest to my readers to give some background insight into some of these lyrics. I have more personal knowledge of the purpose and meaning of my brother's songs, but there are a few others I can shed some light on for you. Naturally, there is not enough space in one book to tell about all the Beatle songs.

Let's start with "Penny Lane." Actually, five separate streets converge at this spot, one of which is "Penny Lane," but we locals call the actual center of this junction Penny Lane. There really was a "shelter (it did rain a lot!) in the middle of the roundabout," complete with a seating area and the customary toilets for the convenience of passengers of trams and buses whilst they were waiting for connections to other parts of the city. On November 11th, Armistice Day, known in the United States as Veterans' Day, many volunteer teenage girls and I, not necessarily pretty nurses, would be provided with a tray of imitation poppies to sell in order to raise money for the veterans. The poppies were in remembrance of a battle fought during WWI at Flanders Field, where—after the battle—the copious amount of bloodshed either made the area look like a field of poppies or poppies sprung up soon thereafter. I heard this story as a child so am not sure which version is correct. If I had time to search the internet I could likely find out. Well, I had a friend find this link, which tells the story of the Flanders Poppy and for those who may wish to learn more here is the link: http://greatwar.co.UK/article/remembrance-poppy.htm.

The barbershop mentioned in the song was where Dad used to go for his haircuts and was named Bartolettis. The bank was on one corner, and the "mac," which the banker never wore, was our name for a raincoat. The fire station also mentioned, however, was located about a quarter of a mile away from Penny Lane junction, at Mather Avenue or Menlove Drive and was across the road from one of our favorite movie theatres. This was the theatre where I'd taken my brothers to see a Gene Kelly movie version of *The Three Musketeers.*

Strawberry Fields, another real place, at one time was an orphanage. Mum would take us there occasionally when her older brother, Uncle Johnny, lived there as groundskeeper and maintenance man. Whenever we visited him, we would take reusable items—the few we weren't reusing ourselves—to donate to the orphanage.

Uncle Johnny was one of the few people I knew who always had a dog. Earlier, I told of my encounter with Nero, his black Labrador. I recall an incident at a time when he had two Old English Sheepdogs: the mother, whose pedigree name was Mumfords Judy, and her six-month-old pup, named Jimmy. They were both very large, and one day when George was just a toddler, we were visiting at Strawberry Fields when the large puppy, Jimmy, at eye-level with George, playfully grabbed him by the collar of his coat, and started to shake him. Fortunately, I had known Jimmy since his birth and was not afraid, so I yelled at him to let go. But this encounter, though brief, was intimidating, so naturally, George, just like his sister, tended to be cautious of dogs for quite a long time after this incident.

This next is about the *Rubber Soul* album. I met a Navy Seal during the '80s when I was living in Sarasota, and he, James Doran, told me this interesting story. He was on the crew of the first nuclear sub, the *Nautilus*. Their first experimental voyage included a six-month exercise beneath the north polar ice cap. A member of the crew received a gift from his sister before they set off. The gift was the newly released Beatles album, *Rubber Soul*. They were permitted to play this on the loudspeakers throughout the vessel during the day. At night, those on duty would roll dice to see which crew member could win the right to use the earphones in order to be able to listen to this music during their duty hours. This was the ONLY music on board, and he told me that although they listened to it constantly, no one ever became tired or bored with it! Some years later, I told this—what I regarded as a remarkable story—to another of my friends. To my surprise, she just said, "Well, of course they didn't get tired of it; most of us have been listening to Beatles music for thirty years now, and we still haven't stopped enjoying it, and I doubt we ever will!"

Judging by the reactions of present day Liverpool Legends audiences, she was obviously quite correct. So much for my amazement at the *Nautilus* story!

George wrote "All Things Must Pass" to help console our Dad. This was in 1970 when our Mum had been diagnosed with an inoperable brain tumor. Our parents had enjoyed such a wonderful, harmonious relationship that the idea of losing his then only 58-year-old wife was devastating. During the time she was hospitalized, Uncle Eddy had gone to Liverpool to 'hang out' with Dad. He called me in Florida in late May and suggested I join him since Mum was so ill. I had been puzzled when I spoke to Mum on her birthday on March 10 of that year. When she spoke to me, her sentences were somewhat mixed-up. I suspected then something was amiss because she had always been so eloquent. So when Eddy called me and told me how sick she was, I realized that the symptoms had been there since March. I made sure my household was in good hands, then quickly booked a flight. Thanks to Eddy's intervention this time, I was fortunate to be able to be at Mum's side during her final weeks.

At about the time I arrived, Dad—due to the stress of nursing Mum alone and trying to spare the rest of the family from worrying—was rushed to hospital and had an operation to remove most of his stomach. He had long suffered from duodenal and other ulcers. His always calm exterior hid the fact that throughout his life he had endured much stress. However, when Mom started showing symptoms of the brain tumor, he had carried on alone, caring for her for quite some time until George discovered just how ill she was and joined Dad and Uncle Eddy in caring for her. I must add here that in Britain there is a national healthcare system, so Mum was able to receive excellent medical care without Dad having the need to call upon a "rich son" to assist. If you revisit the words of "All Things Must Pass," you will understand how George was trying to both prepare and console Dad. In her final weeks, Mum was conscious, but most of her body was paralyzed. She could only communicate by squeezing our hands with her left hand. She retained her kindness and sense of humor as plainly illustrated the day her older sister visited. This sister was very starchy, and always disapproved of *everything*—rather like a certain group of politicos today. Seated at the bedside, she was unaware that Mum—although paralyzed, was fully conscious. My aunt, as usual was giving me a "hard time" about my attire. As was my custom, I held Mum's left hand. My aunt made a scathing remark and Mum gave a squeeze that plainly said: "Don't take the remarks seriously, just have compassion for her."

Once Dad became a patient in the same hospital, we had quite a problem trying to visit them both, yet not let Mum know that Dad was ill, too. This was a very emotional time for us normally, "take-it-in-your-stride-Harrisons."

However, a few years later, the words *"all things must pass"* provided a touch of whimsy when George hung his Gold Album of the same name in the studio on the wall of the toilet, in such a position that anyone seated would be looking directly at it!

During my Daily Beatles Report days, fans who did not understand the British accent in their songs would often ask, "What are they saying?"

"I Want to Hold Your Hand." The lyrics are: "It's such a feeling, I can't hide, I can't hide, I can't hide." This was famously misinterpreted by Bob Dylan as: "I get high, I get high, I get high." During my Beatle report days I was asked about the lyrics of many other songs. Soon I started suggesting to George in my letters that they print the words of the songs within the album. George did not have influence with the "suits," however when Sgt. Pepper album appeared— complete with lyrics—our suggestion was incorporated.

"The Long and Winding Road"—I first I listened to it with George when we returned to Dad's home after Mum's funeral. Together we stood and looked out at the garden, at the roses and lupins and many other plants she and Dad had nurtured. Their garden was quite remarkable. Together we listened to this beautiful melody, holding hands, tears streaming down our faces. That song will always recall that moment.

But typically, as with any serious Harrison's occasion, something really comical had happened to lighten the mood before we went to the funeral. Mum and John Lennon had had a wonderful, full of fun relationship ever since he had lost his own Mother and "adopted" George's. So to honor her, he sent a huge wreath of red roses made in the shape of a cross. It was so large, I think about 8'x5', that the only place it could fit was on top of the hearse. As the vehicle drove down the very bumpy lane from their home, the cross appeared to be leaping up and down as though trying to escape. Dad, my brothers and I were in the first car behind the hearse. Watching the antics of the cross, Dad started to chuckle and said, "I think your Mum is trying to kick that thing off the roof." Knowing how Mum loved "a good laugh" and could not stand "long faces," we realized this was exactly how she would prefer to be making her final car trip. All of us were laughing our socks off! We imagined her proudly telling any new friends in Heaven, "I had my family laughing all the way to my funeral." *(See photo on page 210.)*

There are lots more songs and events I could tell about, but if I try to, I shall never finish this book before my own expiration date, so I shall "Let It Be." There is certainly enough interesting stuff I have not spoken about so maybe, if I have more time, there will be a second edition? Early in 2012 there was some media nonsense about my upcoming "tell-all" book...I will tell only what is appropriate, we Harrisons tend to be discrete, not sensational!

Chapter Seventeen

I WANT TO TELL YOU

*I*t's time now to share some stories that will clearly illustrate why I regard my role as Flying/Global Mum as both a privilege and a significant responsibility. On one hand, there is the friendly interaction with many wonderful individuals, and on the other, so many wild stories to try to tame!

Some years ago, I was asked to sign a book written by Pattie, George's first wife. She and I enjoyed a happy and friendly "sister-in-law" relationship, so when I was shown the page where she mentions me, I was shocked to see that "even she got it wrong." I just now took out her book and re-read what she had said because I wanted to make sure I was not misinterpreting her words.

The direct quotation: "His sister, also Louise, had immigrated to America, but wrote often telling him to get a proper job."

George was already a successful musician when he met and married Pattie Boyd, a model who had a part in the movie *A Hard Day's Night*. So for *anyone* to suggest that George might want or need a proper job, would be quite *insane!* In keeping with my lifelong ambitions, entertaining was the most real activity possible. So this statement in her book had me puzzled and a little upset....

I tried to make sense of this; I knew Pattie had no reason to attempt to "dis" me, and thought back to George's Hamburg days. George and I established an ongoing exchange of letters, back and forth in the early Beatle days. We were equally interested in each other's adventures. In one letter he'd asked my advice, as he had throughout his childhood, this time regarding his choice of careers. Naturally, my well-known Shirley Temple persona was thrilled with his "show biz" endeavors, and I applauded his progress. But remembering Uncle Eddy and how his path through life had been aided and improved due to the business courses he had taken when in the army during WWII, I did suggest that as their income increased, they—all of them—use a little of that money to take a business course to be better able in the future to deal effectively with the many opportunities they were likely to encounter. However, after that one letter, no more was ever said on that topic; but could that be where the "proper job" idea came from?

Of course the way things turned out, they likely would not have had time to take such a course. Looking back, after witnessing the onslaught of numerous "helpers" willing to take them for a ride, it mightn't have been such a goofy idea for them to have some business knowledge under those cute mop-tops. What do you think?

My attorney, Rick Larson, who has worked for me in the past, wanted to know how and when George learned to play the guitar. Obviously I had omitted this information so I'll add it here.

This is the story as our Mum told me in letters and phone conversations. In the mid-to-late '50s Elvis Presley was either on TV in Britain or came to visit (I don't recall which). Naturally he wowed all the British teenagers with his sensuous performance, creating a following of screaming and "swooning" girls. After watching all the excitement for a few days, one evening George tentatively approached Mum and asked in hushed tones if she could maybe afford to buy him a guitar. He reasoned, "I think that's the kind of job I could do." Amused and touched at his innocence, but always sympathetic to our aspirations, Mum started to save until she had the five pounds needed to buy him a "used" guitar. To put this in perspective, at that time five pounds was the amount Dad received in his weekly pay packet, and yes, in those days employees were paid with actual money! She told how with Dad's guidance he learned how to hold and tune the instrument, the correct fingering and so on. Night after night he worked with her and Dad, playing along with the popular songs of the day on their record player. None of the boys could read music in their early days, so that was their only means of learning.

She told how he was so determined he would practice until the tips of his fingers, not yet hardened, would bleed. Mum told how after a few weeks he seemed to lose interest and she merely thought this was due to his sore fingers. There was, however, another explanation; George told me this part. One day he was trying to tune the instrument and he accidentally dislocated the neck from the body of the guitar. Alarmed and concerned (after all, Mum had saved up from her earning for several weeks to purchase this precious guitar) and not knowing how to fix it, he hid it on the top shelf of their bedroom closet. A short while later, one of his older brothers discovered the "disaster" and was able to put it back together for him. Thankful and relieved, he then continued his efforts to become a proficient guitar player. I guess the rest is history?

Another experience worth sharing involves a now-deceased Beatles fan, who at the age of ten was diagnosed with a rare form of cancer known as Von Hippel-Lindau. It struck him first with a brain tumor. Throughout his teen years, he developed benign tumors in many of his organs—the spine, the spleen, the eyes, the ears, etc. Although the tumors were themselves benign, they did disrupt the functions of the infected areas. I met him at a Beatles concert on St. Pete Beach in Florida when he had miraculously survived to be around thirty. His name was Jay Lucien Sicard, and when I founded Drop-In in 1993, he offered to be my computer person. He told me that, had it not been for The Beatles and their music and humor, he could never have "made-it" through all the pain and disability he suffered. He had his own comfortable room in my home, and he remained working with me for about four or five years. He was so frail that my young grandson often carried him up and down the steps into our home.

During the years he worked with me, he made an annual visit to the National Institute of Health, where, as he put it, he became a guinea pig for a week.

As a fundraising effort for Drop-In, we put together a book entitled *This is Love,* featuring about one hundred stories from fans expressing their feelings and telling their experiences regarding the influences The Beatles had on their lives. Although neither of us had attempted to publish a book before, we gave it our best shot.

A 300 limited edition under the name, *FLYING MUM, SEAT O'THEPANTS* was self-published. The stories mailed in from fans were typed by Jay into our computer, then other "Drops" edited and proof-read all the stories. A Beatles convention was up-coming in New Jersey, and we were urged to get the book ready to be sold at that event. Our board president arranged to have the book published, with an extremely elegant green leather cover that included the signatures of all participants etched in gold leaf. We rushed to have it ready. When the published book was delivered, we realized—to our utter horror—due to the time-related stress, Jay had sent from the computer his original typed entry, not the proofread and corrected version of the stories. Jay and I both wrote an apology, which we included with each copy of the book. Back then electronic transmission of documents was still in the future, though in this case it would not have helped.

His own story in the book bore testimony to his bravery and great sense of humor. He told that his favorite Beatles song was "Yesterday" because, due to all his surgeries, "He was half the man he used to be."

Just once during those years I was able to take him along to a Beatle convention in Chicago. I couldn't help being in tears of laughter at his excitement. Though he was so *very* frail, at that convention he seemed to gain super powers! My core of reliable helpers and I came to the conclusion that he'd a jet-engine strapped to his back because he darted so swiftly and energetically through the mobs of Beatle fans. He covered everything worth seeing, far more than I'd had time or the freedom to do! At the frequent impromptu singalongs, Jay belted out his beloved Beatle songs in his crackly, but enthusiastic voice. What a dear soul and what an uplifting experience to have worked with him. How glad I am he was able to enjoy his one Beatle Convention!

Although I feel it's important to be positive and upbeat, I do still take my given role in life very seriously. As my parents' interactions with the fans demonstrated, this role requires a lot of love, patience, and compassion. I learned from our parents the truth that *"the more love you give, the more you receive."* I am extremely grateful to the Creator for giving me this role in life, plus the necessary abilities to respond to those, who, many times share with me a particular trauma or tragedy they have encountered.

Many times when our band has been performing, I will have someone approach me after the show, and—leaning to my ear—whisper their story. One such: A lady told me that a month earlier her mother had died in a car accident. Her mother had been a big Beatles fan, always singing along with her record player whilst tending to her household chores. Her sudden death was devastating to the whole family, and this particular evening was the first time the family had "gone out" since the funeral. They chose the Liverpool Legends Beatles Tribute Show for obvious reasons. This lady told me how much she enjoyed the show and said, "I now understand that so long as I listen to Beatles music, my mother will always be right beside me."

Another person, a man in his fifties, told me, "My childhood was miserable. I was a badly abused foster child, but I had an eight-track player and one Beatles tape. Whenever I was beaten and sent to my room, I would hide under the covers in my bed and play the music to comfort me. Their music was my only consolation and helped me survive. Now I want to thank you and your band for the wonderful evening I just enjoyed." I constantly hear many similar stories and am always thankful to be closely connected with such a positive force as The Beatles.

❧

I could write a whole book about the adventures I shared with this next person; I may still find time to do so, but for now I'll have to make do with just a brief overview.

Judy, Judy, Judy! In 1993, shortly after I started "We Care Global Family," later to be known as "Drop-In," I was invited to a Beatle gathering in Kansas City. The idea behind this "save the world" effort came from fans at a Paul concert when they suggested that an environmental organization especially for Beatle fans would be good. They then said, "So will you start one?" Years after that conversation at the McCartney concert, here I was, in Kansas to encourage Beatle environmentalists to Drop-In. After speaking to the audience, I returned to the table or booth provided for me in the main traffic area. The first person to sign up as a member was a young woman who told me she was a former Marine, had served in Desert Storm and also served as a police officer. We spoke briefly whilst I prepared her membership papers such as they were! Telling me she has always been a sincere Beatle fan, and would be willing to help in any way I needed, she turned to leave to go visit the other displays. At that moment a dozen or more fans arrived at my table to "join," or drop-in. Alarmed, I called to Judy, "If you really want to help, now is a good time. Will you come back behind this table and sign people up?"

That moment turned out to be most fortunate. In the years since that day back in 1993, Judy McGaugh has, at her own expense, accompanied me and provided excellent security at functions all over the United States, Mexico, Britain, and Europe. I wish I had time to tell more about our often hilarious adventures, but I promise if this book goes to a second edition, there will then be a lengthy chapter devoted to Judy, Judy, Judy!

I've dozens of similar stories of the wonderful people I've met through The Beatles' music and their positive messages as well as many stories on how those messages have made troubled lives and traumatic experiences bearable.

Again, if time allows I may include them in another book.

Another extreme kindness I experienced was with regard to a time when I was having a modular home built in the Branson, MO, area. I needed a place to stay for what turned out to be over four months. The owners of a lovely turn of the century-themed hotel named the Victorian Palace offered me, totally without charge, a room in their hotel for the entire time. The hotel was located in a quiet area of town. My room was spacious and comfortable, and best of all—the staff treated me as though I was truly "the Queen of the palace!" This is yet another time in my life when I have been blessed with unselfish, thoughtful kindness. My gratitude and sincere thanks to you, Victorian Palace, Branson.

The next couple of stories I'll relate, (not to "blow my own TRUMP-et'—we've all heard the awesome noise *that* can make) but to demonstrate that following my parents' advice to treat our extended Beatles family with kindness and compassion, has, in many cases, had a good outcome. One lady recently revealed to me that—due to my encouragement some five to six years ago—she gained the courage and confidence to start her own business, which is now doing quite well. Another, who back in 1964 had interviewed me for her high school paper, told me that from that experience she went on to be a pretty successful journalist. Another, an ardent fan in Boston in 1964, had set out to get into a Beatle press conference with little but sheer determination. Apparently I had been instrumental in helping her succeed. She told me that to this day, that was the single most exciting day of her life. This particular story was included in an audio book called *Fab Fan Memories,* which I agreed to host. This audio book was nominated for a Grammy, in the spoken word category—however as expected, Betty White won, in February 2012.

Being endowed with determination and encouraged to, as Dad would say, *"Don't ever give up,"* obviously made me receptive to anyone else who was showing "unflinching determination" to reach a goal. So to anyone else "out there" who considers my intervention to have helped, just give yourself a "pat on the back" and keep on meeting your challenges with that winning determination.

Here's another story I want to tell you. This has needed to be addressed for a long, long time. This very distressing story originated from an article in *People* magazine back in the '90s and continues to this day, resurfacing in the November 2011 George Harrison issue of *LIFE* magazine.

What **really** happened was this: When George visited me in Illinois in 1963, he and our brother Peter stayed at my, then, home at 113 McCann St. in Benton. In the intervening years since I left Illinois, the house has been owned by several other families. In the mid-'90s, the local mining company had acquired the property and was about to tear down the house to make way for a parking lot. It happened that Bob Bartel, a Beatles fan from Springfield, IL, was visiting in Benton on the same day the demolition was scheduled. Bulldozers and a wrecking ball were at the ready. In horror, he approached many authorities, including the Illinois Historical Society, the mayor, and the mining company itself. He protested that this house had historical significance due to my brother's visit and should not, therefore, be torn down. To make a long story short, after many meetings and discussions, it was agreed the house would remain.

Three local couples pooled their resources to purchase and thereby help save the house. The historical society promised the house would become an official historical site in 2013, fifty years after George's visit. The new owners of the home, who already had their own mortgages to pay, wondered what to do with this new acquisition. In their panic, they decided to make it into a Bed and Breakfast. They thought, *"If a Beatle had once visited there, maybe Beatle people would want to stay there, too!"* I was persuaded to help spread the word to bring a little tourism to this economically destressed area. My efforts to publicize the business included an interview with *People* magazine and also an appearance on the *Today Show*.

Somehow the story of my involvement was distorted, possibly because of an editorial lapse on the part of *People*. John Slania, the reporter, accurately told the story of the legal new owners of 113 McCann St., but a caption to one of the photos read, *"...to reach Louise's Bed and Breakfast, call phone #...,"* which unfortunately gave the erroneously impression that I was an owner. **I do not now, nor have I ever owned, a bed and breakfast**. As is usual, the errors escalated, resulting in yet another crazy story that George was so angered by my alleged affiliation with a Beatle-themed bed and breakfast that he refused to speak to me for years.

This false assertion was ridiculous for many reasons:

A) Not only does it attempt to discredit me, but it also makes my brother appear as a petty, spiteful man. That he, who knew full well the number of fabrications regarding anything Beatle related, would take the word of others regarding my actions, rather than check out the story with the subject—myself—does not make any sense. He always called me if he was concerned about anything. He also knew "clearing up Beatle rumors" has accounted for hours—or maybe weeks—of my life.

B) George spoke many times in public of the purity of unconditional love. He believed that unconditional love meant just that: you do not put conditions on your love. Therefore, he would have to go against his own nature as well as his often stated beliefs to have stopped talking to his own sister, even if I *had* been involved with the B&B. Again this story of a rift makes him seem mean spirited, childish and shallow. To see him depicted this way makes me really angry. I know him as the decent, kind and compassionate man who many times went to the trouble to open a window to release a fly, rather than kill it. How would this man treat a sister?

kin ●

When George played in Benton, says Harrison (in Hard Day's Nite, where her brother once stayed), "the whole place was electrified."

Let It B&B

George Harrison's sister Louise helps create a place in the American heartland for Beatles fans to come together

By September 1963, Beatlemania had reached epidemic proportions in Britain, and the lads from Liverpool needed a break. Paul McCartney and Ringo Starr journeyed to Greece. John Lennon and his wife, Cynthia, headed to Paris. And George Harrison spent two weeks in . . . Benton, Ill.

Still unknown in the U.S., Harrison, then 20, went to pay a visit to his older sister Louise. But the trip became a milestone in Beatles lore.

Harrison's trip was the first time any Beatle had set foot on American soil; tiny WFRX, in nearby West Frankfort, became the first U.S. radio station to play a Beatles record, and when the guitarist took the stage at a Veterans of Foreign Wars dance, the 200-person crowd witnessed the first U.S. performance by a Beatle.

To Louise, now 69, the trip also came to symbolize a notable last: "George's visit to Benton was the last time he could walk the streets free

and easy," she says. Five months later, the Fab Four appeared on *The Ed Sullivan Show* and became instant superstars. Over time, tourists began flocking to the small mining town—and to Louise's former home at 113 McCann Street—to see where the Beatle once slept.

Now they can sleep there too. In 1995 Louise and other locals rallied to save the two-story bungalow from being razed to make way for a parking lot. The house was bought by Louise's friends Jim and Daryl Chady and two other investors, Cornelius and Dorothy Schultz, who have turned it into a bed-and-breakfast called Hard Day's Nite. For $60, guests can stay in one of four rooms (each named for a Beatle) and sift through autographed albums and photos—many donated by Louise. "The effort to save the house is an

PHOTOGRAPHS BY TARO YAMASAKI

PEOPLE *10/2/00* **127**

C) He knew full well my financial situation since he was the one providing it. Therefore, he also knew I had neither the resources nor the business knowledge to invest in a B&B.

D) George also knew that I was not overly domesticated; therefore, it would not have been in *my* nature to take on the task of making other people's beds every day!

● kin

example of how wonderful people are here," says Louise, who lives 16 miles away in rural Franklin County. "They call it the heartland because the people have such big hearts."

Raised in Liverpool, the only daughter of Harold, a bus driver, and his wife, Louise, Harrison moved to Benton in 1963 with her then-husband, mining engineer Gordon Caldwell (they have two grown children, Gordon, 43, who runs a Florida window-cleaning business, and Leslie, 41, an Illinois homemaker). Louise spent her free time taking the latest Beatles singles to radio stations across southern Illinois. Most deejays scoffed, but Marcia Schafer, the 17-year-old host of a teen show on WFRX, gave "From Me to You" and "Love Me Do" an on-air spin. During George's visit, she interviewed him live. Now a sales rep for a nearby station, Marcia, 54, remembers George as polite and shy—with one odd feature. "He had this long hair with the bangs," she says. "I'd never seen anything like it before."

On the last two nights of his stay, Harrison jammed on "Roll Over Beethoven" and other tunes with the

"I've always tried to protect [George]," says Louise (with him in '53 in the U.K.).

Four Vests, a local band. "People were banging their fists on tables and stomping their feet," recalls Louise. At one show, she says, an audience member told her brother, "With the right backing, you could go places."

After Louise and her husband divorced in 1970 (Caldwell died in 1995), she moved to Sarasota, Fla., where she started a short-lived nonprofit group devoted to environmental education. But she moved back to Illinois in '95, after hearing of the demolition plans for her old home. These days, Louise, who was divorced from her second husband in '81, stays in touch with her broth-

ers—in addition to George, 57, there's Harry, 66, and Peter, 60, who still live in the U.K., where Peter works for the ex-Beatle. She says she was horrified to hear about George's stabbing last December and "so relieved" he recovered. Though they haven't seen each other in three years, she insists she and George are "not estranged. I receive an income from him." They talk a few times a year, she adds, "but I keep it private."

Except, that is, when it comes to his long-ago visit. She has provided photos for a book, *Before He Was Fab*, on his Benton trip and has plans for a museum adjacent to the B&B, which she hopes will be the town's ticket to ride. Her brother would appreciate the honor, she believes. A few months after his visit, he sent her a letter. In Benton, he wrote, "people were glad to see me—not because I was a Beatle, but because I was me."

● Dan Jewel
● John Slania in Benton

Chaty/Schulz

People.com For more information on Louise Harrison's bed-and-breakfast go to www.people.com or AOL (Keyword: People)

"If I had a magic wand," says Harrison (with grandson Tory Rodgers, 9), "I'd wish George could live open and free, the way he did here."

E) It would be possible for anyone to check the records in Franklin County to find that I never owned 113 McCann St. after I left in the '60s. Even in the '60s it was in my husband's name.

F) Newspaper articles at the time make it clear that although I did try to help save the house from demolition, I soon withdrew from the efforts because I did not wish to participate in the renewed public scrutiny of my brother's previously private and enjoyable visit.

Unfortunately, the concept in both the British and American legal system of "innocent until proven guilty" does not seem to be prevalent today. Haven't we all seen examples of people being wrongly accused of some heinous crime? Without any evidence whatsoever, the "accused" is publicly "condemned."

I considered this particular matter of the B&B a dead issue for many years. Now I realize—with its resurrection in November 2011 *LIFE*—that I should once again try to set this record straight. Addressing this particular episode again is in keeping with my Dad's Shakespearean advice: "This above all, to thine own self be true." *"But Dad, it don't come easy! Why can't others also be true?"*

I recently asked *People* magazine to admit the oversight of the misleading caption in the story they ran all those years ago, but so far have had no luck.... Maybe this statement here will finally end the silly story? (But don't hold your breath, Lou; it is said that "lies get much better mileage than does the truth," and we certainly see that in political election campaigns.)

It would be great if more people could have grown up with a Mum and Dad like ours. But I *am* grateful that we did. Lou, stay calm & carry on!

Chapter Eighteen

CLOSE ENCOUNTERS

I recognize that my name is not known as well as my kid brother's, but due to his prominence on the Planet in the 20th century, it has been my pleasure to meet many interesting and well-known people.

However, I met my first undeniably important person quite some time before George became a Beatle. I was living in Peru with my engineer husband when Prince Phillip made a visit to Lima. As British subjects, my husband and I were invited to the British Embassy to meet the prince. It was an early evening cocktail party, and we took the trip from La Oroya, some 12,000 feet up in the Andes down to Lima at sea level. It was always invigorating to be at sea level after the lack of oxygen one experiences at the higher altitude.

The skilled engineering arm of the world's mining communities was made up of Brits, mainly Scotsmen, who famously were and perhaps still are the best engineers on this planet. It was no accident or mistake that the chief engineer on board the starship *Enterprise* was known as Scotty. During our years in mining we had met quite a few of the other Brits who were also invited to meet the Prince. Many had been employed at the same time as us, at other mining locations around the world, and as a somewhat small, closely knit group, we happily exchanged experiences. As the party wound down, we were briefed by the staff as to protocol. We were all to be presented to His Highness Prince Phillip by the ambassador. Protocol dictates that the royals do not shake hands, a very sensible decision, especially since most people think you have to crunch the proffered hand to show how good a grip you have. I myself have adapted to the fist bump nowadays. Prince Phillip had one hand behind his back, and the other held a glass of champagne. He spoke briefly and pleasantly to each of us and seemed to have been made familiar with our backgrounds. It was a very gratifying moment and one I was happy to write about in my next letter to Mum and Dad.

This happened around 1961/62. So, even though I was actually the first Harrison to meet a member of the royal family, the rest of the family followed soon after!

In 1963, I moved to the United States as a permanent resident alien and spent most of that year writing back and forth to Brian Epstein, George Martin and Dick James, then later in the year connecting by phone to Brown Meggs and Bill Turner at Capitol Records. I met most of these "players in The Beatles saga" in New York in February 1964 when George invited me to spend the week in February with the Boys at the Plaza.

Due to Dr. Gordon's charging me with George's medical care for his strep throat situation, I also met Ed Sullivan on Saturday, February 8. That afternoon I had to tell him I needed to take George back to the hotel. The doctor had ordered him to rest so he would be well enough to participate in the Sunday afternoon's pre-taping of the—newly added—third Beatle TV appearance. Later Sunday night, they performed the first live evening show. Once Ed understood the situation, having earlier been briefed by Brian, he quickly sent for a limo to take George and me "home." He was really very kind, and during the next day's shooting, he seemed just as enthralled with the Boys as most fans. He enjoyed the way they included him as though he was "one of the Lads." He was also very impressed with their wit and polite manners. I would venture a guess that having those Lads on his show was just as much of a highlight for him as it was for them. Later, when I was broadcasting Beatle reports, I spoke several times by phone with his son-in-law, Bob Precht, producer of the *Ed Sullivan Show*.

A couple of months later at the *New Musical Express* awards in Wembley, I met most of the participating stars: The

Rolling Stones, Billy J. Kramer, Gerry and the Pacemakers, and many more whose names I do not recall. More recently, I met Billy J. and his wife, who now live in New Jersey. Gerry Marsden was at one of the Beatle conventions I attended when I had my environmental organization. I hope he is doing better now, but at that time he was suffering with the same affliction I had experienced with husbands. It happens to the best; say no more.

My "other" number one band has always been The Moody Blues. I have met them several times in the past decade or two. One time Justin Hayward brought his wife over to me and said to her, "Tell Lou about the time you ran away from home to go to see George's parents in Liverpool." She told how she hitchhiked to Liverpool when she was a teen and how my parents invited her in, fed her, and helped her get safely home to Birmingham.

As I mentioned previously, shortly after my brother died Nov. 29, 2001, I was invited to New York to be on the morning show with Katie Couric. When I finished the interview, I had the honor, privilege, and pleasure of a phone call from the most beloved, intelligent, decent, and, at that time, badly mistreated politician on the planet—yes, President William Jefferson Clinton. Sadly, as I write this in 2011, our current president is the target of an even more callous attempt to "bring him down." Those with this agenda care not that their heartless plans are also bringing down the entire country. At that time President Clinton called to convey his condolences on the loss of my brother. I'd long known that both he and Al Gore enjoyed The Beatles. I knew that Al Gore had played a Beatles song at his wedding to Tipper. I'd been in touch with them during my days running Drop-In and have letters from them both.

However, on that day, I told the President I would love to meet him, and so he invited me to "come on over." I had a limo from the TV network at my disposal, and I set out to 125th Street in Harlem. I met Maggie Williams, his longtime chief of staff and Jim Kennedy, his aide. Then "Himself"—as they say in Ireland—came and invited me into his private office.

He went on to show me many of his treasured items on the shelves and walls of his office. Many were gifts from foreign countries, whose citizens appreciated him and his wise and cordial leadership.

Since then, I've met with the president several times. Before his library in Little Rock was completed, I offered to put on loan my album *Meet The Beatles,* which was released

THE WHITE HOUSE

WASHINGTON

September 2, 1993

Ms. Louise Harrison
Founder and Executive Director
"We Care" Global Family, Inc.
Post Office Box 1338
Tallevast, Florida 34270

Dear Lou:

Thank you so much for your kind gift. It was thoughtful of you to remember me on my birthday. This has been a significant year for me, and you have helped to make my birthday even more special.

Sincerely,

Bill Clinton

SEP 09 1993

THE VICE PRESIDENT
WASHINGTON

August 3, 1993

Ms. Louise Harrison
4827 Village Gardens Drive
Sarasota, Florida 34234

Dear Ms. Harrison:

I want to take this opportunity to thank you for sending the recordings and for the support and encouragement that you have offered to me. I deeply appreciate your generosity and your commitment to the success of this Administration.

As you know, we are facing many challenges in the coming years. Please be assured that the President and I will be working hard to accomplish those goals of particular importance to the American people--a more efficient government, a cleaner environment, an improved economy, and a better future for our nation. Your participation is essential for the success of our efforts.

Again, thank you for your thoughtfulness.

Sincerely,

Al Gore

AG/wem

when the Boys came to perform on Ed Sullivan. All four of the Lads had signed the album for me. When I took the album to Little Rock, I stayed at the home of Connie and her husband, a couple who had been longtime friends of the Clinton family. Connie presently manages the library gift store. I parked my car on a downtown street on a Sunday morning. Connie and her husband took me in their car to the "under-construction" library. The priceless album was in the possession of the curator of the library, but I'd left my suitcases, billfold, and a lot of Beatle photos in my auto. We visited at the library for about an hour, but on arriving back at my car, found the window smashed and all my "stuff" gone. The local radio and TV media were very helpful in getting the word out, and the police department eventually found my suitcase and my clothes thrown away along a rail embankment. I guess

THE WHITE HOUSE
WASHINGTON

September 9, 1996

Ms. Louise Harrison
4827 Village Gardens Drive
Sarasota, Florida 34234

Dear Lou:

    Thank you so much for the tie and the picture. You were kind to remember my birthday, and I appreciate your continued thoughtfulness and generosity.

    Hillary joins me in sending best wishes.

Sincerely,

Bill Clinton

WILLIAM JEFFERSON CLINTON

August 9, 2006

Louise Harrison
2214 State Route 248
Branson, Missouri 65616

Dear Lou:

Happy 75th birthday! Hillary and I hope you have a wonderful celebration, and we send you our best wishes for health and happiness in the year ahead.

Sincerely,

Bill Clinton

my Walmart clearance rack clothes weren't good enough for the thieves? We never retrieved my billfold, or the Beatle photos, although CNN had news of the robbery streaming all over the planet. I've been fortunate enough in my life that this has—so far—been the only time I've been robbed. It was really uplifting, though, to find how much goodwill toward my "Beatle relativity" there still is in the world.

My younger grandson and I were invited to the official opening of the library. It was a wonderful experience. My grandson met and was photographed with the president, as well as Robin Williams and Ted Danson. More recently, I was invited to the library when the president was there at the book signing for the Ling sisters, of North Korean captivity fame. *(See photos on page 218.)*

During the Clinton administration and my Drop-In experience, I also met and corresponded with Al Gore. I mailed him audio tapes of a total of 170 PSAs which I researched, wrote, produced, and distributed during the '90s. They were called "Good Earthkeeping Tips." George offered his "Save the World" song as a musical background to my tips. So, these PSAs were a double Harrison effort. They aired on 9,200 radio stations, for a total of eighteen months, Westwood One and ABC's Oldies.

I met yet another interesting person many years ago when he was running for senate in Illinois. I was one of the speakers at a rally in Mt. Vernon. When I finished speaking, the mayor came over to me with a young man and said, "Here's a big Beatle fan who would love to have a photo with you." So, as usual, I put on my best smile, and the young man put his arm around me—as most folks do—and Presto! I now have a photo of me and President Obama. *(See photo on page 218.)*

But, oh boy! Did he take on a thankless mess! Our previous administration plunged irresponsibly into an unnecessary and unwinnable war. It has been my experience that no war is actually "winnable" and the previous administration didn't even include the overwhelming financial costs of that war in the budget, much less the loss of innocent lives.

The late Senator Paul Simon was a major supporter of my environmental efforts. In fact he gave me several of his books to read. Senator Percy and Congressman Grey of Illinois were both guests on my *Sound-Off* radio talk show. I met and talked with Tom Hayden of the Chicago Six protest incident. He was married briefly to Jane Fonda. He sent me a copy of

SOUTHERN ILLINOIS UNIVERSITY
CARBONDALE

March 15, 2002
Dictated 3/2/02

Louise Harrison
PO Box 33
Macedonia, IL 62860

Dear Lou:

What is happening on your great idea of Global Interdependence Day?

Let me know what I can do.

Cordially,

Paul Simon

PS/hn

Paul Simon, Director • Mike Lawrence, Associate Director

Public Policy Institute, Forestry 138, Mailcode 4429, Carbondale, Illinois 62901-4429, 618/453-4009
Fax: 618/453-7800, Internet: www.siu.edu/~ppi

his book, *The Lost Gospel of the Earth.* I have worked, either on radio or elsewhere, with many others politicians whose names I do not readily recall.

Another person I met and felt great empathy for was Howard Dean. He had a great following and many very valid policies. I was at the caucuses in Iowa and witnessed all that happened and was appalled at the way the media deliberately destroyed his campaign after the speech with the so-called scream! I heard and witnessed that event and all I can say is the amount of distortion and manipulation of sound that went on was—to my mind—criminal, but I am getting accustomed to the amount of corruption in the American so-called democatic process! That does not imply that I condone the constant twisting of "facts" to suit the agenda of a particular media outlet.

When I was in New York with George for their first "Ed shew," we were descending a spiral staircase somewhere at the TV theatre, and we passed someone on his way up. He stopped and said to George, "Hi, aren't you one of The Beatles?" George replied and gave his name. Then, nodding toward me, he added, "This is my Anglo-American relation!" This stranger then introduced himself as Dizzie Gillespie. Some months later, I read about an interview Dizzie gave where he used that same phrase about Anglo-American relations, and I recall thinking, "I know where he got *that* idea!"

During those few days in New York, I met many prominent people. One gentleman I particularly liked was Dezo Hoffmann, the photographer who took many photos of all of us. However, I think when it got to the point of publishing many of his photos, I ended up "on the cutting room floor." But that was only to be expected; after all, it was all about The Beatles. I had fought hard for many months to see this venture come to fruition. Naturally, I finally met Brian, George Martin, and many others with whom I had been corresponding during the previous months. Brian Somerville and Derek Taylor were the press reps for The Beatles, an extremely hectic and often thankless task.

That same weekend, the Hall family presented George with a twelve-string Rickenbacker guitar, something he had longed for. I missed meeting them at that time as I was busy with the Good Guys, but years later I met their son, and he was kind enough to write about his experience for *This is Love*, the limited (300) edition book I published as a fundraiser during my Drop-In adventure. He also gave me a tour of their guitar factory. I also met Al Aronowitz, a reporter for the *Saturday Evening Post,* who at first I really disliked. Later, when we met again, he became good friends with both George and me. In fact, during the '70s when I lived in Manhattan and had an auto, Al offered to let me keep my car at his garage in New Jersey. Parking garage fees in the City were, and likely still are, outrageous.

I mentioned elsewhere I lived in Manhattan during the '70s and spent a lot of time with George when he was working on the album and film from the Concert for Bangladesh. During this time on his birthday, he thoughtfully called me from Britain in order that I could wish him a happy birthday. The telephone company in Britain would change his phone number every six months because of the volume of calls and lack of privacy. His number had just been changed again so he knew I wouldn't be able to call him. Another interesting story with regard to George's constantly changing phone number involves Leon Russell. It happened I was going to a Leon Russell event—I think at a relatively small pub in I don't recall which city. When I told George I was going to see Leon, he asked me to pass on to him his most recent phone number. This I tried to do, but unfortunately, the Leon Russell henchmen would not permit me to meet with Leon personally in order to tell him the phone number. Naturally, I was not going to give it out to anyone other than Leon. So, possibly for a while, he also could not reach George. If you're reading this, Leon, I tried!

On the many occasions I stayed at George's house, Friar Park, I met quite a few of his pals, including auto racing greats Emerson Fittipaldi and briefly Jackie Stewart, who used to land his helicopter on the lawn. Together, George and I visited the home of Mick Fleetwood, and I recall that evening George would not have any of the trifle, a wonderful British dessert, because it contained sherry. George was in one of his abstinence modes.

Another good friend, Butch Patrick, I first met at the Hard Rock Café in Orlando. We were both gifted with Hard Rock leather jackets. Butch was very supportive of Drop-in and served as an advisory board member. We have maintained a mutually supportive relationship ever since. He has taken the trouble to visit Branson to enjoy an evening with Liverpool Legends, and also joined in the fun for my 80th birthday.

On a number of occasions I have had the very real pleasure to work with Peter Noone, perhaps better known as Herman of Herman's Hermits. The first time I met him was at a concert he gave in St. Louis in the very early days of his career. My daughter, born in 1959, loved his hit "Mrs. Brown You've Got a Lovely Daughter" and, like most parents at the time, we naturally sang it to her. I don't recall when I took both my children to the show (1965), but they both enjoyed meeting Peter. To my daughter's delight, he actually sang the song's title to her. Many years later, Peter and I appeared at several events together. I was impressed that no matter how hectic things were backstage, he always made time to call and chat with his wife and little daughter.

The most memorable event I shared with him took place in St. Pete, Florida, at an outdoor venue in a park. There were many acts booked to play that day. The promoter had put together a wonderful show. Unfortunately, after the first opening acts, the typical summer Florida storms swept in. In the intervening years we have become much more aware of the dangers when an outdoor concert comes "head to head" with an electrical storm. On that day, though, the thunder and lightning was severe, but the rain would come and go. Most of the enthusiastic audience just huddled in their beach chairs, wrapped in tarps or ponchos. They hoped the weather would clear up completely and their "stars" would be able to shine. Peter was the headline act, and naturally the final one. But, as the evening drew to a close it was still impossible to go on stage and plug-in electrical amps and guitars. I had been circulating amongst the audience chatting to them and was aware how much they were looking forward to seeing Peter. As the *end* came near, I had an inspiration. I suggested to Peter that in order to give the potential audience "something" for their patience, maybe he could just walk out between the roped off area in front of the stage, and sing a few songs to them. He eagerly agreed to this solution. He had his accompanist come along to give him the right chord so he could begin. We walked out and I told the very damp, though not dampened, "huddled masses" who had remained all day, "Peter is going to sing a few songs and, if you like you can join in." The performance may not have been glitzy or Vegas style, but for the few hundred patient souls, this was possibly the most thrilling performance they had, or ever would see. Dodging the odd raindrops, Peter and the audience, singing in the rain, sang all his most popular hits with such enthusiasm it almost drowned out the thunder! If I can find them I will include the photos I have of this impromptu event. *(See photo on page 221.)*

Another major family of hit-makers I had the pleasure of meeting and interacting with was "The Beach Boys." From the onset of their recording career they had been one of the few "other" bands besides my brother's that I really enjoyed. I was invited to the event in Hollywood designed to commemorate Carl Wilson, the brother who had died the previous year. There were many notable guests who each spoke at this event. When it came to my turn, I was just announced as "someone who has a few words to say." Taking the playful attitude that I was an "unknown," I started out by saying that I had a brother who had also been in a '60s band. I continued, "I don't know if you have ever heard of them," and at that point a number of people who knew me shouted out "The Beatles." So, "acting" surprised and gratified said, "Oh, some of you *have* heard of them?" At that point the audience joined in the joke. I told how The Beach Boys had an album, "Pet Sounds," which had been the inspiration for an album my brother's band had released. I went on, "But my brother's band called their album a big long complicated name, which is really difficult to remember," Now the crowd roared with laughter and yelled, "Sgt. Pepper's Lonely Hearts Club Band." Again, faking surprise I replied, "Oh, wow, some of you *do* know it?" Then returning to normal, I just went on to chat about the careers of these two remarkable bands. I left the stage to friendly applause. During the rest of the evening I had some wonderful conversations with the members of this kind and talented family and many of the invited guests.

The head of human resources at Universal Studios in Orlando was a board member of my environmental charity. Thus, I made many trips there on business. On one occasion when they were recording an event at the studios in Orlando, I happened to meet the Bee Gees. Actually I didn't really get to know the band, but whilst they were working I was introduced to Dwina, Robin's wife. We became good friends and I visited her at her home both in Britain and in the United States. Dwina, an extremely talented writer and artist in her own right, produces wonderfully whimsical Irish stories, mostly comedic. Looking back, I realize that due to my reluctance to "pry" into private lives, I wasn't really sure then, which Bee Gee was her husband. I know she told me and when visiting, I *did* meet them all.

Michael Moore is another person I admire and was fortunate enough to meet and now consider a friend. While my brother was alive, I was constantly invited to any Beatle related happenings. One was the introduction of the boxed set of Beatle movies released with some fan fair in New York with a showing at the Lincoln Center. It happened I was seated next to Michael Moore. After introducing ourselves, we chatted, naturally about The Beatles. As the showing of the movie progressed, I was able to give Michael many "background" stories that my brother had told me about various scenes. One I recall telling Michael was during a scene in the train corridor: Ringo was upset about something and George was trying to comfort him. In this scene George pulls out a lighter to ignite their ever present cigarettes. This was the solid gold lighter, which George had told me Brian Epstein had given him for his 21st birthday.

Another favorite performer I met was Neil Diamond, I think at the Winter Garden Theatre in New York. An usher escorted me backstage after the show. The first person I met backstage that evening was Otto Preminger, who was really friendly. I've found that most truly "great" people never act like big shots; it is the ones who are insecure and blessed more with luck than talent who behave like "self-absorbed dummies." Before Neil came to greet us, I spoke with a lady who told me Neil was her cousin. As close relatives of a star, we had something in common and we chatted about our experiences. About a week later, I had either a call or a note from her, very kindly saying that "meeting George Harrison's sister was a memorable part of the evening;" naturally I was pleased to have pleased yet another Beatle person.

There are many other notable or well-known people I have met. Some you will find sprinkled throughout the book as they cropped up! (I notice I'm reluctant to use the word "celebrity," I wonder why?) Just two or three years ago I had the great pleasusre to meet Bill Maher. He is certainly a person on my same wavelength!

My encounter with this next undoubted celebrity turned out to be a bit of a "whoops," though he became famous in Sarasota as a different character than the one he'd been known as previously. The incident began at the Patio, part of the Columbia on St. Armands Circle. The band Omni, who had a twenty-five-year gig at the Patio, frequently had visiting stars such as Bob Hope, Tommy Smothers, Paul Shaffer, Graham Nash, Tony Bennett, and others, who would join the band for a song or two. In the '80s I was there often, as I loved to dance. During a break for the band, Sal Garcia, the bandleader—he and his wife Linda were close friends of mine—came to me and said, "Hey, Tony Bennett is here tonight and is going to sing with us later, why don't you introduce yourself and congratulate him on the hit he had of your bother's song 'Something.'" I'd always enjoyed his music and had a lot of his records, so I told Sal, "Okay, good idea."

To backtrack a moment, with a Beatle for a brother, I am usually introduced to other celebs more or less as an equal and know better than to be a "bother." I never ask for autographs, or to have my photo taken with them, which is the reason why I do not have any such photos to show! So this

Louise Harrison

for her exemplary contributions to the world of music

WHEREAS, **Louise Harrison** is a dedicated individual and devoted sister, who has worked tirelessly advocating the music, message, and legend of her late brother George Harrison and The Beatles. She has inspired fans throughout the world and helped introduce the music of the world famous rock and roll bank to new generations of fans; and

WHEREAS, **Louise Harrison's** contributions to the world of music has played an invaluable role in coalescing the civic spirit in Cleveland, Ohio, that led to the creation of the Rock and Roll Hall of Fame and Museum. Her ongoing commitment is sincerely recognized by the Rock and Roll Hall of Fame organization; and

WHEREAS, **Louise Harrison** gives emphasis to her brother's exceptional songwriting and lead guitar talent, his thoughtful and concentrated stage presence being a crucial factor in The Beatle's success, and how the band changed the sound of pop music forever.

NOW, THEREFORE, BE IT RESOLVED that the Board of Commissioners of Cuyahoga, Ohio, salutes **Louise Harrison** for her extraordinary dedication in advocating her brother's music, and her contribution to the civic spirit in our community. We applaud her commitment and wish her much success in all her future endeavors!

Tim McCormack, President

Jimmy Dimora, Vice President

Peter Lawson Jones

Duly adopted this 8th day of August, 2002

evening, Mr. Bennett and his party were about finished with their meal when I approached him. I said, "Hello, I'm Lou Harrison, George Harrison's sister, and I'd like to compliment you...." At that point he waved his hands impatiently and said, "Go away, go away." So, I just moved away. After all, I wasn't exactly hankering for a moment in the spotlight with Mr. Bennett! Sal had seen me near the Bennett party and asked, "How did it go?" So I told him what had happened. Naturally Sal was embarrassed on my behalf. Later when the star was ready to perform, Sal said to him, "I hear you were not very polite to George Harrison's sister" The reply, for which he has been famous in Sarasota ever since: **"If that's George's sister, then I'm Hitler's brother!"** So Hitler's brother lives on in Florida. We've had fun with it, but.... yes, I do understand being a celebrity does get to be tiresome and sometimes one just wants to be invisible. He did make a good version of "Something" even though I couldn't tell him so!

Although some encounters have been mentioned briefly earlier, I have tried to fill in more details in this chapter. Writing this part, I know for certain there is no way I can possibly find time to write about all the interesting people, places and things that have been part of my life. Each time I think I've finished "the story," yet another long forgotten memory pops up. But, I'm still really very busy keeping on "full speed ahead" with many projects. Also, I find telling much of this stuff about myself makes me sound as though I am bragging, but am just telling it as it is. And for me, it's a bit of a bore. After all, I've been there and done that! Other parts, talking about departed family members for instance, are painful. The *most* painful, therefore not mentioned in the book, are the present economic sufferings of those closest to me. Unfortunately most of my global family are experiencing similar sufferings, but I am hoping that our personal situation will improve if this book does well.

So hey! A word to my global family—if you enjoy what you are reading, don't *lend* it to your friends. If they can afford to—suggest they buy it! (Lou, you *are* being cheeky!) Love, Peace and Laughter!

Chapter Nineteen

THE END IS NEAR...
TILL NEXT TIME, CHEERIO!

A s I reach the end of this book, I wonder about the next big
adventure. I've been pretty open with the opinions I've
formed after eight decades of Earth experiences. I repeat, no
one needs to agree with me, but please do *think!* To paraphrase
The Beatles' song "We Can Work It Out," "Think of what I'm
saying. I may be wrong, but then again, I may be right."

There are a few things in my life still too painful to write
about: my son's death in January 2010 and the financial
hardships my close family members and I are experiencing.
But then families the world over are severely stressed these
days, so I am thankful for the attitude we learned throughout
life, which was illustrated in the final scene of *The Life of
Brian* to *"always look on the bright side of life."*

In the introduction, I told how our parents taught us "This
above all, to thine own self be true." I think we followed their
advice as best we could. However, I have noticed that truth
itself is often difficult to define. Maybe you are familiar with
a scenario used to explain the discrepancies in "eye-witness"
accounts of the same event. It goes like this:

A car speeds through an intersection and crashes into
the side of a building. This car was in the process of being
repainted. The left side had only the grey undercoat, but the
other side had been finished with the dark green topcoat.
Okay?

When investigators arrive, they gather eye witness
accounts. Naturally the spectators on the left side of the
street saw a grey car speeding; People watching from the
other side saw a dark green car. Both groups were telling
the truth-from their perspectives. Half a dozen people had

been looking from a sixth floor window when the crash occurred. From their higher vantage point they saw the whole picture—a speeding car, half grey and half dark green. This fabricated scenario is easy to resolve, you merely gather all the witnesses together, examine the car, and all have the same facts/truth.

In real life though, this problem is not so easily solved. Some who saw the grey car, and some who saw the dark green car, refuse to examine the actual crash or evidence. They totally believe with deep conviction that their version was the absolute truth...so help me God! They are so adamant that they are prepared to "damn to hell" anyone who disagrees. For these people there is only *one truth,* or one side of the street, and they have the scoop.

Of course we have not heard from the poor fellow who was crushed beneath the car. He likely saw "something completely different." Okay, so this is an invented story and no actual damage was done. I am sure most of my readers understand exactly the point I am making. If you are confused, too bad! However, if you care to view things from a higher or more detached perspective, you may be more likely to find the truth.

In conclusion, although the Harrison Hug is something that I have mentioned throughout the book, it was based on a comparatively recent incident when my brother asked me to pass on his hug. In the process of reaching back to my beginnings for the purpose of this book, it became very clear to me: I was embraced by The Harrison Hug from the moment I first arrived. My three brothers also grew up enveloped in the warmth of that Hug.

We Harrison kids spent our entire lives wrapped in the security of our parent's hug. So, it is not something new, but IS something that has always been there to comfort and sustain us.

Love, Peace, Joy, Laughter, and all the *good* things we can have, if we make up our minds....

Till next time, Cheerio!

Lou Harrison

AFTERWORD

This is a clarification of the political views expressed in this book. I am a British citizen, also a permanent resident of the United States since March 7, 1963. Although I do pay taxes, I cannot vote (a bit of taxation without representation ☺), I do not belong to any U.S. political party.

Due to my father's guidance, I have always been interested and often concerned about political decisions that impact our every day lives. During the past 50 years, at times I have applauded and at other times been appalled at the policy decisions and laws passed by local or federal government. Depending on how closely these decisions were aligned with the values I learned as a child, I have switched my "silent and unofficial" allegiance back and forth across "the aisles" many times.

At present, 2014, my concerns match the apprehension of many US citizens regarding the non-action and obstruction in Congress, also, the attempted destruction of many hard won social rights such as voting and choice.

I realize and *understand* that no single political party has all the best answers. Though there is widespread corruption, self-seeking and media manipulation of the public, I *want* to believe that most individuals who seek and hold political office incidentally do so motivated by high ideals. Unfortunately, we have witnessed how greed can distort. I can only hope that those who have retained their high ideals will keep fighting the battle so that *love* and *peace* will eventually prevail over *fear* and *greed*.

My sincere love to all of my readers.

Lou Harrison

ACKNOWLEDGMENTS

There are so many friends who have encouraged me to work on this book that it would take many more pages to name all of you. You have my thanks and you know who you are.

However, I do wish to mention and give thanks to Elise Bishop, without whom I could never have finished this book. Elise sat with me day after day, patiently fighting the computer, which kept insisting on "upgrading itself" instead of doing what it was told.

Q. What would we do without technology?
A. Remain sane, maybe.

ABOUT THE AUTHOR

Louise Harrison was born in Liverpool, England, the first child and only daughter of Harold and Louise Harrison. You may not know about Louise, but most of humanity in the latter half of the 20th century have certainly heard of—and know a lot about—her youngest brother George. Yes, he was also the youngest of the four Liverpool lads known as The Beatles!

When Beatlemania burst forth in the early '60s, Harold and Louise Harrison responded warmly to the multitude of Beatle fans worldwide who wrote letters to and about their son, thus becoming Mum and Dad to a warm and loving Global Family of Beatle People. During 1964 and 1965 Louise, living in Illinois, found herself writing and broadcasting daily Beatle reports nationwide, due to public demand for news of The Beatles.

Her distinctive voice with its British accent is immediately recognized by Beatle People all over the world. She has made hundreds of public appearances to greet and hug Beatle People all over the United States, Europe, Canada and Mexico. When her parents died in the late 1970s, Louise became Mum, known by many as "the flying mum," to what she fondly refers to as her Global Family.

INDEX

Caernarvon (Wales) 85
Caldwell, Leslie (see Harrison, Louise) 202
Caldwell, Louise Harrison (see also Harrison, Louise) 56, 57, 168, 185, 186, 189, 190, 196, 200, 202, 203, 204, 205, 207, 208, 215, 216, 217, 224, 237, 238
Canada 6, 21, 136, 147, 153, 200, 307, 359
Capitol Records 28, 160, 168, 171, 181, 255, 336
Captain Planet 280
Carbondale, Illinois 24
Cargill, Patrick 311
Carlin, George 266
Carmi Broadcasting Company 25
Carmi, Illinois 25
Carnegie Hall (New York City) 181
Carney, Art 113
Carney, Cecelia 109
Cashbox (magazine) 24
Cavern Club (Liverpool, England) 150, 207
Cavett, Dick 256
Central Peruvian Railway 148, 152
Cerro De Pasco Mining Company 147, 148, 151
Chakravarty, Kamala 252
Chase, Chevy 316
Cheddar Gorge (England) 290
Chestnut Grove (Liverpool, England) 69
Chicago, Illinois 233, 293, 294, 326
Chicago Stockyard 234
Christie, Lou 234
Cilcennin 85
Clapton, Eric 252, 254
Clinton Library 218
Clinton, William Jefferson (Bill) 218, 292, 337
Colbert, Stephen 14, 70
Columbia Records 28
Comer, Jack 182
Connell, Bud 183, 184, 185

Couric, Katie 292, 337
Cousin Brucie 308
Cox, James 30
Crackerbox Palace 247
Crisp, Frankie 246, 247
Crocodile Dundee 92
Crosby, Bing 234, 247

D

Daily Beatles Reports 184, 191, 359
Danbury, Connecticut 262
Danson, Ted 218, 342
Davis, Russell 20
Daytona Beach, Florida 263
Dean, Howard 343
Dean, Johnny 57
Deauville Hotel (Miami, Florida) 172, 182
Deerfield Beach, Florida 249
Deihl, Bill 188, 190, 191
de Montfort, Louis 108
Diamond, Neil 348, 349
Dick Cavett Show 256, 257
Dick Clark Tours 234
Dixon, Jeanne 228
Dodds, George 243, 244
Dooley, Eugenia 31
Doran, James 319
Dowty Company 134
Do You Want to Know a Secret 22
Drop-In 6, 219, 266, 272, 274, 276, 278, 280, 299, 301, 302, 325, 326, 328, 337, 342, 345, 346
Drysdale, John 214
Dublin, Ireland 43
Duque, Rosalind 26, 35
Dylan, Bob 15, 88, 252, 254, 321

E

Ed Sullivan Show 5, 28, 36, 160, 182, 204, 205, 230, 336
Edwards, Mrs. (teacher) 102
Eldorado, Illinois 39, 156, 201
EMI Records 28
Empire Theatre 117

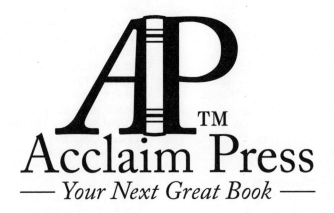